The
Conservative's
HANDBOOK

*Defining the Right Position
on Issues from A to Z*

PHIL VALENTINE

CUMBERLAND HOUSE
NASHVILLE, TENNESSEE

THE CONSERVATIVE'S HANDBOOK
PUBLISHED BY CUMBERLAND HOUSE PUBLISHING INC.
431 Harding Industrial Drive
Nashville, Tennessee 37211

ISBN-13 978-1-58182-662-3
ISBN-10 1-58182-662-1

Copyright © 2003, 2008 by Phil Valentine

Cover design by Roy Roper, Wideyedesign Inc., Brentwood, Tennessee

The Library of Congress has catalogued the first edition as follows:

Valentine, Phil.
  Right from the heart : the ABC's of reality in America / Phil
Valentine.
      p. cm.
  Includes bibliographical references and index.
  ISBN 1–58182–354–1 (Hardcover : alk. paper)
  1. Social values—United States. 2. Social problems—United States.
3. United States—Social conditions—1980-4. United States—Social
policy—1993-5. United States—Moral conditions. I. Title.
HN90.M6V35 2003
361.1'0973—dc21   2003011748

Printed in Canada

2 3 4 5 6 7 8 9 10—10 09 08

To the memory and spirit of

RONALD REAGAN

An inspiration to all conservatives

Contents

Foreword

LET ME tell you what you have to look forward to in the pages ahead. You'll learn the truth about guns and how they save far more lives than they take. You'll see why America's Founding Fathers never intended that there be a constitutional separation of church and state. You'll find holes in the global warming argument big enough to drive a truck through. This book absolutely blisters China and our dangerously cozy relationship with that brutal regime. It makes a strong case against illegal immigration, illuminating points I haven't heard anyone else make. And you're going to love how it sets the record straight on Ronald Reagan and his legacy.

Why is this book so important? Let's face facts. Times have changed so much in the past few years. The world is a much more dangerous place than it used to be—and not just in terms of terrorism and crime. Now there are people fighting for the right to influence our children. These insidious groups demand more support from the mainstream and are making a concerted effort to undo what we conservatives teach our kids. As a father, I have a new perspective on what it means to protect "the children." And I want to know that my values will not be undermined by someone else who holds undue influence over my children. It's my conservative values that will carry them through until they are old enough to form opinions of their own. But just what are those conservative values?

We on the Right often talk about moral clarity. We know how important it is to distinguish right from wrong. What has been needed is a book with *conservative* clarity, one that really spells out all that we believe in and why we believe it. *The Conservative's Handbook* by my good friend Phil Valentine does that and more. This book is so insightful and so well researched that it's impossible to read it and not gain a thorough understanding of conservatism, and perhaps even be swayed to its side. It's a book you can give to your co-workers and your kids and those annoying academes and say: "Here. Read this and you'll know all you need to know about conservatism and why it's right." You see, conservatism is based on logic and facts, after all, and this book is full of both. Conservatism also has a sense of humor. The same wit Phil's listeners have come to expect on his radio show comes through in this book.

I first met Phil in New York at WABC Radio after his successful run in Philadelphia, and we became fast friends. He was deciding where his career would lead him next. The most important issue for him was where to raise his young family. With the oldest of his three sons beginning kindergarten in a few months, Phil and his wife, Susan, chose to move back to Nashville, where they had lived for a decade. His family comes first in each life decision he makes. Phil not only talks and writes about conservative values, he lives them. *The Conservative's Handbook* is not only loaded with truth, it's spiced with Phil's life experiences. These were experiences that took someone who was raised in a Democrat household and forced him to examine his entire belief system.

What he learned was the very same thing Ronald Reagan learned in the early '60s: that he hadn't left the Democratic Party, the Democratic Party had left him. This helped give Phil a unique perspective in talk radio, one that enables him to examine an issue from every angle before drawing a conclusion. It's a perspective that keeps him from toeing the party line or backing a particular elected official if that guy strays from the straight and narrow of what Phil knows is right. That refusal to give in to party loyalty would serve him well upon his return to Tennessee.

Once back in Nashville, Phil hit the ground running and took on Tennessee's Republican governor, who was pushing an unconstitutional state income tax. Although he had campaigned for the governor when he first ran for the office, Phil stuck by his principles instead of going along just to get along. So when the governor broke his promise not to support a state income tax, Phil held his feet to the fire. In fact, he led the charge against him.

Instead of just blasting the governor and the tax plan on the radio, Phil rolled up his sleeves and actually dissected the state budget—page by page. The incredible spending abuses he uncovered were posted on his Web site. A state legislator copied the list and passed it out to all of her colleagues on the floor of the House. Phil's exposure of the arrogant governor and his cronies in the General Assembly set off a firestorm.

Phil marshaled his listeners again and again for protests in front of the state capitol, taking their opposition to the proposed income tax directly to the elected officials. Those of us in other parts of the country cheered them on. We understood how important this battle was. Phil also understood that the issue was bigger than ratings, and he joined forces with rival talk-show hosts in Nashville to fight the tax. Phil, his colleagues, and their army of devoted listeners became the first line of defense against an ever-encroaching, never-ending expansion of government. Whenever he got word that the income tax bill was coming up for a vote, he would rally the troops in front of the capitol. Their battle against a Tennessee income tax—and their ultimate defeat of the levy—is now legendary.

Although it was the income tax fight that attracted national attention, Phil approaches every issue with that same passion. He lays it on the line, covering every hot-button issue of the day. Whether it's AIDS, guns, unions, or God, he pulls no punches. And those issues and many more are inside this book. He explains them all and backs up his positions with facts. *The Conservative's Handbook* is not only a great read, it's a handbook that can be used anytime you want to disarm a liberal. It's informative, entertaining, and one of the most important pieces of conservative work in recent memory.

I also love the way this book is laid out. Each chapter is devoted to a different conservative ideal, and Phil's approach makes the issues easier to understand. He brings each ideal into the open and, like a lawyer in a courtroom, makes an overwhelming case for each one.

My favorite chapter has to be "Liberalism is an ideology doomed to failure." I've been ranting about the failings of liberalism for years. Here, Phil spells out, in no uncertain terms, exactly why liberalism is doomed. He dispels some of the myths surrounding Democrats and civil rights. He reminds us that we've been fooled before and shows what we can do so we won't let that happen again. He tells it like it is regarding political correctness, welfare, and a host of other liberal pet projects. And, best of all, he nails liberals to the wall over their hypocrisy.

I have no doubt that, after reading this book, many of you who thought you weren't conservative will learn something new about yourselves. Those who already embrace the conservative philosophy will be thrilled to have this new tool to use in making your arguments.

We're in a war here in America. It's over the heart and soul of our country, and our very future is at stake. Liberalism is wrong for our country and it's wrong for our future. We have to combat it daily. Phil and I and our conservative colleagues try to do our part on television and radio. We try to spread the truth to as many people as will listen. *The Conservative's Handbook* offers tons of ammunition we can all use in that war. If every American will read this book, there's no doubt we'll win.

—*Sean Hannity*

Acknowledgments

FIRST OF all, a huge thanks to my friend Sean Hannity for writing the foreword to this book. I appreciate so much his support of my radio show and this project. He's as genuine and nice as he appears to be on radio and TV, and I treasure our friendship. His advice over the years has been a blessing.

My producer, Johnny B, is a great talent. When he's not there, the show just isn't the same. He's the best sidekick anyone could ask for. He adds a whole new dimension to our show and my life, and I'm proud to have him as my dear friend.

Thank you to my editor, Ed Curtis, for helping me fine-tune the manuscript, and to Paul Mikos, Jennifer Behar, and all the great folks at Cumberland House Publishing. Their professionalism and enthusiasm made for a great experience. Special thanks to my publisher, Ron Pitkin, for his wisdom and guidance. I also especially want to acknowledge Chris Bauerle at Cumberland House, who first approached me about writing a book. Chris helped put the deal together and walked the project through every step of the way. Thanks, Chris, for all your help.

Steve Brown was the spark that lit the fuse to my radio career in the early days, and I will be eternally grateful.

A very special thanks is in order for my lovely wife, Susan, and my three boys—Carr, Campbell, and Douglas. Without your support, love, and understanding, I would never have finished this book. You've put up with the hours of secluded writing and long nights and weekends. You've given me hours of great material for my show. You've been my anchor and my inspiration, and I love you more than you'll ever know.

And thank you, God, for all with which you have blessed me. I am always mindful of your presence.

Introduction

THIS PROJECT began as *The ABC's of Reality*, an alphabetical accounting of my philosophy intended to bring new listeners of my radio show up to speed on what the show is all about. Soon I had listeners contacting me, telling me that they had copied the list from our Web site and were posting it in their offices and cubicles. I realized that I had struck a chord, that these realities I had outlined through my conservative point of view spoke to a great number of people.

I found myself detailing these issues day in and day out, dispensing morsels of good, solid facts I had unearthed in my daily show preparations. Listeners began e-mailing and calling wanting to know where I had found certain statistics or information. I spent—and still spend—a great deal of time answering these requests.

But it's more than information. It's ammunition. Conservatives find themselves defending their positions against the onslaught of bias coming from Hollywood and major media outlets. Many consumers of this tripe don't bother checking the facts; instead, they regurgitate these little "factoids" at cocktail parties as if they were gospel.

The information we provide on the radio debunks these arguments, yet who could actually recite, line by line, the information, with sources, they had heard just once on the radio? That's when I realized I needed to provide more.

I set about the task of fleshing out *The ABC's*. I referred to my show prep, all of which, since 1998, has been stored in a database. I also keep various paper files on hot-button issues for future reference. The rest entailed filling in the gaps with additional research and referencing all the pertinent facts to combat the "Oh, yeah? Prove it." argument conservatives encounter every day. What emerged was a full-length book that can be used in several different ways.

First, I would recommend a cover-to-cover read. Upon completion, you'll be equipped with the knowledge you need to demolish a liberal argument on a wide range of issues, including but not limited to guns, global warming, drugs, partial-birth abortion, education, political correctness, and the wisdom of Ronald Reagan. This book addresses all of the hot issues of the day as well as "evergreens," as we call them in the radio business, those perennial topics of interest.

Second, you can use the book as a quick and easy reference guide through the use of the table of contents, index, and appendix. Want to destroy a liberal's argument against guns? Simply cite the material listed in this book with the accompanying sources and you'll overwhelm them with facts. Facts may not mean a lot to a liberal, but they can be a heckuva lot of fun for you.

Not only is *The Conservative's Handbook* a conservative philosophy book, it also reconfirms conservatism. Instead of offering just a compilation of op-ed pieces, it fastens the philosophy down to the bedrock of truth. Where liberalism is steeped in emotion, this book is steeped in logic and fact. That's not to say that conservatism can't be emotional. I, like most conservatives, am passionate about what I believe. But many arguments between the two sides degenerate into name-calling and unsubstantiated claims. This book distills those raw emotions and extraneous thoughts into a cohesive argument for conservative principles and values.

If nothing else, I have tried to be consistent throughout. Some issues, like guns and taxes, are unambiguous where the facts meet the argument. Others, like immigration and free trade, require more examination and deeper thought in order to elicit the true conservative position. Contentious as my views may be, I've tried to make a strong case for how conservatives should think on these issues.

If there was one goal I kept in mind while writing this book, it was to cover the full array of fiscal and social issues we Americans face every day, and to do so in a manner that is comprehensive without being overwhelming. Information overload is oftentimes worse than no information at all. I've picked up books as thick as phone books that were chock-full of valuable information, but many times I lost the motivation to tackle such tomes because they appeared so daunting. This book covers a wealth of subjects presented in easy-to-read, relatively short chapters.

Most of all, this book demonstrates that conservatism is *positive*. Conservatism is about hope for the future, not fear of it. It's about confronting our problems head-on with rational ideas on how to solve them, not cowering in a corner waiting for someone else to devise a solution. It's a belief in the individual's power to make a difference. Conservatism is faith. Faith in people. Faith in freedom. Faith in this great country we call home. But conservatism demands thought. It insists on logic and reason in everything we think.

Eighteenth-century English author Horace Walpole noted, "The world is a tragedy to those who feel, but a comedy to those who think." Adolf Hitler observed, "What luck for rulers that men do not think." You may find this book informative, humorous, and possibly enraging—but if it makes you think, then I've done my job.

The
Conservative's
HANDBOOK

1

AMERICA is good.

THERE'S A DISCERNIBLE DIFFERENCE between a *great* country and a *good* country. There's no doubt the United States is a great nation. We are the preeminent superpower of the world. The former Soviet Union, however, was a great nation in terms of military might and its influence around the world. Likewise, China is a great nation as was the Roman Empire, but great is not always good. China, the Soviet Union, and the Roman Empire are all what Yale law professor Amy Chua refers to in her book *Day of Empire* as *hyperpowers*.[1] Chua defines hyperpowers as "societies that amassed such unrivaled economic and military might that they essentially dominated the world."[2] She classifies the United States as a hyperpower too, but that classification does not delineate between good and bad. To be sure, not every nation is all good and few nations are all bad. In order to make that distinction, a country or civilization must be judged by its totality.

A good nation is not measured by its military strength nor its size. A good nation is, in short, a nation that is generally a positive force in the world. The United States is such a place. That's not to say that we haven't made mistakes, but what we have accomplished as a nation—what we have given to the world as a nation—far outweighs our mistakes.

But Weren't the Founding Fathers a Bunch of Racists?

Detractors love to focus on our national warts, foibles, and stumbles. While most of us learned about our country's founding and the brave men who risked their lives to form a more perfect union, too many school lessons focus on the fact that some of the founders owned slaves. Slavery was a contentious issue even during the infancy of our nation. Slave owners like Thomas Jefferson grappled with the contradiction of breaking the chains of oppression from Great Britain while some around him remained in bondage. Jefferson didn't invent slavery; he was merely a link in its ever-weakening chain. While the writer of the Declaration of Independence and our third president never freed his slaves during his lifetime, he helped bring us a step closer to slavery's inevitable abolition.

While some argue that the Declaration of Independence and the Constitution must be viewed as flawed documents because some of their authors were slave owners, they ignore the enormous impact our break with Great Britain had in placing us on a certain path toward abolition. Benjamin Franklin argued that a break with the mother country was necessary if we were to ever end slavery because all prior efforts to end the practice had been thwarted by the British Crown. In fact, after the Revolution, many of the Founding Fathers who had owned slaves chose to release them, including John Dickinson, William Livingston, John Randolph, Caesar Rodney, George Washington, and George Wythe. Franklin along with Founding Father Benjamin Rush formed the nation's first antislavery society. Based, in part, on the work of some of our founders, slavery was abolished in eight states relatively soon after the Revolution. Furthermore, Rufus King, a signer of the Constitution, authored a federal bill prohibiting slavery in the territories of Illinois, Indiana, Iowa, Michigan, Ohio, and Wisconsin. That bill was signed into law by President George Washington.[3]

Slavery was a hotly contested issue at the constitutional conventions. Pro- and antislavery advocates squared off on more than one occasion. Some feared the issue might divide the country before it was fully constituted. Principle gave way to pragmatism, and the nagging issue of slavery was tabled to be fought another day.

Much has been made of the three-fifths compromise during the haggling over the Constitution. This three-fifths clause has been portrayed as a means of dehumanizing blacks in eighteenth-century America. It was, in fact, an *anti*slavery provision. By allowing slaveholders to count only three-fifths of their slaves in congressional calculations, it denied Southern states additional proslavery representation in Congress. Instead of our Founding Fathers being hypocritical taskmasters who only wanted freedom for themselves, they actually fast-tracked the issue of slavery that had been accepted and encouraged under British rule for the prior two hundred years. Richard Allen, a former slave who had been freed after converting his master to Christianity and who went on to found the African Methodist Episcopal Church, reminded fellow blacks of this fact. "Many of the white people [who] have been instruments in the hands of God for our good, even such as have held us in captivity, are now pleading our cause with earnestness and zeal," he told them.[4] Richard Allen recognized, even then, that his country and his people were in a better place, a place where the notion of abolishing the wicked practice of slavery was no longer relegated to the hushed corners of slave quarters but was now being etched into the consciousness of the entire nation.

The Rise of Capitalism

Freedom is the birth mother of capitalism. Today, China practices a limited form of capitalism. So did the former Soviet Union. Both nations, however, begrudgingly adopted their own forms of capitalism as a means of benefiting the state. There is free enterprise in China today, but the communist government, like that of the Soviet Union before it, maintains a controlling interest. A *truly* capitalist society is a free society. And capitalism attracts brilliant minds like a magnet to steel. Names like Albert Einstein,

Mikhail Baryshnikov, and Joseph Pulitzer were drawn to the United States because there has never been a place on earth where so many with so little have accomplished so much.

Through our ingenuity, we gave the world airplanes, refrigerators, and sewing machines. We gave the world roller skates, toilet paper, and rock 'n' roll. We gave it the telephone, blue jeans, jazz, light bulbs, air conditioning, and Coca-Cola. We gave it bubble gum, microwave ovens, cellular phones, calculators, artificial hearts, and the polio vaccine. Skyscrapers would not be practical were it not for Elisha Otis and his elevator. Heck, we invented the skyscraper too. Some people would go through life deaf were it not for R. G. Rhodes and his hearing aid. Imagine where the world would be were we not able to tap into the earth's energy because of Edwin Drake's oil well. The world is so much more productive thanks to Eli Olds's assembly line. Crayons, tea bags, popsicles, cotton candy, frozen food, chocolate-chip cookies, photocopiers, defibrillators, carbon dating, integrated circuits. The list goes on forever. Do you think all this could happen anywhere else but America?

Former British prime minister Tony Blair summed it up nicely. "For all their faults," he said of America, "the U.S. are a force for good. I sometimes think it is a good rule of thumb to ask of a country: are people trying to get in or out of it? It's not a bad guide to what sort of country it is."[5] Our immigration problems, daunting as they may

be, are a testament to our nation's attractiveness. You'll notice that Mexico is certainly not in the position where it
has to worry about a flood of humanity heading south
from the United States.

Just because a nation is free doesn't necessarily mean
it's going to be a magnet for the best and the brightest.
Mexico is a case in point. Mexico is a federal republic very
similar in governmental organization to the United States.
Mexico, however, has been plagued by corruption. The
Global Integrity Index measures "the existence and effec-
tiveness of national anti-corruption mechanisms." It was
founded by Charles Lewis, a former *60 Minutes* producer
who specialized in government corruption. This index
rates Mexico as weak. By comparison, the United States is
rated as strong. The United States ranks at the top of the
index, tied with Bulgaria, a breakaway country from the
former Soviet Union that is now a parliamentary democracy. Mexico ranks thirty-first, behind Kenya, Thailand,
and Russia.[6]

Bribery is legendary in Mexico. Although the Mexicans have made strides in stemming corruption, it's still
not unusual to have to grease the palms of police officers
and government officials. Dr. Shang-Jin Wei is assistant
director and chief of the Trade and Investment Division at
the International Monetary Fund (IMF). Wei has found
that corruption stifles foreign investment and economic
growth. In fact, he says that if Mexico reduced its level of
corruption to that of Singapore, it would have the same

effect on foreign investment as lowering the capital gains tax by 50 percent![7] Mexico is rich in natural resources and is the second-largest supplier of oil to the United States, but it remains a third-world country because of rampant corruption. Were Mexicans to eliminate their corruption, there's no reason they couldn't be on par with the United States and Canada, and millions of Mexicans wouldn't find it necessary to break into *our* country.

But capitalist nations don't just happen by mistake; they happen by design. The United States was founded as a capitalist nation. That's why calls to end capitalism by those on the extreme left aren't just wild ramblings from disgruntled socialist misfits. These people are anti-American. Capitalism and America are inextricably intertwined; in fact, capitalism is the shortest path to individual freedom. One cannot be simultaneously free *and* dependent on the government. Our freedom to be all we can be is what makes the United States unique. It's also what makes us good.

Through the Eyes of a Foreigner

Does the rest of the world hate us? You'd think so by listening to many on the left. Certainly we've had our ups and downs in world opinion, and Uncle Sam's eye has been blackened a bit by the Iraq War. But America's relationship with the world is not represented by a single snapshot in history. National relationships are cultivated and nurtured over time. Suffice it to say that our relationship with Great Britain has seen its ebbs, but the Brits remain one of our strongest allies in the world, as do the Canadians.

Toronto television commentator Gordon Sinclair captured America's good in a 1973 editorial. What he said about the United States back then still holds true today. "Germany, Japan and, to a lesser extent, Britain and Italy were lifted out of the debris of war by the Americans who poured in billions of dollars and forgave other billions in debts," Sinclair observed. "None of these countries is today paying even the interest on its remaining debts to the United States." Regarding France, one of our most vocal critics, Sinclair noted, "When France was in danger of collapsing in 1956, it was the Americans who propped it up, and their reward was to be insulted and swindled on the streets of Paris. I was there. I saw it."

Sinclair recognized the unbridled altruism of the American spirit. "When earthquakes hit distant cities, it is the United States that hurries in to help." He noted that no one lifts a finger when Americans suffer their own natural disasters. "Our neighbors have faced it alone," Sinclair concluded, "and I'm one Canadian who is damned tired of hearing them get kicked around."[8] Sinclair was right, of course. When the tsunami hit Indonesia in 2004, the U.S. government stepped up with $656 million in aid, in addition to sending our military to the region on a humanitarian mission. What's even more remarkable are the private donations from American citizens that topped

$1.8 billion.[9] More than a third of Americans gave to private charities to help the victims of the tsunami.[10] Yet, according to a Pew poll, even after all our generosity, only 38 percent of Indonesians have a favorable view of the United States.[11]

The United States is by far the single largest donor of foreign aid in the world. Unlike some countries that force philanthropy through tax policies, Americans donate the bulk of their money through the private sector. Of all the foreign aid the United States provides, 79 percent of it comes from private foundations, corporations, voluntary organizations, universities, religious organizations, and individuals, according to the annual *Index of Global Philanthropy*. In 2005, U.S. foundations gave more than each of eleven of the twenty-two developed-country governments, including France, Germany, Japan, and the United Kingdom.[12] So much for the greedy American capitalists.

Spreading Democracy

It can be argued that it would be in our best economic interest *not* to spread our form of successful government around the planet. Free nations mean competitive nations. Still, being the altruistic country we are, we've not been swayed in our mission to nudge the rest of the world toward freedom. According to the World Bank, the United States leads the world economies based on purchasing power parities. Canada is number two, followed by Australia, the United Kingdom, Germany, and Japan.[13] Did you notice the connection? All of these top economic powers owe their form of government—either directly or by influence—to the United States. Technically, the United States is a representative republic, but "democracy" has come to represent any form of free government that springs from the people. That concept lay dormant for centuries until it was resurrected and embodied in our Declaration of Independence. Over the past two and a half centuries, this notion of self-government has spread like wildfire around the planet.

Although we remain the preeminent economic powerhouse of the world, that title is not guaranteed in perpetuity. Nations like China have the sheer numbers of people power to dominate the world economically if they would only cast off the chains of communism. The productivity a billion and a half people could muster if only they were free is incalculable. There's no doubt that democracies make better economic partners, but spreading democracy and capitalism to places like China and the Middle East will also, most assuredly, make for a safer world.

Sean M. Lynn-Jones, the editor of *International Security*, the International Security Program's quarterly journal at Harvard, laid out an impressive argument for spreading democracy long before the Iraq War. Lynn-Jones argued that democracy is good for the citizens of new democracies. He noted that democracies are less likely to use violence against their own people, they enhance long-term economic performance, democracies never have famines, and they historically don't wage war against other democracies nor do they support terrorism.[14] Spreading democracy, in essence, is spreading good. Our attempt at spreading democracy in the Middle East may not have been the most popular decision we ever made, but it is the only thing that will ultimately lift that region into long-term prosperity.

Why Religious Extremists Hate America

Just take a stroll around Las Vegas and it's easy to understand why Muslim extremists find our nation so repulsive. Pornography is big business. The United States is the number-one producer of pornographic videos. More than 40 million American adults regularly visit Internet pornography sites. Every thirty-nine minutes a new pornographic video is being made in the United States. Even Christians are not immune. Fifty-three percent of men enrolled in the group known as Promise Keepers admit to weekly accessing pornography. Yet while the United States may be the top producer of pornography, we are not its number-one consumer. China, Japan, and South Korea all rank above us in consumption. While there are 4.2 million pornographic Web sites on the Internet, they make up just 12 percent of the total.[15] That means that 88 percent of the Web sites are something other than pornography. It's easy to focus on the bad, but the Internet, like our country at large, is primarily good.

Muslim extremists see this obvious decadence and assume that's what our military is fighting to protect. Even the nutcases who follow Fred Phelps and his Westboro Baptist Church (so-called) believe our military is protecting and defending homosexuality. This despicable group pickets the funerals of our fallen soldiers with signs that read, "God Hates Fags" and "God Hates the U.S.A." Like Muslim extremists, Phelps's crowd misunderstands the mission of our military forces in Iraq and Afghanistan. We're not fighting to protect pornography or homosexuality or decadence. We're fighting to protect freedom. This nation was founded on the principles that our citizens are free to make their own choices, even when those choices are bad.

The problem with Muslim extremists, like so many liberal extremists in this country, is that they see the issue of good vs. bad as black and white, with no gradations. War is never good, but it's sometimes necessary. Can anyone argue that the United States shouldn't have teamed up with the Soviet Union to defeat the Nazis? When choosing sides in conflicts, either to protect U.S. interests or to promote a path to freedom, our choices are sometimes between the lesser of two evils. We've certainly made some missteps in supporting certain groups and governments in the past. Some of those decisions have come back to haunt us, but at the time we made the best decision based on the circumstances. For example, our support of the mujahideen in Afghanistan was critical in our aim to cripple the Soviet Union. We had no way of knowing that one of their number, Osama bin Laden, would later wage war against the United States. Our goal was to liberate the Afghan people from the grip of Soviet expansionism and, by doing so, accelerate the downfall of the Soviet Union.

Despite our success in helping to drive the Soviets out of Afghanistan, despite our coming to the aid of countless millions in Indonesia, Muslim extremists still see us as evil incarnate. There is nothing we can do to convince them otherwise. We are infidels that must be destroyed. It doesn't matter how much humanitarian aid we provide. It doesn't matter how much military support we provide. To a certain segment of Muslims, there is no gray area.

You may be asking yourself, "Then, why should we continue to try to be an influence of good?" The answer is simple. No matter their religion, no matter their ethnic background, people everywhere yearn to be free. Oppression is oppression, whether it's coming from a communist regime or a radical Islamic theocracy. The oppressors are the minority. Their stranglehold on the people is strong. It took us almost seventy-five years to bring down the Soviet Union. We're now chipping away at the Red Chinese. Understand, people are oppressed, not by will, but by fear. As the shining light of freedom in the world, it is incumbent upon us to share what we've discovered for ourselves with the rest of the world. We must do this, not because we want to force our will on everyone else, but because, as fellow human beings, it's our obligation to try to free people from bondage, just as we freed our own. Because we have learned the hard lessons of freedom through our blood, sweat, and tears. Because we're a nation of hope, a nation of dreams. Because America is good.

2

BELIEF IN GOD is a cornerstone of our republic.

ONE OF THE MOST misused phrases in American culture is "separation of church and state." We hear this all the time. We can't have a Nativity scene in the town square because it violates the constitutional separation of church and state. We can't have a prayer before a football game because it violates the constitutional separation of church and state. The city manager of Eugene, Oregon, banned Christmas trees from public buildings, believe it or not, because they violated the constitutional separation of church and state—or so he said.

Hear me on this one, people. There is NO such thing as separation of church and state in the U.S. Constitution. It is nowhere to be found in the entire document. The First Amendment simply states, "Congress shall make no law respecting an establishment of religion, or prohibiting the free exercise thereof." It articulates a freedom *of* religion, not a freedom *from* it. The polemical history of the First Amendment grows more and more contentious.

Original Intent

To understand what the Founding Fathers meant, you have to understand the times in which they lived. Back when the Constitution was crafted, individual states had their own state religions. Their individual state constitutions laid down the law regarding church and state. Not only did the states not separate the two, many required that they be joined. North Carolina's constitution said, "That no person who shall deny the being of God, or the truth of the Protestant religion, or the Divine authority of the Old or New Testaments, or who shall hold religious principles incompatible with the freedom and safety of the state, shall be capable of holding any office, or place of trust or profit, in the civil department within this state."[1] Several states, instead of requiring an officeholder to be a Protestant, merely required a professed belief in God.

These established state churches continued as late as 1833. That's almost fifty years *after* the Constitution was ratified! The Founding Fathers were careful not to step on this right of the states to choose their own religion. They even spelled it out in the federal agreement between the states, promising that Congress would never try to usurp their power by establishing its own national religion. They also promised that the federal government would never pass a law prohibiting the free exercise of religion. So, instead of a separation of church and state, there is a clear *protection* of religious expression outlined in the U.S. Constitution. The separation is clearly between the states and the federal government. Don't get me wrong. I think having a state religion in any of our states today is a bad idea, but the Constitution clearly leaves that decision up to the individual states, not the federal government. That's why all these rulings from the U.S. Supreme Court on local school matters, like having prayers at ball games, are a violation of the very Constitution they swear to uphold.

Knowing all that, the obvious question is, where did we get all this "separation" business to start with? How did we get from point A to point B, only to look back and find ourselves so far away from original intent? The problem can be summed up in one phrase: legal precedence. Instead of basing rulings on the Constitution, the Supreme Court oftentimes bases its rulings on prior Supreme Court rulings. What inevitably happens is that we find ourselves incrementally further and further away from original intent until the rulings bear little resemblance to what our nation's founders had in mind. The point where we jumped the track on this separation-of-church-and-state issue can probably be traced back to a Supreme Court ruling in 1947.

In *Everson v. Board of Education*, Justice Hugo Black opined that the First Amendment forbids any interaction between church and government. He said that Jefferson's "wall [of separation] . . . must be kept high and impregnable." That was a reference to President Thomas Jefferson's 1802 letter to the Baptists in Danbury, Connecticut. The state religion in Connecticut at the time was Congregationalism, and they had petitioned the president for aid in religious disestablishment, which Jefferson himself had advocated as governor of Virginia. The Danbury Baptists were disappointed when the president failed to intervene on the grounds that the federal government was strictly forbidden from interfering in state matters.

Although Jefferson used the phrase "a wall of separation between church and state" in that letter to the Danbury Baptists, you have to look at the letter in context. The full statement reads, "I contemplate with sovereign reverence that act of the whole American people which declared that their legislature should 'make no law respecting an establishment of religion, or prohibiting the free exercise thereof, thus building a wall of separation between church and State.'" The "State" to which he referred is clearly Congress, which he calls the "legislature." And, of course, he's right. The First Amendment clearly prohibits Congress from getting involved in the establishment of a national religion, and the reason is obvious. Congress is prohibited from doing so because that right was reserved for the states and the states alone.

It's also interesting and instructive to note that this president, who is so widely quoted regarding his "wall of separation," did absolutely nothing to help the Danbury Baptists with their plight. Jefferson's inaction on this matter is a distinct indication that he regarded this as a state matter, not a federal one. Furthermore, advocates for wiping our government clean of religion read too much into the establishment clause. There's nothing mysterious about it. The framers of the Constitution weren't writing in code. They meant, literally, that Congress shall not establish a religion. In other words, Congress doesn't have the power to pass a law making Catholicism the official national religion.

"Oh, but they must have meant something more," these advocates insist. No! If they'd meant more, they would've said more. If they'd meant that state legislatures had no business establishing state religions they would've said, 'Neither Congress *nor the state legislatures* shall make any law respecting an establishment of religion.' But they most unambiguously did not. Congress is the only entity restrained by the establishment clause. Not state legislatures. Not local school boards. Congress.

Other Jeffersonian Writings

It should also be noted that, even though Thomas Jefferson was a bright guy and a deep thinker, he had nothing whatsoever to do with framing the Constitution. He was the Declaration of Independence guy, remember? During the time that the Constitution was being drafted and debated, Jefferson was in Paris as ambassador to France. But since Jefferson is the Founding Father of choice on this issue, just for grins, let's take a look at some of his words of wisdom on the subject. "The God who gave us life gave us liberty at the same time; the hand of force may destroy, but cannot disjoin them."[2] He also said, "If ever there was a holy war, it was that which saved our liberties and gave us independence."[3] That, of course, was an obvious reference to the Revolutionary War, which he regarded as a war ordained by God. Surely this was not something uttered by a man who was antireligion.

However, knowing that individual states had their own laws regarding religion in holding office, it is instructive to see how Jefferson felt about states' rights too. He wrote in 1791, "I consider the foundation of the Constitution as laid on this ground: That 'all powers not delegated to the United States by the Constitution, nor prohibited by it to the States, are reserved to the States or to the people.' [X Amendment] To take a single step beyond the boundaries thus specifically drawn around the powers of Congress, is to take possession of a boundless field of power, no longer susceptible of any definition."

Once Jefferson's letter to the Danbury Baptists is understood in the context of his reasoning regarding the federal government's limited role in affairs of the states, it becomes quite clear that he never intended to extract religion from public life. The fact that he attended a religious service at the Capitol the very day he wrote his famous letter to the Danbury Baptists is itself a testament to that. No doubt Thomas Jefferson would be appalled by the way his words have been twisted to make him the poster child for the separation-of-church-and-state movement.

The Separationists

Still, the antireligion zealots continue their quest to rid our society of any religious symbols that can even remotely be tied to "the state." I refer to these folks as separationists. These separationists have so bastardized the establishment clause that they now consider any hint of religion in any sector of government to be a violation of the Constitution. The separationists have been at work for years trying to strip "In God We Trust" from our money and "one nation, under God" from our pledge. They succeeded, briefly, in June 2002 when the Ninth U.S. Circuit Court of Appeals in San Francisco found the recitation of the Pledge of Allegiance in public schools to be unconstitutional because of the 1954 insertion by Congress of the words "under God." The public outcry was so intense that even liberals like Barbara Boxer of California were taken aback. "From the beginning of our country, God has always played a role," Boxer said. "All you have to do is look at some of the churches in the thirteen colonies to know that God has always played a role in the foundation and continuation of our nation."[4]

On June 14, 2004, the U.S. Supreme Court reversed the lower-court decision, ruling that Michael Newdow, the atheist who challenged the recitation of the Pledge of Allegiance in schools, did not have legal standing to do so.

Newdow was in a custody battle over his then third-grade daughter, and since he did not have custody, he could not speak for the girl, the Court said. In 2007, Newdow came back with a string of other lawsuits, including one on behalf of a New Hampshire couple and another on behalf of parents with children in three Sacramento-area school districts.[5] I find it odd that someone who professes there is no God would be so threatened by Him. I suspect it has little to do with his daughter or his lack of religion and more to do with his seeking the limelight.

I often wonder how these separationist fanatics manage to drive past a house of worship with a cross in full view without recoiling in Draculan horror. God forbid they should have to drive down *Church* Street. Unfortunately, these atheistic rabble-rousers are winning the PR war. They've convinced otherwise intelligent people that there truly is a constitutional separation of church and state. Their "separation of church and state" is now ingrained in the American psyche, and they've managed to succeed with the help of their willing accomplices in the news media. One is desperate to find a story on this issue that doesn't throw out as "fact" somewhere therein the phrase "constitutional separation of church and state." As someone who's read the Constitution, it frustrates me to no end, because that phrase just isn't in there. Not in the *United States* Constitution, anyway. It is, however, in another constitution. The former Soviet Union's constitution.[6] How ironic.

This movement to obliterate religion from anything related to government has also been unwittingly aided by the sometimes overzealous religious right. Their righteous indignation—oftentimes justified, mind you—has been the source of scorn in the media, leading many people to resent religion's perceived intrusion into the body politic. The truth is, religion and religious people have been integral parts of the political landscape since this country's inception. The Founding Fathers' quotes are replete with references to God and faith. The separationists would have you believe our Founding Fathers were agnostics or atheists, but nothing could be further from the truth. Jefferson may, in fact, have been a deist, but not by today's definition of the word. Jefferson believed in a creator but preferred to believe that God set things in motion and men were pretty much left to their own devices.

Further evidence of this so-called separation, so say the separationists, is article 6, section 3, of the U.S. Constitution. The separationists love this part, claiming it proves that there's a separation of church and state. Article 6, section 3, states, in part, "no religious test shall ever be required as a qualification to any office or public trust under the United States." Well, of course not. With potentially thirteen different state religions, it would be impossible for anyone to agree on a religious test for *federal* service. The Founding Fathers were, again, making sure that the federal government didn't overstep its boundaries. Again, I direct your attention to the North Carolina constitution, which specifically requires such a test. It is quite obvious, given the full picture, that the Founding Fathers intended that the federal government not usurp the powers that were clearly left in the hands of the individual states.

Back to Basics

There is good news, however. The pendulum seems to be swinging back toward the side of sanity on this issue. In December 2001, the U.S. Supreme Court refused to hear a case involving a Jacksonville, Florida, high school that allowed its seniors to choose "chaplains" to give inspirational addresses at graduation. In *Adler v. Duval County School Board*,[7] a group of students, egged on by their clueless parents, sued to stop the policy. They lost. The Supreme Court refused to hear the case, thus allowing the policy to remain in place.

Although this case was largely ignored by the media, it shot an enormous hole in the argument of the separationists who have not yet been able to determine the difference between school-sponsored religion and students' free speech. I venture to say that none of our Founding Fathers ever envisioned courts putting muzzles on students at school graduations.

Another atheist lawsuit was shot down by the Supreme Court in June 2007. The High Court threw out an atheist group's lawsuit against the government's faith-based initiative that funnels taxpayer money to religious groups that help with assorted social ills. By a five-to-four decision, the justices ruled that the group had no standing in the case. They said it was unreasonable for someone to claim harm as a taxpayer over a relatively small portion of the federal budget. While not ruling directly on the church-state issue, it indicated the Court is less concerned about keeping church and state separate than it has been in the past.[8]

In an odd twist, the Supreme Court on the same day made two rulings that seemed to contradict one another regarding displaying the Ten Commandments. In June 2005 the justices held that a Ten Commandments display on the grounds of the Texas statehouse was constitutional while displaying posters of the Decalogue in two Kentucky courthouses violated the First Amendment. The issue of constitutional versus unconstitutional seemed to hinge on how much time had passed since each was displayed rather than the Constitution itself. Justice Stephen Breyer was the swing vote in each case. "The determinative factor here, however, is that 40 years passed in which the [Texas] monument's presence, legally speaking, went unchallenged," Breyer wrote. "Those 40 years suggest more strongly than can any set of formulaic tests that few individuals . . . are likely to have understood the monument as amounting . . . to a government effort to establish religion." His logic completely sidestepped the constitutional issue. The High Court historically has taken extreme liberty in interpreting the establishment clause to mean that it applies to any and all government entities.

Clearly, it only applies to the federal government. Had the justices bothered to do any research, instead of worrying about what prior courts have said, they would have learned that the Founders were protecting the states from an overbearing federal government. The Court's rulings in the 2005 Ten Commandments cases may have served to keep the monument grabbers at bay, but they did nothing to clarify the original intent of the Constitution.

Still another landmark decision by the Supreme Court came, ironically, in the same week as the now-infamous Ninth U.S. Circuit Court of Appeals ruling on reciting the Pledge of Allegiance in school. In a case out of Cleveland, Ohio, the High Court ruled in favor of using vouchers for private and parochial schools. The justices ruled that allowing tax dollars to be used in a religious school did not constitute an establishment of a religion but was merely a case of "true private choice."[9] This flew all over the separationists, who are repulsed by the idea of using any public money for anything religious, even if it benefits children.

This should give you an ugly glimpse into the liberal mind. Everything's supposedly "for the children," until you talk about giving them and their parents a choice in their education. A friend of mine summed it up perfectly. He said that back in the '60s we had George Wallace standing in the schoolhouse door, refusing to allow black children in. Now we have liberals standing in the doorway, refusing to let them out.

It's odd that the separationists read so much into one phrase but don't read the rest of the Constitution. An excellent example is the pledge issue. As long as the majority doesn't trample on the constitutional rights of the minority, the majority rules. The vast majority of people in this country are for keeping God in the pledge. There's no harm done to the minority by reciting it in school, so the majority rules. I had an atheist call my show the day after the pledge ruling by the lower court was handed down. I asked him what his problem was with having his child recite it, and he said he didn't want his kid indoctrinated by the state. Now follow me on this: If he believes there's no God and that when he dies, it's all over—that he has about as much chance at an afterlife as a dead tree rotting in the woods—what does he care whether his daughter recites a pledge that mentions God? Is he afraid she might become a believer? And if so, what would that matter if he's convinced that it's not true anyway?

You see, I believe these people don't care about what their child is reciting. They care about what *your* child is reciting. They detest God and religion. It's their intention to completely undermine your religion and your beliefs because they somehow feel threatened by them. And that's a violation of *your* rights. If they choose not to believe in God, that's fine. I choose not to believe in atheists.

In an institution that bases many of its decisions on legal precedent, only time will tell if future Supreme Courts will continue this slow turn back toward interpreting the

Constitution instead of legislating from the bench. One thing's for certain: the writings of our Founding Fathers leave no doubt that belief in God was, and is, a cornerstone of our republic, and they would be terrified for us if they could see just how far we've tried to distance ourselves from it.

3

CHARACTER is the single most important attribute in a leader.

ANYBODY WHO TELLS YOU that character isn't important apparently slept through the Clinton administration. Aside from the obvious sexual indiscretions, Bill Clinton committed a series of acts that seriously jeopardized national security. One of the more serious was a waiver he granted that allowed Loral Corporation to provide the Chinese with critical missile guidance technology, a move made over the objections of his own Justice Department. Bernie Schwartz, Loral's CEO, not coincidentally, was Clinton's and the Democrats' largest campaign contributor, giving, along with his family, more than $2 million.[1] After a four-year investigation, Loral Corporation was slapped with a $20 million fine, the largest fine in American history, for violating the Arms Export Control Act by "turning over technology to China that allowed it to improve the guidance systems for its missiles."[2]

Flash forward to 2007, and the Chinese have successfully tested a missile that blows satellites out of orbit.[3] Thanks, Bill. Now the Chinese have the capability to take down every satellite we have. That's like gouging out the eyes of the American military. Can you imagine what that means to the security of our nation? Practically everything we do, militarily, depends on satellites. And they laughed when Ronald Reagan wanted to develop a missile defense system using weapons in space to shoot down enemy missiles. They're not laughing now. This is what happens when someone with no scruples gets the keys to the Oval Office.

Bill Clinton's behavior while in the White House will have negative repercussions in America for many years to come. Polling data toward the end of his presidency demonstrated, beyond a shadow of a doubt, the high level to which the character issue had been raised. When asked how important it was for the president to provide moral leadership for the country, 73 percent said it was very important. Another 19 percent said it was somewhat important.[4] Another survey showed that 90 percent of Americans believed that we had major problems with morality in this country or were in an absolute moral crisis.[5] When asked to compare their own moral standards to those of Bill Clinton, 69 percent said their standards were higher.[6]

The good news was, the majority of American *adults* recognized Bill Clinton for the cad he was. But what about the kids? How many of them were irreparably damaged by Clinton's cavalier attitude toward immorality? Only time will tell. We didn't fully understand the impact of the free-love '60s until that generation's children became teenagers. I was on the younger cusp of that group, and I'm thoroughly convinced that my generation's disregard for authority has come back to bite us.

While most bemoan a generation of kids with no respect for themselves or others, I maintain that we don't have a sorry crop of children. Instead, we have a bumper crop of sorry parents. Time was if a child came home after getting in trouble at school, he or she got in double the trouble with their parents. Now parents blame the teachers, or worse, sue them. We have a whole generation of children who don't know how to take responsibility for their own actions because their parents are trying to right the perceived wrongs of their own tortured childhoods by solving all of life's problems for them. They still cling to the rallying cry of the Flower Power era, "If it feels good, do it."

The first time the realization of the damage done to the presidency became so strikingly clear to me was in the fall of 1994. I was attending a fund-raiser for Tennessee's soon-to-be-Senator Fred Thompson. The guest of honor was former President George H. W. Bush. When Bush took to the podium, a wave of nostalgia engulfed me. I remember vividly looking up at him and thinking, *Oh, that's what a president looks like.* I had truly almost forgotten how dignified the office could be. I realized at that point just how low Bill Clinton had taken the presidency. Little did I know that he'd take it even lower—much lower.

Ross Perot made a statement back during his first run

for the presidency that has stuck with me. I don't remember the exact circumstances surrounding the remark, only that years before he had apparently fired an executive of one of his companies because of infidelity. The reporter remarked that adultery was a private matter that had no bearing on a person's ability to do his or her job. Perot fired back in his classic style, "If your wife can't trust you, neither can I." That simple but crystalline statement is so true. Not that good people don't screw up every now and then. They do. But serial adultery is a character flaw that speaks volumes about a person.

Compromising Position

Character not only affects the way an elected official does his or her job, the lack of it can be used as a lethal tool by that person's enemies. During the height of the Monica Lewinsky scandal, I wrote a commentary for our Web page, entitled "Why Character Matters." In it, I brought up an angle everyone seemed to be missing. What if Linda Tripp, instead of taking her information to Ken Starr, had taken it to the Chinese embassy? For all we know, the Chinese may have known all about Monica Lewinsky long before the affair went public and used it as leverage against Clinton. That may account for the sloppy manner in which his administration handled sensitive material that ended up in the hands of the Chinese.

The point is, infidelity can greatly compromise people in office. Ironically, some of our leaders were conspicuously quiet during the Lewinsky scandal. As it turned out, some had a lot to be quiet about.

Former Speaker of the House Newt Gingrich finally fessed up to having an affair with a congressional aide twenty years his junior even while he was pursuing impeachment against Clinton. He told *Focus on the Family*'s James Dobson in 2007, "I drew a line in my mind that said, 'Even though I run the risk of being deeply embarrassed, and even though at a purely personal level I am not rendering judgment on another human being, as a leader of the government trying to uphold the rule of law, I have no choice except to move forward and say that you cannot accept . . . perjury in your highest officials.'"[7] Gingrich rationalized his character flaw as something irrelevant to the whole Clinton scandal. He's correct in that Clinton elevated his own transgression by lying under oath. But Larry Flynt was sniffing around Washington with his dirt diggers, and those who had something to hide were getting nervous.

Here's a footnote to the Clinton impeachment trial. I was actually called to Washington to discuss some information I had discovered with the House managers who were conducting the trial. The point I made to the House managers was simple, but everyone had overlooked it. The big question was whether or not the president's conduct rose to the level of an impeachable offense. The Constitution states that a president can be removed from office upon conviction of "treason, bribery, or other high crimes and misdemeanors." I pulled the sentencing guidelines from the Justice Department and found that perjury ranked higher in terms of severity than bribery, which is listed in the Constitution. It stands to reason that if bribery is an impeachable offense then anything more severe would be impeachable too.

I shared my discovery in a House managers meeting the day before the impeachment trial started in the Senate. The night before the last day of the trial, I received a call from Florida Congressman Bill McCollum. He had an attorney for the House managers on the line with us. They told me that they had investigated my little tidbit of information and that I was right. They were very excited about this revelation and would be presenting it the next day at the trial. Much to my chagrin, when McCollum began to address the matter, he rambled on about geese landing on the reflection pool of the Capitol and other such flowery notions and his time expired before he could make the point I had shared with him. Shortly after that, the trial was abruptly called to a halt and a vote was taken. Clinton was acquitted on the charges of perjury and obstruction of justice. Two months later, however, Clinton was cited by Federal District Judge Susan Webber Wright for civil contempt of court for his "willful failure" to tell the truth during the Paula Jones sexual harassment lawsuit. In other words, Clinton had lied under oath and should have been convicted by the Senate. We'll never know if the information I presented to the House managers would've made a difference. I think it's safe to say that the skeletons in the closets of some lawmakers corrupted the process, making an even stronger case for why a politician's character is so important.

The political landscape is littered with fatally flawed elected officials whose personal life finally caught up with them. President Warren Harding, who oversaw one of the most corrupt administrations in the history of our republic, was known to have had affairs with at least two different women. One, a German sympathizer during World War I, blackmailed him. She reportedly was paid off by the Republican Party.[8]

It's impossible to know how many commanders in chief had their private lives used against them. Consequently, it's equally difficult to assess the damage caused by infidelity. It wasn't until years after his death that Jack Kennedy's sexual indiscretions and alleged links to organized crime—and the ways in which they compromised his presidency—came to light. One point is clear, however. JFK's reckless private life ultimately affected judgments he made as president.

Thomas C. Reeves, a then-supporter of Kennedy and author of the book *A Question of Character* (1991), wrote: "Given the facts now available, it is clear that Kennedy abused his high position for personal self-gratification. His reckless liaisons with women and mobsters were irresponsible, dangerous, and demeaning to the office of the chief executive. They were irresponsible because of the enormous potential for scandal and blackmail they posed. Had Kennedy lived to see a second term, the realities of his lechery and his dealings with Sam Giancana (Mafia boss) might have leaked out. Impeachment might well have followed such public disclosure. The real Kennedy . . . lacked greatness in large part because he lacked the qualities inherent in good character."[9]

A Sign of Things to Come

But the peril of compromise isn't the only reason character is important in a leader. Character flaws are warning signs of deeper trouble. For instance, Gennifer Flowers was the proverbial canary in the coal mine for this nation in the Clinton administration. Richard Nixon gained fame by prosecuting Alger Hiss in the famed Pumpkin Papers case. Accounts of some of Nixon's comments during that period displayed an insatiable appetite for power long before Watergate, an indication that he might take drastic measures to maintain his grip. Warren Harding's immoral personal life had a profound effect on his presidency. His poor judgment brought down an entire administration. Presidential train wrecks rarely happen in a vacuum. They are years, often lifetimes, in the making.

Nixon's insecurities about the 1972 election ultimately cost him the presidency. He ended up winning by 520 electoral votes to George McGovern's 17, hence the Watergate break-in didn't need to happen. We may never know "what the president knew and when he knew it" regarding the actual break-in, but we do know that he went to great lengths to cover it up. As is often the case, the cover-up became more of a crime than the actual crime being covered up. It just proved once again that leaders who are corrupt to the core will do anything to stay in power.

Warren Harding's infidelity was a harbinger of things to come in his administration. He surrounded himself with seedy and unscrupulous men who came to be known as "the Ohio Gang." Some of these men, old drinking buddies, actually, did jail time for defrauding the government. The Teapot Dome scandal became the undoing of his administration. Harding, by executive order, had transferred control of the naval oil reserves at Teapot Dome, Wyoming, and Elk Hills, California, from the Navy Department to the Department of the Interior. Without first seeking competitive bids, Albert Fall, Harding's secretary of the interior, leased the Teapot Dome fields to oilman Harry Sinclair and the field at Elk Hills to a man named Edward Doheny.

These deals became the subject of a Senate investigation that discovered that Doheny had loaned Secretary Fall $100,000 interest free. When Fall retired, Harry Sinclair also loaned him a large sum of money. Of course "loan" is a loose interpretation. The Senate determined they were bribes. Fall was convicted of accepting bribes and sentenced to a year in the pokey and fined $100,000. Sinclair beat the bribe rap but was sentenced to prison for contempt of the Senate along with the nasty practice of employing detectives to tail members of the jury in his case. The oil fields were eventually restored to the U.S. government by the Supreme Court.[10]

Harding was never accused of any wrongdoing, primarily, I suppose, because he died before the investigation was completed. While on a Western tour to defuse the controversy, he got food poisoning, which triggered a lethal stroke, though some suspect he was actually poisoned by his wife. No, she wasn't rumored to have killed him because of his affairs, which lasted until his death. Like some Greek tragedy, the buzz of the day rumored that Flossie, Harding's wife, had offed him to save him from embarrassment by the Teapot Dome scandal.

Like Nixon, Clinton's efforts to cover up his boorish behavior were more serious than his initial transgressions. Underscoring just how corrupt our political system has become, Bill Clinton would have been convicted in his impeachment trial had it not been for certain senators with character flaws of their own. The threat of their exposure in effect emasculated these lawmakers, rendering them impotent in our nation's quest for justice. The fact that Clinton was found in contempt of court in the Paula Jones matter *after* the impeachment trial confirmed the very guilt the House managers had argued before the Senate. The Senate's lame excuse of not wanting to put the nation through the removal of a president was a worthless and pathetic attempt to excuse their own incompetence.

When Senator Tom Harkin stopped the trial almost as

it began and admitted to the assembled press corps that the House managers were trying to box them in with the facts, I knew that no more desperate statement had ever been uttered by an elected official. Yet when it came time to make the crucial decision, the Senate did not have the stomach to go in for the kill. One wonders just what Larry Flynt and company had dug up on them. Character, or the lack thereof, had once again altered the course of history.

Looking for Mr. Milquetoast

So, what's the solution? Aristotle wrote in his masterpiece, *Politics,* "Hence the ruler ought to have moral virtue in perfection."[11] Plato's *Republic* suggests that leaders should give up their private property and forgo having families in order to devote their full attention to the common good.[12] Do we demand that our presidents come to us having lived the lives of monks before we allow them to take the oath? Of course not. We should expect our presidents to be human but free of troublesome character flaws that might endanger the nation at some future point.

Refreshingly, George W. Bush admitted his flaws up front. He made it clear from the beginning that he'd once had a drinking problem that he had overcome. (Martin Sheen cried that nobody with a drinking problem could overcome it on his own—the classic liberal dependency mind-set.) When confronted on the eve of the 2000 election with a story of a DUI arrest many years before, Bush quickly faced the music. He made no excuses but fully owned up to the story instead of spinning it or characterizing it as a dirty trick cooked up by his opponents, which, of course, it was. That's all the public expects from its president: someone human enough to have a reasonable number of skeletons in his or her closet and enough character to learn from those mistakes.

Lack of Character Kills the Candidate

Al Gore, as he ran for president in 2000, dodged and denied his wrongdoing in the Buddhist temple scandal. Buddhist monks who had vowed a life of poverty were suddenly coughing up a thousand dollars a head. When it came to illegal White House fund-raising, Gore claimed that "no controlling legal authority" prohibited him from raising campaign money from his vice presidential office. No controlling legal authority? What the heck does that mean? His misdeeds and subsequent lying to cover them up came back to bite him in the buttocks in the 2000 presidential election. With a good economy—although it was already beginning to falter—along with the incumbency advantage, Gore should have blistered Bush. Instead, he lost the election in a squeaker that took weeks to untangle.

I'm convinced the agony Gore had to endure during the excruciating period of endless chad inspections was the direct result of his bad karma. It certainly was not lost on Gore that Florida's recount would have been a moot point had he won his so-called home state of Tennessee. Those who knew him best, however, liked him least, and Tennesseans sent a loud message to Gore and to the nation that he could no longer be trusted. The man who had dreamt of being president from birth could only watch as the Holy Grail of politics was snatched from his grasp for one simple reason: character.

Gore's lack of character is peculiar in the sense that he lied even when he didn't need to. Perhaps he was just practicing or trying to keep up with his boss. Maybe there was a lie quota that the Clinton administration wanted to meet. Gore's résumé, whether you liked him or not, was impressive enough without having to embellish it. When he told CNN reporter Wolf Blitzer that while in Congress he "took the initiative in creating the Internet," he demonstrated that he was willing to lie just for the heck of it. Maybe he was suffering from an inferiority complex, living in Clinton's shadow. Who knows?

The lying continued almost up until the eleventh hour of the 2000 campaign, with Gore claiming that his mother-in-law paid three times as much for the same arthritis medicine he gave his dog. The story was totally made up.[13] He also claimed to a group of union members that his mother had rocked him to sleep as a tot singing a famous union song, which he then proceeded to sing. The only trouble was, the song was written for a television campaign when Gore was twenty-seven.

Who can forget the most egregious and shameless lie Gore ever told? It was during the 1996 Democratic convention. I was there covering it for my station. Gore gave one of the most emotional speeches I've ever heard. Hardly a dry eye remained in the building as he recounted his sister's agonizing death from lung cancer, the result of years of smoking. Gore claimed that upon his sister's death in 1984, he vowed to dedicate his life to antismoking efforts. Yet four years after her death, as he made his first run for the White House, Gore bragged to tobacco farmers about how he worked in tobacco as a young man. He solicited, and got, thousands of dollars from the tobacco companies and continued to raise the crop on his family farm. Some antismoking effort.

Fortunately, the American people saw through the lies, and we were spared a Gore presidency in 2000. He promised to come home to Tennessee to "mend fences." But his idea of mending fences was to buy a $1 million-plus residence in one of the richest neighborhoods in the country, Belle Meade in Nashville. Democratic candidates in Tennessee ran from him in 2002. Later that year he announced that he would not be a candidate for president in 2004. Obviously, he was paying attention to the polls that showed even the hard-core Democratic infatuation with him had died.

Gore has reinvented himself in recent years. (I guess if he can reinvent the Internet, he can do the same for himself.) His Academy Award and Nobel Peace Prize have raised his stature in the eyes of many. Yet these accolades were based on lies too. (We'll explore that in more detail in our junk science chapter.) He's certainly not finished as a public figure and has, in fact, enjoyed much more respect than he likely would've garnered as a former president. Although his deception may have cost him the presidency, it has paid off in the long run. It can certainly be argued that he became much better at it. Maybe he took the advice of the late comedian George Burns, who said, "Acting is all about honesty. If you can fake that, you've got it made."

4

DRUG LEGALIZATION will cripple America.

THERE HAS BEEN A movement afoot for quite some time now to legalize drugs in America. What may surprise you is that a number of conservatives have advocated legalizing drugs as a means of reducing the crime associated with them. This is one of the few points on which I disagree with the Libertarian Party. (Another is the legalization of prostitution.) Some might say that a Libertarian is actually a conservative who likes to smoke pot. There may be a measure of truth to that, but most Libertarians merely want less government interference in their lives. The legalization proponents, Libertarian and otherwise, call drug use a *victimless crime* and point out all the problems associated with locking up people for something that will only destroy the user. Some of these advocates of drug legalization would have you believe that we have to try something else because our war on drugs has been a dismal failure. Let's look at the facts, and you decide if the current approach qualifies as a failure.

In 1979, more than 14.1 percent of Americans had used an illicit drug at least once during the previous thirty days. By 2006, that figure had dropped to just 8.3 percent, with the vast majority of that being marijuana use.[1] The same survey showed that 16.3 percent of youth aged twelve to seventeen were users of illicit drugs in 1979. That figure had been reduced to 5.3 by 1992. However, usage rose through the 1990s to 10.9 percent in 1999, still far below its high-water mark in 1979. By 2006, it had dropped to 9.8 percent. Again, the vast majority of that group (6.7 percent) was marijuana use. I don't know what yardstick you use to measure success, but it would stand to reason that when drug use is cut in half and clearly more than 90 percent of your citizens don't use them, you're *winning* the war on drugs.

Many people scoffed at Nancy Reagan's Just Say No campaign, but it had a real impact on the youth of America. In 1979, the percentage of kids ages twelve to seventeen who had *ever* used an illicit drug stood at 31.8 percent. By 1992, that number had been cut by more than half, to 15.1 percent. The Clinton administration put the youth drug problem on the back burner. Subsequently, the percentage of kids ages twelve to seventeen who had ever used an illicit drug climbed to 23.7 percent by 1997.[2] The number of Americans over the age of twelve who had used drugs in the previous thirty days plummeted from 14.1 percent in 1979 to 5.8 percent in 1992. It's crystal clear that the war on drugs, when waged with a combination of tough law enforcement, sound education, and strong leadership, can and does have a major effect on the problem.

Speaking of leadership—or the lack thereof—remember when Bill Clinton said he'd tried pot but didn't inhale? It became the butt of jokes across the country. Instead of dealing with the issue honestly, in a way that would encourage young people to stay away from the stuff, Clinton tried to dodge a political arrow with an answer that was, well, less than credible. Our young people got the message. Between 1991 and 1998, previous-month pot use among high school seniors jumped from 13.8 percent to 22.8 percent. Among tenth-graders, usage rose from 8.7 percent to 18.7 percent, a 215 percent increase. Eighth-graders' previous-month pot use skyrocketed more than 300 percent, from 3.2 percent to 9.7 percent![3] Yes, people may have made fun of Nancy Reagan's approach, but the facts show that it got results. The facts also show that a lack of leadership results in a substantial increase in the problem.

Drugs vs. Alcohol

Once confronted with the truth about the war on drugs, the fallback line of many in the prolegalization camp is that alcohol does far more damage than illegal drugs. They then point out that alcohol is a drug and we legalized it. Why not be fair and legalize all drugs? I'm not going to argue that alcohol is not destructive, because it certainly can be, but there are several problems with the alcohol-versus-drugs argument. First of all, in the case of alcohol, that toothpaste is already out of the tube and there's no putting it back. We tried that, remember? It was called

Prohibition. Too many people had gotten a taste of the spirits and they wanted it back. Second, if we legalize drugs, we will expose them to millions of people who, otherwise, would never have touched them.

Having gone to high school in the 1970s, I'm not naive about the lure of drugs. Most of my friends were smoking pot on a regular basis, but I never got involved. I credit a strong family influence for most of that, but I claim at least partial responsibility for having enough sense not to do it. However, it stands to reason that if you expose more people to drugs, more people will use them, especially if they're legal. Keep in mind that more than 90 percent of Americans haven't used drugs in the past thirty days. There's a good reason for that. Most people have never laid eyes on drugs in person, for starters. The strongest deterrent, however, is that they're illegal and most people aren't curious enough to risk going to jail.

The third, and most important, reason why drugs should not be legalized is that they're much more addictive than alcohol. Don't believe me? Consider this: in 2006, 125 million Americans had consumed alcohol in the previous thirty days and 17 million Americans were hooked on or abused booze. That's an addiction and abuse rate of about 14 percent. Now, consider that in that same year 20.4 million Americans took an illicit drug in the previous thirty days, yet 3.8 million were hooked. That's an addiction rate close to 20 percent. Cocaine users were addicted at a rate of about 75 percent. Heroin users were addicted at a rate of 95 percent.[4] In other words, cocaine users were five and a half times more likely to get hooked than alcohol users, and heroin users were almost seven times more likely to become addicted.

Let me put it another way: If the same number of people who had tried alcohol in 2006 had also tried heroine or cocaine, instead of just 1.7 million coke heads in this country, we'd have 94 million. Instead of 323,000 heroin addicts, we'd have almost 119 million! The devastation would be enormous.

Legalization **Won't** Solve the Problem

The notion that there would be less crime if we legalized drugs is counterintuitive. Sure, there would be no more drug arrests because drugs would no longer be illegal, but that's like saying there wouldn't be a problem with bank robbery if we just legalized it. The problem wouldn't just vanish. In fact, it would get much worse, only there would be no law to stop it. Understand that the arrest itself is not the problem. People look at drug busts on TV and say that if we legalize drugs, we won't have anymore of that. They are looking at the *arrest* as the problem when, in fact, a drug arrest is part of the *solution* to the problem.

Drug use—and its devastation on the individual and society—will only get worse with drug legalization. Previous-year illicit drug users are sixteen times more likely than non-drug users to be arrested for larceny or theft.[5] (Incidentally, alcohol users are only nine times more likely to steal.) People who steal to buy drugs, by and large, are not the most productive people in society. More than a quarter of the inmates in state prisons doing time for robbery committed their crimes to buy drugs. Nearly a third of the convicted burglars committed their crimes to buy drugs.[6]

Some argue that the price of illegal drugs would come down considerably if they were legalized. That's probably not true. Cigarettes are cheaper on the black market than at the corner convenience store. The legal ones are more expensive, and part of the reason is because cigarette taxes are so high. But let's say, for the sake of argument, that prices went down. How low is cheap enough for somebody with no money? For people hooked on drugs, many of whom don't have jobs, the price of drugs is inconsequential. If they cost anything at all, many would have to steal to buy them.

Now, let's go back to the example earlier in this chapter of the potential number of addicts America would have to contend with if drugs were legalized. Current data show that roughly 1.2 million people are hooked on cocaine or heroin.[7] Consider how many more robberies and burglaries there would be if we had 213 million addicts on the street![8] Does this sound like a victimless crime now?

The Solution

So, what is the solution to the drug problem? First, let's put the problem in perspective. Contrary to popular belief, not everyone is doing drugs. The good news is, as I stated before, more than 90 percent of us do not use drugs on a regular basis. That leaves less than 10 percent of the population to deal with, which is roughly 30 million people. A sizable chunk, no doubt, but not an epidemic by any stretch of the imagination. Still, the widespread repercussions push way beyond the boundaries of the self-inflicted addict. Crime touches us all. Many innocent people are robbed or killed in crimes related to drugs. Those of us who aren't direct victims become indirectly affected when we must alter our daily activities because of fears for our own safety. Our loss of freedom is in direct proportion to the rise in crime. Much more must be done.

There are two fronts on which the drug problem can be attacked: the supply side and the demand side. We should certainly stiffen penalties on the demand side, but the real focus should be on supply. Right now, the median sentence for drug trafficking in a state court is just sixteen months behind bars.[9] That's barely over a year—for drug trafficking! That doesn't count all the guys who brought enough high-powered legal talent to court to get them off. U.S. District Court is more heavy-handed with drug traffickers. The median prison sentence there is fifty-seven months.[10] Even so, they're not heavy-handed enough. The only way to come close to eliminating the problem is to get serious about putting drug peddlers away.

My solution is this: mandatory sentencing of six months at hard labor for the first offense of felony drug trafficking. During that six-month period those convicted would work from sunrise to sundown, turning big rocks into little rocks, digging ditches, or performing similar tasks. No cable TV. No girlie magazines. No workouts in the gym. Just hard labor. You have a lot of time to think when you're digging a ditch.

Second-offense felony drug traffickers would face a mandatory sentence of life in prison. It's that simple. No plea bargains. No reduced sentences. No more chances. When first-time offenders leave the big house after their six-month ordeal, it would be explained to them in no un-certain terms that what they just endured will be their life if they screw up again. They would return with absolutely no chance of ever leaving. You can bet there would be very little recidivism. Unfortunately, many lawmakers are too squeamish to enact such tough laws. Some argue that we don't have enough prisons to hold all the drug criminals. But if we get this tough, we won't need more prisons, we'll need fewer.

Put yourself in the shoes of a young drug-dealer-in-training. He sees the drug dealer with the fancy car and the cool clothes, and it all looks rather appealing to him. When the dealer gets busted, he's right back out on the street. No consequences, right? Well, what would happen if the guy never came back? Or, if it's his first arrest, what would happen when he comes back after six months with a horror story about the hell he's been through? It would-n't take long before the young drug dealer wannabe gets the message. He'd learn that there actually *are* consequences to his actions.

Right now, the fortune outweighs the risk. But when the risk begins to outweigh the fortune, you'll see a lot fewer people willing to enter the drug-dealing business. That means a lot fewer people getting arrested and a lot fewer people in prison.

Law Enforcement Corruption

Something that serves to undermine the whole war on drugs is police corruption. Drug cartels manage to get to police officers and drug enforcement agents, eating away at the infrastructure of law enforcement like a cancer. Punishment needs to be swift and severe. Any law enforcement officer convicted of taking a bribe should be sentenced to a minimum of ten years in prison. No exceptions. Right now, officers face no more than three years in prison,[11] with countless ways to plea bargain and wiggle out of the sentence. Similar consequences should await the guard who facilitates the use of drugs inside a prison. As it now stands, such offenders face only twelve to eighteen months in prison.[12]

There's nothing sorrier than a bad cop, someone who has gained the public's trust enough to be given a badge and then betrays that trust. A bad cop is the proverbial fox guarding the hen house. Our society should send a loud and clear message to anyone with designs on taking advantage of us that we take a very dim view of it. In fact, I wouldn't have a problem with sending these cops to the same work camp as the drug dealers for the first six months of their sentence. They can serve the rest in a maximum-security facility—if they survive the first six months.

It's all about our level of tolerance, and if we resolve ourselves to be intolerant of police corruption, it will change. If we turn a blind eye, it won't. Until then, we can't expect a whole lot from the folks inside the prison if those who put them there and those guarding them aren't any better. The same goes for judges or any officer of the court, for that matter. If you corrupt the process, you should suffer the consequences. This problem is much too important to tolerate anything less.

The Cost of Legalization

Finally, let's consider the cost of legalizing drugs. The pro-legalization crowd points to the enormous expense of waging war on drugs. The federal government spends more than $14 billion per year,[13] a considerable amount of money, but let's imagine an America with legalized drugs. With government sanctioning, prices would go down and drugs would be much more readily available, so without question, drug use would rise.

Currently, we know that drug and alcohol abusers are five times more likely to file a worker's compensation claim. They incur 300 percent more health-care costs than nonusers. They're a third less productive and absent from work three times as much.[14] All of this costs money. The actual monetary cost to society is enormous, surpassing $97 billion, and almost half of that burden falls on the back of the U.S. government. Translation: that's you and me, our tax dollars. Costs include drug-related crimes and trauma (such as motor vehicle crashes), as well as government services like criminal justice and highway safety. Not to mention the various social insurance mechanisms, such as private and public health insurance, life insurance, tax payments, pensions, and social welfare insurance.[15]

That's almost $100 billion a year wasted because less than 10 percent of the population uses drugs on a regular basis. Most of that group is made up of pot abusers. The heroin and cocaine abusers make up less than 1 percent each, and that's where most of the expense is incurred. So we have $14 billion for the war on drugs compared to $97 billion in damage caused *by* drugs. It's not too difficult to see how that $97 billion price tag will balloon if the other 90-some percent of Americans are exposed to drugs. In 1979, more than twice as many Americans were using drugs. Double that $97 billion figure and it becomes more and more evident that the war on drugs is a bargain. It's also crystal clear that legalizing them would spell disaster for America.

5

ENTREPRENEURS are our economic lifeblood and deserve every penny they make.

CLASS WARFARE. IT'S BECOME the weapon of choice for the left-wing crowd. Class warfare is nothing new. In fact, it dates back thousands of years, even to Joseph and his coat of many colors. It's jealousy, pure and simple, and it's such a powerful, consuming emotion that it is easily exploited. We've all fallen victim to it. A colleague gets the promotion that should've been yours. A neighbor trades up to a new car that should've been yours. It's one of the baser instincts, like fear, which the political Left has learned to wield like a mighty sword to slice the electorate in half.

Wealth is attained in many ways. Some inherit it. Some hit it big in the entertainment business or professional sports. But few are loathed more by the Left than the entrepreneur who strikes it rich. Entrepreneurs leave the cozy confines of the office and the health insurance package behind to follow the dream of being their own boss. If they have a vision and work hard, then maybe, just maybe, they can strike it rich. It's the final American frontier, in many ways, and the leftists would prefer to keep it untouched.

The Richest Man Enriched Us All

Bill Gates and Paul Allen were two such entrepreneurs who started out together in 1975. The two of them devised BASIC, the first programming language written for a personal computer. That same year they opened up their first retail store in Los Angeles. In 1976, they registered the name Microsoft and formed a partnership. In the next few years they produced several software packages, one winning the ICP Million Dollar Award. IBM came to them in 1981 and asked them to develop MS-DOS, to be used on the company's soon-to-be-released "personal computer." Paul Allen resigned from Microsoft in 1983 and Gates continued to steer the ship through the uncharted waters of the PC software business. In its eleventh year, Microsoft launched Windows and, shortly after, went public. Within a few years Bill Gates had become the richest man in the world.

Imagine for a moment what the world would be like had Gates and Allen *not* started that little company back in 1975. They had no idea how successful they would be or even *if* they would be successful, but the world is undoubtedly richer for their efforts. This book was written on a computer driven by Windows software, for instance. Most computer users can accomplish their day-to-day tasks much more easily and much faster because of Microsoft. Bill Gates is hated by many for the billions of dollars he's earned, but it is impossible to calculate the impact that Microsoft has had on the world economy.

Punishing Microsoft, as the Clinton administration so viciously tried to do, also punished our nation's economy. I believe the economic downturn that began in 2001 was at least exacerbated by—if not caused by—the relentless pursuit of Microsoft by the Clinton Justice Department. Because the left-wingers couldn't stand that Bill Gates had become so wealthy, they tried to bring him down and, in the process, damaged our economy, which had a ripple effect around the world.

In the end, who do you think was harmed by the Microsoft witch hunt? Oh, Bill Gates may have lost a few hundred million, but he still has billions to spare. The people who were hurt most were those who live on the margin of our economy. Those are the people who were thrown out of work. This is always the case when government tries to punish people for getting rich. Ironically, Gates is a Democrat and has given to many left-wing causes. It's rather amusing, isn't it? The Kennedys, whose fortune was made in bootleg whiskey, are acceptable rich folks, but Gates is not.

The Hypocrisy of Limousine Liberals

Think it's easy being an entrepreneur? Consider this: between 1990 and 1997, businesses were going belly-up at a rate of nearly seventy-nine thousand per year.[1] We're talking about one of the best economic periods this country has ever seen, yet almost seventy-nine thousand businesses bit the dust. That's a lot of folks just like you and me who took a chance on "the next big thing" and fell flat on their faces. Most of us will never have the guts to try it, yet many of us resent those who *do* try and succeed. These naysayers play right into the hands of the class-warfare provocateurs.

Speaking of such, on Election Day 2000, I got a call on-air from Rob Reiner, the activist actor most famous for his portrayal of "Meathead" on *All in the Family*. Apparently Al Gore's pollsters could see the handwriting on the wall and knew they were about to lose his home state. In a futile act of desperation they sicced Reiner and Cher on me. Reiner began ranting about how the rich should be made to pay their "fair share." I noted that they were already required to give a greater percentage of their hard-earned money to the government than the average taxpayer, but that point had no chance of rising above the din of his righteous indignation. Here was a man who was reared in the lap of Hollywood luxury and handed life's riches on a silver platter, and he talked about the rich as if they were someone else.

One question became obvious. At a rare moment when Reiner took a breath from his hysterical harangue, I attempted to raise it. I asked him—in all seriousness—why he didn't form a movement in Hollywood to give away everything to the government, since bigger government seemed to be his answer for everything, leaving just enough to live a modest lifestyle. He boiled over with rage at the suggestion and screamed that Hollywood was the most giving community on the planet, then slammed down the phone. Obviously, I had hit a nerve, but he missed the point entirely.

There certainly are many generous wealthy people who give to their favorite charities. That was my point, exactly. These charities are so much more efficient in helping the people who really need it than the government is. Why groan and moan that the government needs more money when private charities do a much better job of taking care of the less fortunate?

The Nashville Rescue Mission, one of my favorite charities, does remarkable work with the homeless. As is the case in most other cities, drug and alcohol addiction play a large part in the plight of the homeless. The mission understands that you have to change the entire person to solve the problem, not just treat the symptoms. It requires each homeless person to attend a church service in order to receive a free meal and a place to stay overnight. Some on the left have accused the mission of violating the rights of the homeless by placing such conditions on its services. However, nobody has a *right* to a free meal and a bed. Right off the bat, the Nashville Rescue Mission teaches that you don't get something for nothing.

Homeless men and women have the option of enrolling in the mission's program, which instills in them a sense of self-worth, teaches them the skills they need to return to normal society, and helps them stay clean and sober by establishing a lasting relationship with God. One of my dear friends went through the program. It literally saved his life. The moral of the story is, the mission does this miraculous work without a dime from the government. It has positively confounded the liberals.

If the government would quit picking our pockets every time we turn around, then more money could be given to the charities that are so effective in helping with society's problems. It seems that Rob Reiner, of all people, would understand that fact, but instead, he insisted that the people who actually drive the economy and create the wealth in this country should have more of their money confiscated to feed an unwieldy, bloated government.

Good Ol' Yankee Ingenuity

The Rob Reiners of the world haven't the foggiest notion as to what really makes this country tick. It's the Edisons and the Fords and the Gateses who make this country great. If you look closely at the important advances in technology over the past hundred years or so, you'll find the vast majority of those advances are the result of *American* entrepreneurs. Why is that? Is it because Americans are genetically superior? No. Many of these entrepreneurs had just immigrated to this great land with barely more than the shirts on their backs when they struck it rich. What allowed them to succeed is America's unique system of government, a system whereby you can dream, create, and build—and still keep most of what you earn.

To borrow a line from the movie *Wall Street*, "Greed is good." As crass as that may sound, greed is basically the oil of the entrepreneurial engine. Perhaps it's more palatable if we call it ambition. Whatever you call it, it's what drove the people en masse to dig for gold, which in turn led to the development of California. It's what made Texas the oil capital of the country. It's what built the computer age and the Internet. A dream of success with limited government intrusion—that's what makes America a beacon to the world.

Still, there are some who've made their fortunes in this country who then turn to bite the hand that feeds them. One glaring example is Ted Turner. Turner took over his father's billboard business, which was badly in debt, and turned it into a winner. With that capital, he was able to build his empire. First a couple of television stations, a sports franchise, then CNN.

I worked for one of Turner's TV stations prior to CNN. Back then I would've sworn Ted was a conservative. Something happened along the way. Maybe it was Jane Fonda. Maybe it was rich man's guilt. Whatever it was, it transformed Ted into a socialist. You think that's too harsh? Here's what he told a gathering in Shanghai in late 1999: "I'm a socialist at heart." He then went on to castigate Oracle Corporation chairman Larry Ellison for his yachts. "I'd rather use money for the benefit of mankind rather than spend it selfishly," Turner admonished.[2] Hold the phone! Doesn't Ted own yachts? Doesn't Ted own multimillion-dollar homes and a gazillion acres in Montana, Nebraska, South Dakota, and New Mexico? In fact, he's the largest private landowner in the country!

Speaking of that, Mr. Socialist, who is worth about $2.3 billion,[3] coughed up a measly $500 donation to a volunteer fire department that fought a blazing forest fire that consumed some twenty-six thousand acres, mostly on ol' Ted's Nebraska ranch. The fight cost the fire department about $42,000 in wear and tear on equipment.[4] Typical of left-wingers, Ted is rather selective when it comes to giving. He gave $1 billion to the United Nations to spend on furthering another Turner passion, one-world government, but he could only manage $500 for the folks who saved his ranch. Go figure.

People ask me on my radio show what the difference is between socialism and communism. My response is usually, "The firing squad." Although that's not too far from the truth, the real difference is the degree of government control. Communism's control is absolute. Socialism's control is pervasive but just short of smothering. The reason Ted Turner—and other wealthy leftists, for that matter—have such an affinity for socialism is because there is always a ruling class and they intend to be part of it. You see, if America had been a socialist nation back in the '70s, Ted would never have been able to amass his vast fortune. Now that he has, it's easy to extol the virtues of socialism.

If Turner and his rich socialist friends were true socialists, they would give their worldly goods to the government and let it run their lives. Instead, they want to rule
the socialist government. Ted Turner may look altruistic,
and he may feel great about himself for giving $1 billion
to the UN, but he still has more than $2 billion left,
hardly a socialist's pension. I suspect Ted's real initial motivation for cozying up to the one-worlders was to get CNN
into every corner of the globe. Although he no longer controls the network, it's still a matter of pride with him.
Dealing with all those irritating governments has become
a hassle. It would be much easier to do business with a single world government.

The "Finite Money" Argument

When I was doing talk radio in Philadelphia, I worked
with a guy who genuinely believed that there was a finite
amount of money in this country; thus, anybody who got
rich was doing so by taking money away from the poor.
I'm serious. He truly believed this—and he's not alone.
There are countless Americans who actually think that they
are poor just because Bill Gates came in and ran off with all
the money. Not that I need to convince you, because if
you're reading this book, you obviously have more sense
than that, but just to make the point, consider the poverty
level. It has remained pretty steady over the last thirty years,
yet Gates was able to rise from nothing to be one of the
richest men on earth and the poverty rate hardly budged.

The very fact that inflation exists deflates these folks' argument. If there's a finite amount of money, then how could a salary of thirty thousand dollars in 1990 be worth almost thirty-five thousand dollars five years later? A new car in the early 1900s cost about six hundred dollars. Try getting a new car for that today. So if everybody's making more and everything costs more, how can there be a finite amount of money?

A lot of this nonsense comes from people who are too lazy to get off their own rear ends, so they make excuses as to why they haven't made it. These are the same malcontents who sit around bellyaching about the boss instead of trying to *be* the boss. The truth is, being the boss entails more work than they're willing to do. I saw an interview with Bill Cosby once. He was asked if he thought he'd been lucky. He said, "Yeah, and the harder I work, the luckier I get."

Those who buy into the "finite money" argument are looking at currency as the wealth when currency is only a symbol of the wealth. You can be filthy rich and never see a dollar. Let me explain. If I draw a fifty-thousand-dollar-a-month paycheck from a company and it's direct-deposited into my bank account, then I buy a house full of new furniture with my credit card and they draft my bank account for the furniture, do I have new furniture in my home? Yep. Did any hard currency exchange hands? Nope. Am I rich? You bet. Even though my wealth, in this example, is on paper, it's the general agreement that those figures on that paper have value that makes the whole process work.

Entrepreneurs are indeed our country's economic lifeblood. They take the risks. They may get rich, they may go broke, they may land somewhere in between. If it were a sure thing, everyone would be doing it. It's those people with a dream and a burning desire to make it come true who provide opportunities not only for themselves but also for the many people they will employ if their dream becomes reality. America is great because of the entrepreneur, and the entrepreneur is great because of America. We aren't *guaranteed* the right to happiness in this country, but we're sure guaranteed the right to *pursue* it. Instead of trying to find ways to dismantle entrepreneurs once they've made it, we should allow them to reap more of the fruits of their labor. It's those fruits that encourage other entrepreneurs. If we are to survive and flourish as a country, then we *must* encourage them. If we *discourage* them, our days as a prosperous and free nation are numbered.

6

FAMILIES are the basic building blocks of society.

THE "AVERAGE FAMILY" THAT used to dominate network television sitcoms is no more. It's sad but true. Ozzie and Harriet, Lucy and Ricky, Rob and Laura—they're now the exception rather than the rule. Don't blame Hollywood. Most of the TV sitcom families still consist of mom, dad, and the kids. The reality is, the vast majority of families no longer look like that. Get ready for a cold slap in the face. Fewer than 25 percent of families consist of a father, mother, and a child or children.[1] Fewer than 25 percent! That startling statistic should frighten us all, regardless of our marital status. Is there something wrong with a person just because he or she has gone through a divorce? Of course not, but a happy, sustaining marriage is something we should all at least *aim* for if our society is going to survive.

In addition to the chilling stats on divorce, the number of couples "living in sin" has skyrocketed since the days of Ward and June. In 1960, there were roughly 439,000 cohabiting couples in the United States. By

2008, that number was more than 5 million. Today, more than half of all couples that marry live together first. Between 1965 and 1974 that number was less than 10 percent. Ah, but living together will help ensure a stronger marriage, right? That's what many people think. Or, maybe that's what many men convince women is true, but it just ain't so. That old cliché of trying on the shoes before you buy them doesn't hold water. More than 67 percent of cohabitating couples who eventually tie the knot end up in divorce court compared with 45 percent of all first marriages. Those who talk themselves into shackin' up will argue that they're just as much a family as a married couple, but living together does not a family make.[2] When there is no legal commitment, this so-called family is just one argument away from disintegrating. Those who maintain that they don't want to get married because marriage will ruin the relationship are spewing hogwash. If you're not willing to make a long-term commitment, you're fooling yourself (or your mate) about just what kind of relationship you're in.

Believe it or not, the commitment is not about you. It's about your mate and any children you might bring into the family. Think back to when you were a child. What was the most important thing to you? Security, right? We all crave security, and a legal commitment provides a good measure of it. I remember thinking that nothing would ever change. I thought my parents would always be there. I thought my parents' friends would always be there. I thought my little town would always be there, unchanged. If you were one of the unfortunate ones who had to live through your parents' divorce when you were young, you know what I'm talking about. All of a sudden, things aren't as etched in stone as you thought. My mother's sudden death when I was twenty-one was my wake-up call. Although I was an adult, I was still clinging to the security of consistency.

A legal, marriage commitment offers security to your mate and your children. You might think a verbal promise is just as binding, but in reality it's not. If your best friend borrowed fifteen thousand dollars from you, would you accept a verbal promise to pay it back? Even if you answered yes, you have to admit that you'd sleep better at night if there were a signed agreement between the two of you. Not that anything would happen to cause you to lose that money, but the contract provides a certain level of security.

Some things are unavoidable. Sometimes divorce is one of them, but there's no question that children are better off when their parents patch things up and stay together. If you don't believe that, check out the shelves of your local library. They're brimming with books on how children can cope with divorce. Aside from the obvious emotional advantage of mom and dad staying together, there are just some things kids get from one parent that they can't get from the other. That doesn't mean that one parent is deficient. It merely means that men and women bring different attributes into child-rearing, just as they do into a marriage. Although an active noncustodial parent can still contribute a lot of that, there's just no substitute for a happy family. The sad fact is, many kids never have the benefit, for even a short period, of having both parents under one roof. They start life, right out of the gate, in a single-parent home.

Illegitimacy Is at the Heart of the Problem

Time was in America when out-of-wedlock births, especially among white women, were almost unheard of. In 1960, just 2.3 percent of all children born were born to white unwed mothers. Oh, how times have changed. During the 1960s, that figure began to climb. By 1999, 26.7 percent of white children were born illegitimate.[3] By 2005 that figure was 31.7 percent. (I've never cared much for the term *illegitimate*, since it insinuates that the innocent child is somehow to blame, when in fact it's the parents who are in the wrong.)

Unfortunately, the news in the black community is even sadder. In 1960, the illegitimacy rate among blacks was 23 percent. By the end of the twentieth century, that number had soared to 68.8 percent. More than two-thirds of black children born in America are born out of wedlock. The silver lining to the black illegitimacy rate is that it has declined a bit since peaking at 70.5 percent in 1994.[4] In 2005, that number was 69.3 percent. Overall, the out-of-wedlock birthrate in the United States is around 37 percent of all births.

It's hard to say how many of these kids born out of wedlock have a father they even know, but it's a good bet that "Dad" didn't stay too close to home. What changed between 1960 and 1999? I have a few theories.

The Sexual Revolution

The first is the so-called sexual revolution of the 1960s. People became more promiscuous during that era. It was the "feel good" generation, and little thought was given to the consequences. "Free love" was the mantra of the sexual-freedom crowd. What a crock that turned out to be. Don't get me wrong. I'm as big a fan of sex as the next guy, but the fundamental premise behind the sexual revolution was fatally flawed.

Freedom never comes without a price, and some paid dearly for their new-found freedom. Divorces began to skyrocket because feeling good took precedence over marital commitment. (There's that word again.) People thought they were finding happiness, but in reality they were merely escaping their humdrum lives for a moment. What they gave up, many for a lifetime, was the security of a monogamous, loving marriage.

Probably the single most important catalyst of the sexual revolution was the oral contraceptive. "The Pill," which was introduced in 1960, was supposed to set women free. Instead, it gave unmarried sexual partners a false sense of security. The darn thing didn't always work or the woman forgot to take it. Dad rationalized that it wasn't *his* fault, so why should he let a little thing like responsibility ruin his life? Besides, he had a career to think about.

Back in my parents' day, there was a considerable amount of shame attached to getting a girl pregnant. In retrospect, shame was a good thing. It caused men to be a little more noble. I look back at some of the friends I had growing up. Once I was old enough to do the math, it wasn't too difficult to figure out that their parents had to make a tough decision once upon a time and they opted for the honorable option of making a go of it as a family. Many of them stayed married their entire lives.

The deep, dark secret that the Left wants to keep hidden—especially the feminists—is that being single is not the source of happiness for many people. Many of the more rabid feminists preach that women don't need men, that men are superfluous and are only needed as sperm donors. This completes their "women are victims" picture, which serves to lure more ladies into their fold. I've got some bad news for them. All of this runs counter to the truth.

Michael Argyle, an Oxford-based psychologist, spent the last twenty years of his life methodically researching what made people happy. Are you ready? The single institution that made the most people happy was marriage.[5] That was followed closely by that second piece of propaganda promulgated by the right wing—church. Oh, yeah. Did I mention that Argyle's research also showed women were happier than men? How can that be? Women are supposed to be victims, the Left says. How dare they be happy, and happily married, to boot. And going to church at the same time. Don't you know the feminists want to keep this information quiet? If this ever gets out, it could ruin them.

Illegitimacy vs. Abortion

My second theory is *Roe v. Wade*. (You knew I'd get to that eventually, didn't you?) If the Pill was the spark that started the fire of the sexual revolution, *Roe v. Wade* was the gasoline. Heck, with that many options there was no reason *not* to have sex, right? Between 1973, when *Roe* was made law, and 1985, the teenage abortion rate went from 23.9 per 1,000 girls under age twenty to 45.4, essentially doubling. Then something interesting happened: the abortion rate began to fall. By 1996, it was back down to 30.3 abortions per 1,000 girls under age twenty.[6] By 2007, the abortion rate was just under 20 abortions per 1,000 girls.

So, what happened? Why the sudden reversal of the trend? Well, during that period the out-of-wedlock birth rate took off. The stigma attached to illegitimacy had begun to melt away. And why not? Everyone from Madonna to Murphy Brown was getting in on the act. It was the "in" thing.

This left conservatives like me in a quandary. Fewer abortions is a good thing but increased illegitimacy is not. You've heard of the dumbing down of America. Well, this was the *numbing* down of America. All of a sudden, women were being praised for keeping their babies, which admittedly is a better option than abortion. But what about the third option? What about keeping the baby *and* getting married?

Now the shoe was on the other foot. It was the woman who was complaining that she had a career to think about and she didn't want to be tied down to a man. Unfortunately, the vast majority of women having children out of wedlock couldn't afford a round-the-clock nanny like Madonna and Murphy Brown had. It's hard enough holding down a job, but holding down a job *and* raising a child alone is more than most people can handle. Something has to give.

Too often, it was the child who suffered. Don't take my word for it. Let's go back to 1960, when the illegitimacy rate was low and the violent-crime rate stood at 16.1 per 10,000 incidents reported. By 1991, that figure was 75.8 violent crimes per 10,000 incidents.[7] Teen suicides rose from 3.8 per 100,000 fifteen- to nineteen-year-olds in 1964 to 11.1 in 1990.[8] I can give you figures until your eyes glaze over, but you get the picture. Indeed, there are many other circumstances that factor into this disturbing jump in the numbers, but common sense will tell you that a father at home would make a difference.

Uncle Sam Became Daddy Sam

My third theory as to why the illegitimacy rate has soared concerns the government, namely, the government has become the de facto dad in many households. It's become routine for many women to turn first to the government instead of to the father when they become pregnant. In too many cases, it's a given that the government will provide food and shelter for the family, relieving the father of any *responsibility*. (There's that word again.) Instead, the government should be tracking down the father and insisting that he take an active role in the life of that child. The government not only doesn't insist on paternal responsibility, it oftentimes discourages it.

When I worked in Philadelphia, I had a black producer. I mention that he was black purely to illustrate how black males have come to be treated in some segments of society and some parts of the country. He and his lovely wife both worked. They had been married a few years and decided to have a child. She gave birth to a wonderful little boy, and Dad was there for the birth. Later, as Mom rested, Dad went down to the nursery to see his son. The hospital staff would not allow him to go near the child without the mother's permission! It was *his* child! I note this distinction because my third son was born in Philadelphia too. I, as a white man, was never questioned when I wanted to hold my son.

But before we go judging the hospital too harshly, we have to, again, remember that startling statistic. Almost 70 percent of black children are born out of wedlock. So, there was a good chance that my black producer friend was not married to the mother, thus placing him under a cloud of suspicion that he might have motives contrary to the mother's wishes. Unfortunately, the hospital's actions were a sign of the times.

From a family standpoint, we look back to the '50s with fondness. With all the technological advances, I prefer to live in today's world. However, there's no question that the family as an institution was healthier back then. The family unit truly is the building block of society. As the family goes, so goes society. That much is irrefutable. One sure way to repair much of the social decay in this country is to repair that basic building block. That's why governments and companies for years have offered special privileges to the family in the way of benefits like health and life insurance. Many have forgotten—or perhaps never knew—why that is. These benefits are there to encourage the family unit because families are good for society and good for companies.

Families are also good for individuals. I refer back to that dirty little secret that married people, by and large, are happier than single people. The Michael Argyle study that I cited earlier is certainly not the only evidence of that. A Dartmouth College study showed a lasting marriage brings as much happiness as an extra $100,000 of annual income.[9] Married people are also healthier, according to the experts.[10] In fact, they advise men who are in less than perfect health who aren't married to get married in order to increase their longevity. That's why it makes no sense to offer folks who are shackin' up full family benefits. Why encourage anything less than the traditional family? It's good for the individual. It's good for the company. It's good for society.

I will say that, although I think it's a bad idea, I'm firmly in favor of allowing companies to make benefit decisions on their own. They're in the competitive market and they have to do whatever it takes to remain competitive. People screamed and hollered when Disney started offering same-sex benefits. As wrong as I think that is for society, I certainly understand the company's reasons for doing it. They would never tell you this, because it's far too politically incorrect, but there are a disproportionate number of gay people in the entertainment industry. I know it's a stereotype, but it's true. There are many gays who are artistically inclined. In order to attract the best and the brightest, Disney felt it necessary to offer gay-partner benefits.

That may be understandable for a private-sector business; however, there's no excuse for governments to fall in line. In fact, it is the responsibility of governments to set an example. That example should be a family made up of a married man and woman with or without children. As a constitutionalist, however, I should add that I believe individual states should make the decision whether or not to sanction gay marriage. There's nothing in the Constitution that gives the federal government any say-so over marriage. That's why I've opposed any attempt to amend the Constitution. It doesn't need it. States were meant to make these decisions on their own. If Vermont, for example, wants to be the gay marriage magnet of America, then have at it. The only amendment to the Constitution I would recommend would be if the full faith and credit clause of the Constitution were interpreted to mean all other states had to recognize Vermont's gay marriage. Some argue that it does already. I would argue that it doesn't. For example, some states allow citizens to have gun-carry permits. Unless states have reciprocity agreements, you cannot expect another state to allow you to carry a gun. The second part of article 4, section 1 states: "Congress may by general Laws prescribe the Manner in which such Acts, Records and Proceedings shall be proved." In other words, Congress has the authority to stipulate what laws states have to recognize and what laws they don't.

That's not to say I favor any state's recognizing gay marriage. I don't. I simply believe that power belongs to the states. I also believe the gay marriage movement is not so much about gays having equal rights. A business partnership can already be set up to cover most, if not all, of the complaints from gays who claim not to have the same rights as married couples. The real reason is acceptance of gay marriage as legitimate by society. Remember, there's a big difference between tolerance and acceptance. We tolerate a lot of things we might find distasteful. Acceptance means we think there's nothing wrong with it. The number of people who believe that homosexuality is morally wrong still outpaces those who think it's morally fine, but just barely. Homosexual unions are gaining favor in the eyes of many Americans, and they are but another issue that's chipping away at one of the building blocks of society.

To those in favor of governments offering same-sex benefits and legally recognizing gay marriage, I would ask, why stop there? Why not allow three or four or more folks to get married? Why not allow brothers and sisters to get married? The answer I always get is, "That's ridiculous. You can't allow that." Why not? Two guys or two girls getting married is just as ridiculous to some people.

Let's not take our eye off the ball. The basic activity we should be encouraging as a society is the procreation and rearing of children in the healthiest environment possible. Only a man and a woman can procreate, at least the last time I checked, and study after study after study has concluded that raising a kid with a mom and dad in the house is the healthiest environment. That doesn't mean that every other combination is necessarily wrong. It means that mom, dad, and the kids make up the ideal family—and that's what governments should be encouraging for the overall welfare of society. It's not a judgment call (although I'm more than happy to make those too). It's simply a fact. And the sooner we realize where we went wrong, the sooner we can get about the business of correcting our mistakes.

7

GUNS are good.

THE NOTION THAT GUNS are evil is one of the most dishonest and hypocritical arguments of the Left. The fact that Rosie O'Donnell ranted and screamed about banning guns, then employed an armed bodyguard for her kids, should have given any intelligent person cause to distrust the anti-gun crowd. "Whether or not my family is in need of armed guards," she told *People* magazine, "that doesn't change my position on gun control."

Ironically, Rosie maintained that she and her three children needed protection because of threats made against her as a result of her outspoken stance on gun control.[1] In other words, if she and her family are threatened, then they should be protected with guns. However, if you and your family are threatened, you should not be allowed access to guns. Very nice.

Guns Save Lives

The gun-haters start with the basic premise that guns are bad. You shouldn't have them in your house because they're dangerous, they say. I should let you know right from the start that handguns are used for protection against criminals in America more than two million times per year. That's up to five times more often than they're used to commit crimes and nearly 128 times the total number of murders in the United States.[2] Those stats alone are good enough to blow any anti-gun argument out of the water, but there's more. According to the National Crime Victimization Surveys, people who use guns to defend themselves are less likely to be attacked or injured than people who use other methods of protection or don't defend themselves at all.[3]

Robert A. Waters chronicled many such stories in his book *The Best Defense*. In one of the most gripping accounts, Waters tells of a psychotic serial killer who brutalized his victims before killing them. One woman was found dead with a gun shoved in her vagina. Wayne Nance was one of the most sadistic killers in American history, and he attempted to make a couple in Missoula, Montana, Kris and Doug Wells, his eleventh and twelfth victims. That proved to be his fatal mistake. You see, Nance had chosen a couple who kept guns in the house.

Nance had been stalking Kris, and when Doug surprised him outside the couple's home, the killer shot him in the back of the head. Dazed and bleeding from a deep scalp wound, Doug struggled with his assailant from the garage into the house. Amazed that Doug was even still alive, Nance pounded him with a length of pipe and finally prevailed. After grabbing Kris and tying her to the bed frame in the couple's bedroom, Nance took Doug to the basement and tied him to a post. Doug, a gunsmith by profession, had earlier placed an antique lever-action Savage Model 99G Take-Down rifle near his workbench in the basement. He knew that if he could get to it, he and his wife might have a chance.

Doug had been shot, bound, and beaten nearly to death, but Nance still stabbed him in the chest with an oak-handle kitchen knife, puncturing one of his lungs. The killer then left to have his way with Kris, most assuredly intending to kill her afterward, as he had done with so many of his other victims. Somehow, Doug managed to muster enough strength to break loose from the clothesline that bound him. He grabbed the Savage, loaded it, and waited, knowing that if he headed upstairs for the bedroom, Nance would surely use Kris as a shield. Doug banged the butt of the rifle against the wall to get Nance's attention. The ploy worked. Nance raced back toward the basement stairs, and as soon as he came into view Doug let him have it with the Savage.

In the meantime, Kris had managed to free herself except for one arm. Hearing the shot, she feared that Nance had killed her husband. Doug managed to stumble up the stairs, and when he saw the wounded Nance begin to rise, proceeded to pummel him with the butt of the rifle. As Nance crawled toward the bedroom, Doug continued to beat him with the gun until the butt splintered. By then, Nance was in range of the still-tethered Kris, who began to kick and punch him. Nance pulled his gun from its pouch on his belt and fired at Doug, missing him. His second shot caught Doug just above the knee, but Doug kept coming, beating Nance with the barrel of the rifle. In the process, he knocked the lamp off the bedside table, plunging the room into darkness. Doug heard another explosion, and as he lunged for the table where he kept a pistol, he hit the switch for the overhead light. When he grabbed the handgun and trained it on Nance, who lay on the floor convulsing and twitching, Doug saw that the criminal had shot himself.

Wayne Nance died a few hours later. Doug Wells miraculously recovered from his wounds, and his wife, Kris, was not physically harmed.[4] Care to wonder what would have happened had Doug Wells not had a gun in the house? Want to guess how many other innocent victims Wayne Nance might have slain had Doug Wells not killed him? This is but one example of literally millions of times that guns have saved lives, something the anti-gun nuts don't want you to know. But now you do.

The anti-gun advocates have been galvanized in recent years by the highly publicized school shootings, which they point to as the reason we need more gun control. That's an emotional response and not one based in fact. These shootings are indeed tragic, and steps *must* be taken to stop them, but banning guns is not the answer. Actually, banning guns is *adding* to the problem. Research shows that people who commit these heinous murders have absolutely no regard for *any* kind of law, much less laws that prohibit them from carrying a gun onto a particular property. The only thing that will stop them is somebody else with a gun.

By now you're probably familiar with the 1997 school shooting in Pearl, Mississippi. What you may not know, and what wasn't widely reported, is that after the shooting started, an assistant principal ran outside to get his own gun from his automobile, which by law had to be parked a thousand feet from the school because there was a firearm in it. He then held his gun on the killer, physically immobilizing the shooter before he could cause additional harm.[5] In the school-related shooting in Edinboro, Pennsylvania, which left one teacher dead, a citizen who happened upon the scene held a shotgun on the offender while the young man was reloading his gun, preventing him from killing again. The police didn't arrive for another ten minutes.[6] Yet, the anti-gun crowd screams for more gun control. Thank God someone with a gun was present at Pearl and Edinboro. Imagine how less tragic Columbine could've been if only some responsible citizen with a gun had been there to stop it.

The Virginia Tech massacre was one of the most tragic school killings in U.S. history. The horror perpetrated by the nut who took out thirty-two people before taking his own life could have been avoided if someone had been allowed to bring a gun on campus. Virginia Tech was a gun-free zone. We now see what kind of deterrent that turned out to be. The day of the mass killing in 2007, I interviewed a Vanderbilt University official. I suggested that those with carry permits should have been allowed to bring their guns on campus. He emphatically disagreed, maintaining that guns create a dangerous atmosphere. Well, yeah, if you're crazy. But if you've gone through a background check and a safety course, you have a very good chance of saving lives if some nut cuts loose on a school campus. This is something liberals just can't quite fathom. About fifteen months before the Virginia Tech killings, the Virginia General Assembly considered a bill that would have lifted the ban on licensed conceal-carry permit holders carrying their weapons on college campuses. Ironically, a spokesman for Virginia Tech celebrated the bill's defeat, saying that killing the bill would ensure public safety at Virginia Tech. The liberals just don't get it.

What is particularly confounding is the media's refusal to recognize the role guns play in thwarting crime. At the Appalachian School of Law in January 2002, a gunman killed three people before, as the *Washington Post* reported, "Three students pounced on the gunman [Peter Odighizuwa] and held him until help arrived."[7] They failed to mention that these students "pounced" after holding a gun on the assailant, forcing the gunman to drop his.[8]

Another account from the Associated Press seems to purposely omit the part about the guys subduing the gunman with their own guns: "Todd Ross, 30, of Johnson City, Tenn., was among the students who were outside when Odighizuwa (the gunman) left the building. Ross said the suspect was holding his hands in the air and dropped the gun at his prompting."[9] The story didn't mention that the "prompting" was done with the business end of a gun. One would have to go out of his way *not* to report that a gun saved lives at Appalachian School of Law. I guess the truth is too politically incorrect to be printed. Apparently, it doesn't fit some of the left-wing reporters' agenda—an agenda to rid this country of guns.

That's really what all this comes down to. If there were not a concerted agenda on the part of many in the news media to rid the United States of guns, you would have equal attention given to other forms of murder. Glaring examples of the double standard can be found in some of this country's most high-profile murders. Something overlooked by many in the so-called crime of the century, the O. J. Simpson trial, was that Nicole Simpson and Ronald Goldman were not murdered with a gun, they were stabbed to death. That may be an obvious point, but it shifted a lot of the focus. In every high-profile murder case involving guns, you get the usual plea from the gun-snatchers to ban all guns. The September 11 terrorists used box cutters to take over the planes. Where was the outcry to ban knives and box cutters in the wake of those murders?

It's the Shooter, Stupid

In Florida, they went so far as to actually put a gun on trial. I'm not kidding. The headline from the *Palm Beach*

Post read, "Gun used to kill teacher on trial." The widow
of a teacher slain by a student brought a lawsuit against
the gun's distributor claiming the gun was a dangerous,
defective product that led a notorious life of crime.[10] The
gun! Leading a notorious life of crime! Reasonable people
understand that the gun didn't kill the teacher, the student
did. However, in many cases like this one, there are always
those quick to blame someone else.

I suspect money was a strong motivator in that case
too. The kid who pulled the trigger is serving a twenty-
eight-year sentence and, in all likelihood, doesn't have a lot
of cash. The gun distributor, on the other hand, is a richer
target. Why not sue the distributor? The widow had already sued the pawnshop that sold the gun and the family
friend who owned the gun. The pawnshop and the man's
insurance company settled out of court for a combined
sum of more than a half-million dollars. Granted, she had
a legitimate beef with the gun owner, who stored the gun
in a cookie tin. Not very smart when you have kids in the
kitchen and they tend to scrounge around looking for . . .
what? Right, cookies. The gun owner probably had it
coming, but the distributor? The distributor can no more
determine how a gun is going to be used than a dealership
can determine if a car it sold will be used by a drunk
driver. Several courts have said as much.

A Maryland Supreme Court in 2002 ruled in the ac-
cidental shooting death of a three-year-old boy that
"There was no malfunction of the gun; regrettably, it

worked exactly as it was designed and intended to work and as any ordinary consumer would have expected it to work."[11] A disturbing number of small kids are killed by drowning in buckets of water. That may sound strange, but little toddlers curiously peek over the edge to see what's in the bucket, fall face-first into the water, and are unable to pull themselves out. Tragic, indeed, but are we going to start suing bucket makers now? Guns are intended to kill the bad guys, or at least scare them off. When they're used any other way, then they're not being used in the proper manner. Perhaps the government will begin requiring orange stickers with words to that effect stuck to the handle of all guns.

An Armed Zone Is a Safe Zone

After the highly publicized multiple-victim public shootings, some states made it more difficult for average citizens to obtain a gun and protect themselves. However, prior to Columbine, fourteen other states passed carry-permit laws between 1977 and 1995, bringing the total to twenty-one states. In those states, the per capita multiple-victim public murder rate dropped by 89 percent. The multiple-victim public injury rate from firearms dropped 82 percent. Not surprising is the fact that the vast majority of these types of killings—more than 90 percent—many years occur in states *without* carry-permit laws.[12]

It's quite interesting to note that there were sixteen school shootings in America from 1977 to 1995. That's an average of less than one per year. In 1995, a federal law was passed banning guns within a thousand feet of a school, including permitted concealed handguns. In the two-year period between 1997 and 1998, there were *five* public school shootings. It is also interesting to note that during the 1977 to 1995 period in which sixteen shootings took place in schools, fifteen of those were in states *without* right-to-carry laws. There were nineteen deaths and ninety-seven injuries in states without the law, while one death and two injuries were reported in states with the law.[13]

Economist John Lott, formerly of Chicago School of Law and later a professor at Yale, has done, to date, the most extensive research into the gun issue. Although Lott was not a gun advocate when he started, he has become one of the Second Amendment's most ardent supporters after his research provided empirical evidence that gun ownership by responsible citizens has a dramatic effect on reducing violent crime.

"Right after the Columbine attack," he told *Reason Magazine*, "a friend of mine dropped off his kids at a public school in Seattle, and he e-mailed me afterward, because there was a big sign in front of the school that said, 'This is a gun-free zone.' The question I had was, if I put a sign like that in front of my home, would I think that people who are intent on attacking my home would be less likely, or more likely, to harm my children and my wife? You may be trying to create a safe area for your family, but what you've ended up accidentally doing is creating a safe zone for [criminals], because they have less to worry about."[14]

In the vernacular of law enforcement, we have created a "soft target" for criminals at our nation's schools.

Most law enforcement officers will tell you that they cannot prevent, nor can they be there to stop in progress, a school shooting. Their job is to investigate the crime and write up the report. As cited in Pearl, Mississippi, and Edinboro, Pennsylvania, ordinary citizens with firearms prevented the killers from murdering more people than they did. These ordinary citizens were on the ground where the crimes were taking place and acted responsibly and heroically. The police arrived later.

Even in the case of the Santana High School shooting in California, it was an off-duty deputy dropping his children off at school who stopped the murderer. As they took the kid into custody, they found his .22-caliber pistol was fully loaded and cocked. Had the off-duty cop not been there, this twisted kid surely would have killed or wounded more students.

So, what is the solution? It's obvious. So obvious, in fact, that few are willing to utter it for fear of being labeled a "gun nut." But I have no such fear. I have kids in public school and I want to make sure they're safe. There is no possible way to prevent a school shooting. What we must hope for is a speedy resolution if one happens. Each school must have what I've termed a designated defender—a teacher or principal who is trained to handle a firearm. His or her name would be kept secret, except to faculty, and the DD's gun would be locked safely away, with only that person and the principal having a key. The DD of each school would go through a rigorous background check, like those undertaken for carry permits. The DD would also go through a police-administered firearms safety and proficiency course.

On the heels of the Santana High School shooting, I had a gentleman who used to be a police officer in Memphis and Nashville call in to my show. At the time of the Columbine shooting, he had retired from the police force and was teaching school. One day in the teachers lounge, one of the other teachers suggested that, since he was a cop, he bring his gun to school to protect them in the event a shooting occurred at their school. One of the other teachers piped in that he was no longer a cop and therefore no longer qualified to handle a gun! Is it the badge that makes him qualified to handle a firearm, or is it his training? I think you know the answer. There's a preconceived notion with many in America that unless you're carrying a badge, you shouldn't be carrying a gun. That idea is a scary one but, on top of that, it's a foolish one.

Many private citizens are more than qualified to handle a firearm responsibly, but their states don't allow them to carry one for personal protection. I can't speak for other states, but I know that in Tennessee, with the thousands of citizens who have carry permits for their guns, as of this writing only a couple have been used in the commission of a crime, including one that involved the gun's owner chasing and firing at a guy who had just robbed him. That's a better record than the police! That's not a dig at police officers, by any means. They have a tough job and I, for one, appreciate all they do. The point is, police officers are citizens too. They are neither more nor less upstanding than the ordinary citizen who takes a gun-safety course, subjects himself to a background check, allows himself to be fingerprinted, and obtains a gun carry permit. The time has come for us to toss aside our fear of armed citizens and start protecting our children.

Take the Guns, Increase the Crime

The anti-gun lobby loves to point out that America is the murder capital of the world. They draw the fallacious conclusion that it's because of the guns. If that's so, then Switzerland should be the bloodiest place on the planet. Switzerland has no standing army. The country is, instead, defended by a militia composed of almost every male citizen. In fact, the government issues rifles to these citizens, who keep the rifles in their homes, yet Switzerland remains Europe's most peaceful country.[15] England boasts one of the lowest murder rates in the industrialized world, and many hold it up as an example of what gun control can do. But England's murder rate has always been very low.

A country's murder rate is more a product of its society than anything else. If a lack of guns was the reason, then, logically, Switzerland would have the highest murder rate of any industrialized nation. In reality, England's homicide rate of 1.4 murders per 100,000 citizens is 16 percent *higher* than Switzerland's.[16] Interestingly, after banning handguns in June 1997, England saw its murder rate rise.[17]

In 1996, Australian lawmakers passed sweeping legislation banning guns. Their intent was to make Australia a safer country. What they did was make it a soft target for criminals. Within just a few years of the gun ban, homicides were up 3.2 percent in Australia. Assaults were up 8.6 percent. Armed robberies climbed nearly 45 percent! In the Australian state of Victoria, gun homicides climbed 300 percent![18] Does this sound safer to you?

The twenty-five years prior to the gun bans saw crime in Australia dropping steadily. Thanks to the gun ban, Australia now ranks number one in the world in victimization by violent crime, according to The International Crime Victims Survey conducted by Leiden University in Holland. Coming in at number two was that other infamous gunphobic society, Great Britain. By the way, the United States didn't even make the top ten of industrialized nations whose citizens were victims of crime. Better than 30 percent of Australia's citizens have been victimized by violent crimes, and in England and Wales the rate is 26 percent. Holland, Sweden, and Canada all had higher percentages of their citizens victimized by crime than America did (our rate was 21 percent).[19] Ironically, and not surprisingly, these countries have much more stringent gun laws than America.

Guns and Kids: The Myth

Oh, but banning guns is *for the children*. That's what the Left loves to say when they're trying to appeal to your emotions. They do this because they know the facts are against them. But that doesn't stop some on the left, who just make up their own facts to promote their anti-gun agenda. On March 2, 2000, Bill Clinton went on NBC's *Today* show and claimed that thirteen children were killed by guns every day. His definition of a "child" was anyone under age twenty. Webster's defines a child as "a boy or girl in the period before puberty." Firearm death statistics for juveniles and young adults ages fifteen to nineteen jump dramatically from those of *real* children age fourteen and under. In fact, it's a jump of 569 percent!

Let's look at firearm deaths in relationship to other forms of injury deaths for kids fourteen and under. *Real* children are much more likely to die in a fire, drown, or die in an auto accident than they are by gunshot. To be more specific, almost twice as many children die by drowning and more than four times as many die in auto-mobile accidents than are killed with guns.[20]

There were 17,034 murders in America in 2006. Less than 3 percent, or 477 of those, were kids under age thirteen. Of those 477 children murdered, how many do you think were killed with a gun? Would you believe 120?

That's right, just 25 percent of the children under thirteen who were murdered were killed by a firearm. Seventy-five percent were killed by some other means. More than twice as many of these children were killed by bare hands than with a gun.[21]

Important Enough to Make the Constitution

Stop and think for a moment about how important our right to bear arms was to the Founding Fathers. Of all the belongings of their day that were important to them—a home, clothing, a horse—guns are the only inanimate objects in the entire Constitution that are singled out for protection. Why? Thomas Jefferson said, "The strongest reason for the people to retain the right to keep and bear arms is, as a last resort, to protect themselves against the tyranny in government." It was George Washington who said, "The very atmosphere of firearms anywhere and everywhere restrains evil interference. They deserve a place of honor with all that's good." If you think their thinking is a bit outmoded, contrast their statements with this statement by Adolf Hitler: "The most foolish mistake we could possibly make would be to allow the people to carry arms. History shows that all conquerors who have allowed their subjected peoples to carry arms have prepared their own downfall by so doing."

If guns are, in fact, bad, suggest to the next gun snatcher you argue with that policemen should be stripped of their guns. "Why, that's nuts," they'll respond.

Well, if guns are bad, then nobody should have them, right? The fact is, guns are *not* bad. Guns are good. The problem is, some people are bad. These people will use guns, knives—even their bare hands—to carry out their crimes. It's up to good people to protect themselves and their families from these bad people. And there's no better way to do that than with a gun.

8

HYPHENATED LABELS are divisive and destructive.

In this country we have no place for hyphenated Americans.

—*Theodore Roosevelt*

EVERYWHERE YOU TURN, SOMEONE is being identified by his or her race or ethnic background. African-Americans, Italian-Americans, Asian-Americans. Funny thing is, these labels are usually attached to people by other people who aren't even Hyphenated-Americans. The same goes for many of these politically correct causes.

Take the cause of abolishing Indian names for sports teams, for example. One of the chief . . . (I'm sorry; that's politically incorrect.) One of the *principal* instigators in that movement in South Dakota was a woman named Betty Ann Gross. Doesn't sound Indian to me. In March 2002, she withdrew five civil rights complaints she had filed with the U.S. Department of Education, citing a lack of support from the Indian community. Vernon Belle-court, cofounder of the American Indian Movement, speculated that Gross was "able to swallow her personal convictions on this issue in the interests of political pragmatism." You see, she decided to run for mayor of her small hometown. Suddenly, all this turmoil she had stirred up didn't seem so important.[1]

Betty Ann Gross is not alone in stirring the pot just to cause trouble. The whole hyphenated-label movement, I'm convinced, was dreamt up by similar rabble-rousers who never had a personal stake in the issue. I'm certainly not suggesting that people of one ethnic group or race shouldn't come to the aid of another if they witness injustice. During the '60s, many whites threw themselves into the cause of civil rights for blacks. That was a just cause and one for which some of these whites gave their lives. What I'm saying is, people shouldn't *create* injustice where there is none.

Americans First

I saw a survey a few years back that polled *African-Americans* to see how they preferred to label themselves. You know what the majority said? Black. Just plain old black. The left-wingers have been falling all over themselves to come up with a *sensitive* label, and most black folks would rather not use it. When you think about it, these hyphenated labels are really oxymorons. I mean, either you're African or you're American. Either you're Italian or you're American. Unless you have dual citizenship, you can't be both. Me? I guess I could claim to be an English-Italian-Spanish-American, since, as best as I can figure, that's where my ancestors came from. Maybe I could shorten it to Euro-American. That sounds more cosmopolitan, doesn't it? I'm an American, in case anybody wants to know how I want to be labeled. A white guy, if you want to get real specific.

Don't misunderstand. There's nothing wrong with celebrating your heritage. I love big Italian families and Mexican families and so on and so forth. Irish families are particularly proud folks. It's fun tracing your family roots. Of course, in my case, it's like the guy who spent three thousand dollars tracing his genealogy and then another three grand covering it up. I only had to go back a couple of generations before the family skeletons started falling out of *our* closet. No, being proud of your heritage is fine. Where I have a problem is when people start leading with their race or ethnicity. They want you to know upfront that they're one of those hyphenated people, somehow special in some way. It's rather irritating, really. Nobody likes to have their face rubbed in it.

I remember during Black Awareness Month in high school, different black students would get on the intercom before classes started and tell the story of some notable black person. It was great, and quite interesting, until the end when they would announce with a defiant tone, "He was a *black* man." Any ground they had gained in bridging the gap between the races was instantly washed away with a torrential tide of attitude. Can you imagine if I had gone on the intercom to tell the story of George Washington? He was our first president. He became known as the father of our country. And George Washington was a *white* man.

Hyphenated labels have that same effect. They insinuate an importance to the background of a person that's, quite frankly, not that important. Newspapers are famous for using hyphenated labels. What do I care if someone's African-American or Asian-American, unless it's relevant to the story? Either I'm familiar with the person they're writing about, in which case I probably already know if they're black, or I don't know them. If that's the case, I don't need to know their racial background unless it's pertinent to the story. By the way, did you ever notice that they never refer to anyone as a Scandinavian-American? Newspaper people are very selective in their labels. Why would it be more important to know that someone is an African-American than, say, a German-American? Why? Because the news media, especially the print medium, are obsessed with race.

What Is a Black Leader?

While we're on the subject, let's talk about one of my pet peeves. I have, for some time, been disturbed by the term *black leader*. The title *leader* is usually reserved for those who are either elected to an office by the people, or those who choose to take the reins of a movement. Martin Luther King Jr. emerged as the foremost spokesman against the egregious inequality of blacks in America. His courage in the face of incredible adversity, which included ridicule, imprisonment, and, ultimately, the giving of his own life for the cause, earned him the title *civil rights leader*. Other movements have produced their own leaders. The late William F. Buckley Jr., through *National Review* magazine and his authoritative books on conservatism, became a leader of the conservative movement. Gloria Steinem emerged as a leader in the feminist movement.

For every movement there are leaders, but being black is not a movement. Somewhere along the way *civil rights leaders* became *black leaders*. Somewhere along the way, either through media labels or self-anointing, they crossed the line from leading a legitimate movement to claiming to speak for a whole race of people. When you really think about it, the notion of someone being a black leader is quite condescending and, actually, an insult to all black people. It connotes a presumption that all black people think alike, which is the ultimate in stereotyping.

As a conservative, I certainly respect and admire many leaders in the conservative movement. I study their writings and opinions and I acknowledge their contributions. But as a white guy, I have no white leaders. Being white is not what I believe in; it's the race to which I happen to belong. There is no white person who speaks for me. Those who presume to do so are immediately castigated by me and others as racists.

Why, then, do the media continue to use the label *black leaders?* First of all, you must understand that most people in the news business are simply regurgitating what they read. There are very few original thinkers in news. A term or phrase emerges from one of the major newspapers or wire services, or is planted by a particular group, and everyone begins to use the new phrase as if it were their own idea.

A great example of that came in the 2000 presidential campaign. Some talking points handed down by the Democratic leadership maintained that George W. Bush lacked gravitas. Remember that? Mario Cuomo used the term on one of the TV news shows, and all of a sudden everyone in the news business was using it—most having no idea what it meant—as if they'd been using it their entire lives. It's been much the same with the term black leaders. What's ironic is that many of the people held up as so-called black leaders have never been elected to anything nor have they served our nation's government, while those who have are discounted if they happen to be conservative.

Nowhere is this more clearly illustrated than in the NAACP. Its treatment of Clarence Thomas, for one, was appalling. If this were actually an organization dedicated to the advancement of black people, it would have supported Thomas during the confirmation hearings for his appointment to the U.S. Supreme Court. Instead, its goal is to advance a political agenda. Since Thomas is a conservative, he isn't really black in their eyes. To me, that's blatant racial stereotyping.

I have since renamed the group the NAAPC, the National Association for the Advancement of Political Correctness. This group no longer even remotely resembles the respectable, pioneering civil rights organization it once was. Instead, it has degenerated into a left-wing propaganda arm for the ultraleftists in Congress who plot and scheme to trap minorities in government dependency in order to hold on to a voting constituency. Ironically, Clarence Thomas and his family were card-carrying members of the NAACP. Once he began researching history and conservative thinking, he broke the chains of conventional black thinking.

One of the people I admired most in America when he was on the national stage was Colin Powell. Think what you will about some of his positions on some social issues, I believe he was one of the most honorable, distinguished, and conscientious leaders in America, yet you never heard of him being referred to as a *black leader*. Now, let's see. The man was black, and he was a leader. If anyone ever qualified for that title, it should have been Colin Powell, right? Here's the problem. The decidedly left-leaning news media, which print and report these stories, have been conducting their own racial profiling in the newspapers and magazines and on the airwaves all across America. If a black person doesn't fit their profile of how a black person should think or act, they don't get the title.

How many times have you heard J. C. Watts, the distinguished former congressman from Oklahoma, referred to as a black leader? How about Clarence Thomas? Or Condoleezza Rice? These are American success stories, people who have risen to the top, but because they're not liberal, they're not considered black leaders. In the end, that's a good thing. It's a good thing because the aforementioned people have done something that Al Sharpton and Jesse Jackson will never do. They've transcended race. They are leaders for *all* Americans, and they just happen to be black.

Check out this logic: Clarence Thomas isn't really black because he's conservative, but Bill Clinton was "the first black president." Clinton was dubbed "our first black president" by author Toni Morrison in a piece she wrote for the *New Yorker* magazine in 1998. Some left-wing black activists picked up the moniker and ran with it. Morrison wrote: "Clinton displays almost every trope of blackness: single-parent household, born poor, working-class, saxophone-playing, McDonald's-and-junk-food-loving boy from Arkansas." Others added that because he was liberal and had experienced oppression by those who sought to persecute him, he was really a black man. How ridiculous is that? I'm surprised the NOW crowd didn't declare him "the first female president." I guess Monica Lewinsky dashed any chance he had of being named "the first gay president."

Contrary to what the news media would have you think, black people and mass-appeal leaders are not mutually exclusive. When I look at Colin Powell, I don't see a black man. I see an American hero. However, many in the news media, especially newspapers, don't consider someone legitimately black unless he or she toes their liberal line. This largely white fraternity of journalists is who labels the likes of Jesse Jackson a black leader. That's right, the newspaper business is a largely white fraternity. The vast majority of newspaper reporters and editors are white, despite their chastising of conservatives for not supporting quotas.

According to the American Society of Newspaper Editors, even though blacks make up somewhere around 14 percent of the United States population, American newspaper newsrooms are only 5.36 percent black![2] (And only 4.41 percent are Hispanic.) What hypocrisy! These print journalists would never dream of calling anyone who was white a *white leader*, because that person, it would be assumed, would be speaking for them. They're much too smart and educated and urbane to have someone speak for them. They're perfectly capable of speaking for themselves. No one would get away with lumping *them* into a category just because of the color of their skin. Why, to have someone claim to speak for white people and include them would be an insult to their intelligence, yet they do it regularly to black Americans in newspapers all across this country. It's all a part of the condescending nature of liberalism.

There is an implied presumption that the people they choose to cast their pity upon are too stupid to help themselves; therefore, the government must step in to save these people. Yet, when it comes to doing something that

would really help someone—like giving them a job—
newspapers are woefully lacking. Such is the hypocrisy of
liberalism, which we'll cover in greater detail later.

Separated by a Hyphen

Ultimately, I believe that hyphenated labels are meant to divide, not unite. Whether they're used by people who fit the
label or people wanting to sound sensitive, they are used to
separate people from the herd, to single them out. That's
certainly not what desegregation was all about. That's one of
the reasons I thought the Black Awareness Club in my high
school was so destructive. We had spent so much time and
energy desegregating the schools, then someone came along
and wanted to start a club for blacks only. I thought it was
wrong then, and I think it's wrong now. That's why I attended the club meeting and ran for president.

During my speech to the club, I reminded them that
they didn't need the Black Awareness Club to make them
aware that they were black. I asked them how they would
feel if someone were to start a White Awareness Club. I
also reminded them that our parents had worked together,
begrudgingly sometimes, but together they worked to tear
down the walls that separated us. Now these students were
again erecting those walls. I urged them not to slide backward toward segregation but to move forward, not as
blacks and whites but as one student body. I finished my
speech and walked out with a couple of white folks who
had been brave enough to join me. I was pleased when

several black students walked out behind us. We didn't change a lot of minds that day, but I believe we got them thinking about it.

The principal of our school thought I was going to start a race riot, but I believe I gained the respect of many of my black classmates. They understood where I was coming from and appreciated the spirit. Hyphenated labels only serve the same purpose as the Black Awareness Club. They unnecessarily pick at old wounds. If you drop everything before the hyphen, you identify people as what they really are—Americans.

Hyphen Equals Victim

Another reason some use hyphenated labels is to portray themselves as victims. A guy named Willie from Memphis called my show once. I had been going off on hyphenated labels, and he called to set me straight. He said that his people had been dragged here in chains, and he didn't even know his real last name since it had been given to him by white slave owners. Because of all that, he argued, he could never get a fair day in court. He owned property and said he lost every case he'd ever tried against tenants. Upon pressing Willie, I learned that the people he sued had been black, too, namely, black women. After I'd pulled that little tidbit out of him, he proceeded to tell me that the only people in America who hadn't been victimized were white men and black women. In other words, his whole argument collapsed.

I offered Willie some unsolicited advice. The chip that he was carrying around on his shoulder was hurting absolutely no one but him. How his ancestors got here is irrelevant. It's indisputably tragic, most assuredly regrettable, but wholly irrelevant. How Willie's or my ancestors got here doesn't mean a thing in everyday life. It's what we do with our own lives that counts. We can sit around making excuses for ourselves, but we'll never change the past. However, too many people allow the past to affect their future. You may be saying, "Easy for you to say, white boy," but think about it. Is Willie's chip ever going to affect me? Willie thinks he's born to lose because the white man has screwed him over. Will that ever hurt me in any shape, form or fashion? Who's the only person it's going to hurt? That's right. Willie. And until Willie changes his attitude, he's never going to have much success in life.

It's funny, because another black listener named Art called right after my conversation with Willie. He agreed with me 100 percent. He had just moved to Memphis recently and apparently had quite a lucrative career. He commented that he'd never seen so many victims in one place.

Those who choose to continue to use hyphenated labels continue to widen the divide between races and ethnic groups. That curse is now being broadened to religious groups. Some in the news media refer to Americans who practice the religion of Islam as Muslim-Americans. Should I now begin referring to myself as a Baptist-American? Again, leading with our differences only promotes discord.

What makes America great is its reputation as a melting pot. I believe it was comedian Dennis Miller who offered some sage advice when he said, "America's the great melting pot. Then melt, dammit!"

9

ILLEGAL IMMIGRATION is dangerous to this country.

ASIDE FROM THE FACT that illegal immigration is, well, illegal, the influx of illegals into this country has repercussions not only here but also in the countries they left behind. I certainly have no problem with controlled legal immigration; this great country of ours was built on it. But when illegals flood across our borders, they jump ahead of the law-abiding immigrants who have gone through the proper channels and followed the procedures necessary to enter this country. I understand the frustration endured by those trying to obtain legal permission to come here, but entering any other way sets a whole host of problems in motion.

We have immigration laws for a reason. They were designed as a filter to allow us to pick and choose who we want in this country and why. If we have a shortage of doctors, for instance, legal immigration affords us the opportunity to bring in qualified doctors trained in the fields for which they're needed. No doubt that in the last decade or so, manual laborers, like construction workers and service personnel, were in high demand. That demand enticed workers to crash the border and businesses to hire them. However, sustained illegal immigration can be quite detrimental, and not just for the reasons that might be apparent.

The Ignored Victims of Illegal Immigration

There are basically two groups illegal immigration hurts the most. The first is the working poor in America. These are people who want to make it on their own. They want to earn a living, yet their education and work skills limit them to lower-paying jobs. The problem is, these lower-paying, low-skill jobs are being scooped up in ever-increasing numbers by illegal aliens. Maricopa County, which includes Phoenix, hired Harvard economist George Borjas to conduct a study on the economic impact of illegal immigration. He found that illegal immigration had a great effect on the working poor. Wages for entry-level workers were 4.7 percent less than what they ordinarily would be if illegals were not part of the equation. In total, he found that illegal immigration cost workers around $1.4 billion in 2005.[1] Some unscrupulous employers can pay less than minimum wage to these illegals because, let's face it, who are they gonna tell? These employers can't get away with that with American citizens.

Of course, not everyone who hires an illegal alien is unscrupulous. Many are just trying to survive in a competitive world. Many of these illegals will work harder for less money. To some businesses, it makes sense to hire them if you can get away with it. The problem is, many of our citizens won't take these low-paying jobs. Why? Because, too often, they can make out better on public assistance. The illegal aliens sometimes live several families to a dwelling. To many of them, the arrangement is only temporary, as they wire much of what they make back home where the dollar buys so much more. To others, the living conditions here, no matter how deplorable we may find them, are much better than in the country they left.

If we really wanted to discourage the skimming of American dollars from our economy then we should be taxing money wired by noncitizens out of the country. If you can't provide a valid U.S. birth certificate and proper corroborating ID, then you pay the tax. Or how about, if you don't have the proper ID, you can't wire money at all? This would certainly help cut down on the practice.

The homebuilding industry, like many other manual-labor industries, has been overrun in many parts of the country by immigrants, many of them illegal. When we renovated our home in late 2001, the vast majority of workers were Mexican. I talked at length to one of the only American subcontractors who refused to hire Mexican immigrants. He was resentful about how they had taken over the construction industry and had almost run him out of business. (Just for grins, he would show up at the site wearing a "La Migra" T-shirt, Spanish for *immigration agent*.)

My first instinct was to say that the free market was in play and it determined how much customers were willing to pay for a particular project. There's a degree of truth to that; however, when you factor in illegal workers, it tends to artificially deflate the price of labor. In other words, it short-circuits the free market system. Here's why: illegal workers are in no position to haggle over how much they're paid. By their very status, they're at the mercy of the employer. Therefore, those who hire illegal aliens can pay far less than they would have to pay an American citizen, thus holding down their costs and underbidding anyone else who doesn't hire illegal aliens.

Some say this is the very reason we should open our borders and quit making criminals out of those who want to better their lives. That sounds well and good, but they're forgetting something. One of the primary responsibilities of our government is to control the borders. The reason we have the Immigration and Customs Enforcement (ICE) to start with is to protect our citizens from outlaws fleeing their own country. It's also to protect us from disease that may be carried into this country by an immigrant. Not to mention the need to control the flow of people so they don't become a drain on local, state, or federal governments. Sneaking into this country illegally or overstaying your visa short-circuits that whole process.

There's also a reason not to legalize illegal aliens that is completely ignored by the pro-illegal immigrant crowd, and that's the second group harmed by illegal immigration: those countrymen the illegals leave behind. Take Mexico, for example. The underlying reason most Mexicans come here illegally is because the living conditions in their own country are abominable. Allowing them to escape their own country's problems does a disservice to their countrymen. Illegal immigration works as a release valve, taking pressure off of their government to change its policies.

Why do you think the Mexican government is eager for us to grant amnesty to illegal aliens while at the same time cracking down on anyone trying to enter Mexico from Central America? They don't have jobs for them in Mexico. If they were to be deported back to Mexico, it could cause an uprising and, God forbid, change. These same people who risk life and limb coming across the border into America might be well suited to forcing change in their own country. Instead, they've chosen the path of least resistance and we as a nation have contributed to maintaining the status quo in nations like Mexico that are sorely in need of reform. We unwittingly prolong the misery and the abject poverty because we allow a few to escape when we can't possibly take in the whole country. The illegal immigrants will continue to stream across the border until Mexico gets its act together.

As we've learned through our disastrous welfare program here in America, the worst thing we can do is to prop up Mexico. Instead, we should be concentrating our efforts on helping the Mexicans improve their own lot, not through foreign aid but by advising them on how to structure their government so as to encourage capitalism and self-sufficiency. You may or may not have noticed that hundreds of thousands of people travel back and forth across our border with Canada, but we don't have a problem with illegal Canadian immigrants. The reason is, of course, because the standard of living in their country is very close to ours.

When Congress was debating amnesty for illegal aliens in the spring of 2006, some religious leaders saddled up next to the illegal aliens as they brazenly protested in the streets of America. One Catholic leader explained his reasoning for joining the protest on the National Mall in Washington by scolding the then Republican-led House of Representatives for passing a bill that would clamp down on illegal immigration. "The difficulty," he said, "was that it made all these people who are illegal, criminals." It made illegal people criminals. Wow. That idiotic statement came from Cardinal Theodore McCarrick, head of the Washington, D.C., archdiocese. In an interview with Cybercast News Service, he added, "There's a big difference between being illegal and being criminal."[2] There is? Do tell. Where I come from, being illegal *is* being criminal. Under federal law, it's a misdemeanor to enter this country illegally the first time. Subsequent illegal trips across the border are felonies. Those who choose to align themselves with illegal aliens are aligning themselves with felons. Those who choose to harbor illegal aliens are harboring felons.

Which brings me to the Elvira Arellano story. Arellano first broke into our country in 1997. She was deported not once but several times, and she repeatedly returned. In

2000, she made it back over the border just in time to give birth to a son, Saul. By 2002, Arellano was working at Chicago's O'Hare Airport. Oh, and by the way, she used forged documents to get her job. According to ICE, Arellano was "working illegally for a janitorial services business whose employees had access to security sensitive areas."[3] Because she used a stolen Social Security card, she was convicted of a felony and sentenced to three years' probation. After serving her probation, she was once again kicked out of the country, only this time she didn't leave. ICE tracked her down and began deportation proceedings. That's when she began a melodramatic bid for sanctuary. She took refuge in the Adalberto United Methodist Church in Chicago. "I was desperate," she told the *Los Angeles Times.* "I remembered how Joseph and Mary were given sanctuary. I asked my church for sanctuary, and they agreed." Joseph and Mary were given sanctuary? Joseph and Mary weren't given sanctuary. They were looking for a room in an inn. "If Homeland Security chooses to send its agents on the Holy Ground to arrest me," she said, "then I will know that God wants me to be an example of the hatred and hypocrisy of the current policy of the government."[4] Hey, here's a thought, Elvira. Maybe it means that God wants you to go home and obey the law.

Anyway, the church in Chicago took her in, and she stayed there for a year. Yes, she was there for a solid year, thumbing her nose at ICE the whole time. Illinois Democrat Representative Luis Gutierrez and Senator Dick

Durbin joined the act. They sponsored a bill that singled out Arellano for special consideration. They cited a "medical emergency" for allowing her to stay. You know what this medical emergency was? Little Saul, they claimed, suffered from ADHD. Yes, I know, that's ridiculous. That's what the rest of Congress thought too. They shot the bill down.

With all this celebrity status, it was only a matter of time before Arellano's ego got the best of her. Eventually, she couldn't resist the opportunity to travel to Los Angeles as a centerpiece for an illegal alien protest. After the rally in LA, she was picked up by ICE and deported. Of course, she went kicking and screaming, protesting the injustice of having to leave her young son behind. How about this for an idea, Elvira? How about take him with you? Apparently, the thought never occurred to her. It didn't occur to her handlers at the church either. They decried the immigration raids, condemning them for tearing families apart. Please. They blamed the government, but actually they are the ones at fault. The woman was a convicted criminal. The woman broke into our country. If they cared anything about the child, they would've insisted she take him with her. After some time back in Mexico, it became apparent to Arellano that she was not going to be allowed back into the United States. At that point, she sent for her son, and they were reunited back in Mexico.

Barbara Coe is the founder of the California Coalition for Immigration Reform. The group's mission is to put a stop to what she described as "the immigration invasion destroying our nation." Coe fully grasps the situation and the simple solution to this business of tearing families apart. "These churches are harboring criminals, and they should lose their federal nonprofit tax status, which strictly forbids engaging in political activity with tax dollars," she said. "If their point is to prevent separation of undocumented families, I have a simple solution: These families can take their entire families with them."[5] Exactly. If that means packing up your family and going home, then start packing.

It's also the obvious solution to all these so-called anchor babies. These are babies whose mothers entered the country illegally and then gave birth, just like Elvira Arellano. The courts have ruled that these children are automatically citizens, citing the fourteenth amendment, which ensures that all slaves and their descendants are considered to be citizens. Until that issue is resolved, the solution is simple. *You* are not a citizen, despite the citizenship status of your child. You have two options: either leave and take the child with you or leave the child behind to be put up for adoption. In any case, you're going to have to go. That may sound harsh but it's the only way to deal with these people trying to take advantage of a loophole in our law. One would think that any caring parent would take their child with them.

The New Conquest

Aside from the obvious danger of terrorists crossing our borders, which we'll cover in a later chapter, there's another issue that is threatening to boil over while our attention is diverted. As most Americans look overseas for our next conflict, I believe the next big problem is brewing right here in our own backyard. It's the issue of losing control of parts of the Southwest United States. Think I'm overreacting? There's a movement in that part of the country called *la reconquista* ("the reconquest"). It is a calculated effort on the part of some Mexican immigrants, illegal and legal, to gain political control and return to Mexico the areas of the United States lost by the Mexican War of the mid-1840s.

Understand that the war was precipitated by Texas, which had already fought for and won its independence from Mexico (Remember the Alamo?), wanting to gain U.S. statehood. The Mexicans attacked and we pushed them all the way back to Mexico City, occupying that city for a short time. Instead of taking over the whole country, which we rightfully could have done, having been attacked, we settled for territory north of the Rio Grande, which included the region now known as the Southwest United States. That included California. Just a couple of years later, gold was discovered there (darn the Mexican luck). Apparently they're still hacked off about that.

These reconquistas are quite bold and explicit in their desires. "California is going to become a Hispanic state," reconquista movement leader Mario Obledo warned, "and anybody who doesn't like it should leave!"[6] That's a view held by many Hispanics inside and outside America. In 1997, former Mexican President Ernesto Zedillo told the

National Council of La Raza, "I have proudly affirmed that the Mexican nation extends beyond the territory enclosed by its borders."[7] Art Torres, chairman of the California Democratic Party observed that "Proposition 187 (a California measure to deny government benefits to illegal aliens) is the last gasp of white America in California."[8] And who do you think made this little jewel of a statement? "In the near future, people will look upon California and Mexico as one magnificent region." None other than then-governor Gray Davis of California.[9]

Yet with all this overwhelming evidence, many on the left believe this whole reconquista business has been dreamed up by a bunch of racists. *The Nation*, a socialist rag that labeled me "Tennessee's most poisonous media personality," calls the reconquista movement "the biggest nativist myth of all."[10] *Nativist* is what the libs have come up with to paint anti-illegal immigrant advocates as Klansmen. The word actually means "the policy of protecting the interests of native inhabitants against those of immigrants."[11] It's meant as a pejorative, but it completely misses the point of the illegal immigrant backlash. Most people have no problem with legal immigration; it's illegal immigration that concerns them. Leftist mouthpieces like *The Nation* draw no distinction between illegal and legal because they see borders as evil instruments constructed by oppressive governments. They're for open borders, and they're useful idiots in the ultimate plan of the reconquistas. Or maybe they're just useful idiots without the "useful" part.

The Absolut Vodka people apparently believe the reconquista movement is for real. In March 2008 they launched the "In an Absolut World" campaign. This campaign targeted specific audiences to tap their "ideal world." For example, they ran ads in gay magazines that conveyed the message that "gay marriage is a celebrated reality" in an Absolut world.[12] Advertisements in Mexican magazines showed an early nineteenth-century map of Mexico and the United States in which the American Southwest was part of Mexico with the caption "In an Absolut world." You don't think their marketing firm didn't do some research on their target audiences? Absolut abruptly pulled the ad after an avalanche of complaints from Americans, but their press release explaining why they yanked the ad actually told us why they ran it in the first place: "In no way was this meant to offend or disparage, nor does it advocate an altering of borders, nor does it lend support to any anti-American sentiment, nor does it reflect immigration issues." The Web site statement went on to say: "Instead, *it hearkens to a time which the population of Mexico may feel was more ideal* [emphasis added]."[13]

It's not like the mainstream media don't see the signs, literally, of reconquista. A huge billboard caused quite a flap in 2005 in the Los Angeles area. A Spanish-language television station advertised their newscast with "Los Angeles, CA" printed at the top. But CA was crossed out. In its place? The word *Mexico* in bright red letters. Stuart Fischoff, a professor of media psychology at California

State in Los Angeles, said the billboard was like "sticking a finger in your eye" to immigration reformers. "The joke here is, 'We're taking back California,'" Fischoff said. "Underneath the joke is part of the truth."[14]

Make no mistake about it. These reconquista folks have definitely not forgotten the Mexican-American War, and they're bound and determined to win back the Southwest and California for Mexico through our own democratic elections. Now, is that to say that every Hispanic elected official should be looked upon with suspicion? Of course not. But firm loyalties need to be established and motives need to be determined by the voters or we could find ourselves with a huge mess on our hands. I can't imagine that these reconquistas actually think that we'd stand idly by for such nonsense, but they brag that their dream is not too far from fruition.

Language Can Unite or Divide

The reconquista movement is all the more reason why English should be the official language in America. A dominant second language becomes a wedge that drives people apart. One need only look north to Quebec to see how language can divide a country. Canada came very close to a split several years back because of the chasm created by a dual-language society. We should take a cue from that volatile situation before it becomes a reality here. Several states have adopted English as their official language, and we should federalize that idea before it's too late.

That's not to say that all other languages should be banned everywhere in America. Take the case of a Houston cabbie who took his "English Only" sign a bit too far. A Colombian passenger was talking on his cell phone in Spanish during his ride from the airport to his hotel. The cabbie stopped the vehicle, pulled the man's suitcase from the trunk and tried to physically force him from the backseat, ripping the guy's suit in the process. The cabbie was cited for assault.[15] He obviously needs to switch to decaf.

I've traveled abroad a few times and I appreciate the English-speaking tourist assistants. However, if I were to move to a country like, say, France, I would learn French instead of insisting that everyone speak my language. However, I can't imagine being thrown from a cab in Paris because I didn't speak French. It's really the defiance and arrogance of some immigrants that frosts me. It's as if they're expecting us to bend over backward to accommodate them instead of having the courtesy to learn the language before they move here. I think requiring a working knowledge of English before granting a work visa to the United States would be a splendid idea. It sure would make it easier separating the legals from the illegals. It would also make it a heckuva lot easier getting my order straight at the drive-thru.

The Cost of Illegal Immigration

The cost of illegal immigration is staggering in monetary terms and in lives. A 1997 Rice University study placed the net cost at $20 billion. That included the cost of education, incarceration, food stamps, housing, and a host of other costs amounting to around $33 billion. They figured the amount illegals paid in taxes was around $12.6 billion. Subtract that from $33 billion, and the total cost comes to $20 billion. That estimate did not include the cost of unemployment benefits for those who lost their jobs due to illegal immigrants, nor did it consider the lost taxes from those unemployed.

The Federation for American Immigration Reform (FAIR) took the Rice study and extrapolated it using figures that took into account the explosion of illegal immigration since 2004. They came up with a net cost to federal, state, and local governments of $45 billion. They figured the indirect costs would have increased as well, adding another $10 billion, thus arriving at a net cost of $55 billion annually.[16]

ESR Research released a 2008 study that placed the number of immigrants in the United States, legally and illegally, at 37 million. They estimated the federal costs alone equaled $346 billion. Part of that equation included $100 billion in federal taxes lost "from the reduction of native incomes caused by immigrant workers." They estimated a third of that 37 million to be in the United States illegally. That put the number of illegals at just over 12 million, which is actually on the low side of most estimates. Even with that conservative number, that would mean a cost to the federal government alone from illegal aliens to be somewhere in the neighborhood of $115 billion! Edwin Rubenstein, a former director of research for the Hudson Institute, said, "This is another nail in the coffin of economic growth. There is absolutely no reason immigration policy shouldn't be discussed on its economic merits."

The human cost of illegal immigration is downright frightening. According to the Violent Crimes Institute, there are an estimated 240,000 illegal immigrant sex offenders in the United States. That's 93 sex offenders and 12 serial sex offenders crossing into the United States *every day!* Each sex offender averages 4 victims. That's close to a million victims just from this one study, which covered only a period of eighty-eight months. Of the cases reviewed in this study, 35 percent were child molestations, 24 percent were rapes, and 41 percent were sexual homicides and serial murders.[17]

While illegal aliens continue to stream across the Mexican border, this mass of humanity includes a disproportionate number of killers. The federal government doesn't keep tabs on such things, but Congressman Steve King (R-IA) conducted a study of government records and cross-referenced them with arrest records and prison population estimates, among other sources, and came to a startling conclusion. On average, 12 Americans are murdered daily by illegal aliens. That's 4,380 per year. Or, to put it another way, that's more people killed each year than we lost in the first five years of the Iraq War. Did you see the CodePink nuts protesting against illegal aliens? Neither did I. But it gets worse. King's study estimates another 13 people are killed by illegals in traffic accidents each day, primarily from driving drunk.[18] That's a total of 25 innocent Americans snuffed out each day—9,125 per year—because we won't secure our borders. It's a national outrage. That's a 9/11 happening every four months. That's a 727 jetliner full of people going down every week. Of course, American stooges take to the streets to protest on behalf of these people because, after all, as they love to say, "no person is illegal." Oh, no? Tell that to the families of the 10,000 people killed each year. Tell that to the women who were raped. Tell that to the little children who were molested by these thugs we allow to walk across our border unabated.

More than $115 billion in taxpayer money and nearly 10,000 lives lost each year because we have too many people putting profit ahead of principle. Congress is unlikely to do anything about it. Although we have some great folks in Washington doing their best to fix the problem, they're swimming against the current. Those who control this issue in Washington only see illegal aliens as the menial labor around them that cleans and cooks for them. They're insulated inside the Washington Beltway from the carnage on the highways, the rapes, the murders, the child molestations, the loss of jobs, and the degradation of whole neighborhoods. They don't see MS-13 moving in and taking over, American culture being supplanted by a third-world culture, and hospitals closing because they're overwhelmed by illegal aliens. Don't expect Washington to do much. The solution will come from those closest to the problem. The problem will be solved on the state and local levels; those who have witnessed firsthand just how out of control this situation has become.

Demagnetize America

The answer to the illegal immigration problem is two-pronged. First, more government workers must be assigned to the caseloads of people wanting to immigrate to this country legally. It should not take years for qualified candidates to weave their way through the process. One of the reasons you find so many people taking the illegal route is because the legal one takes forever. There are dozens of hoops to jump through. Not that we shouldn't require an adequate amount of hoop jumping—those background checks and reference checks save us headaches later. But the process could be hurried along with a larger concentration of personnel to handle the load.

I mentioned earlier that we have the prerogative as a nation to admit people who will fill a certain need, like doctors. We do have a need for labor that is willing to work at or around the minimum wage, so once we've screened these people adequately, they would be an asset to the country. It used to work this way. As a child, I remember what were then called migrant workers. Lawyers used to refer to them as *migraine* workers. These people would work seasonally up and down the East Coast, then head back to Mexico. The problem started when we literally let our guard down—the border guard—which brings me to my next point.

Concurrently with speeding up the immigration process, we need to get serious about protecting our borders. (More on that in a later chapter.) I would also call for the immediate repeal of the Posse Comitatus Act and station our military along the border. Once we've beefed up the Immigration and Customs Enforcement to expedite the processing of applicants who want to enter this country, the only excuse people would have to crash the gate is if they had something to hide. I hear politicians and pundits alike say that the solution to the illegal immigration issue is complicated. It's not. In fact, the solution to the problem is rather simple. Demagnetize America. The magnets are the jobs and the government benefits. You cut those off, and the illegals go home. Oh, but how are we going to deport 12 million to 20 million people, I hear some ask. We didn't pay to import them, we should not have to pay to deport them. They came because of the magnets; they'll go home once those magnets are turned off.

As it stands right now, an illegal alien can hop across the border, get a driver's license, free health care, and student aid at state-run universities. In many cases, illegal aliens have more rights than citizens. For example, I have to show birth certificates in order for my kids to attend public schools in Tennessee. If you're illegal, they can't require that of you. I would put a stop to free services for illegal aliens beyond basic life-saving measures. Anything beyond that just begs for more of the same.

If you start feeding cats that aren't supposed to be in your yard, what are you going to get? Right, more cats. We have to stop making ourselves a magnet. We can do that by cutting out the enticements to come here and by cracking down on illegals who do. Sounds pretty simple, but you'd be surprised at how many people go ballistic when you suggest such a thing, especially if you're a politician.

Take Tom Tancredo from Colorado, for instance. As a congressman, he swore to uphold the Constitution and the laws of the United States. When he saw a picture on the front page of the *Denver Post* of an eighteen-year-old student who had entered the country illegally six years earlier with his family, he pushed federal officials to deport the boy and his family. The *Post* had run a story exploring the possibility of Colorado following the lead of California, New York, Texas, and Utah in giving in-state tuition breaks to illegal aliens.

Both Democrats and Republicans ridiculed Tancredo for daring to uphold the law. The young man in question was, after all, an honor student, they exclaimed in horror of his daring to follow the law. "That's not the issue at all," Tancredo argued. "The issue is: What do we tell all these thousands of immigrants who are here legally and who are sweating it out to do it the right way?"[19] The Immigration and Naturalization Service (before changing its name to Immigration and Customs Enforcement) initially refused to act but finally agreed to send a letter of warning to the family. Now, that's going to really scare the illegal aliens, isn't it?

Tancredo's actions on the issue of illegal aliens won him a dressing down by Karl Rove, President Bush's senior adviser, who warned him to "never darken the door of the White House again." President Bush purposely failed to introduce him to the crowd during a 2002 rally in Colorado.[20] Perhaps the president sees him as a liability, but the greater liability to the Republicans—and to the country, for that matter—is to ignore the problem, or worse, pander to the illegals and their sympathizers.

During the heat of the illegal alien amnesty debate in 2007, Karl Rove let the cat out of the bag as to why he was pushing so hard for illegal immigration. "I don't want my seventeen-year-old son to have to pick tomatoes or make beds in Las Vegas," Rove said at a Republican women's luncheon.[21] It's that type of snooty attitude that makes us increasingly dependent upon cheap, illegal labor. Picking tomatoes or making beds is *exactly* what Rove's son needs. Okay, not necessarily those specific jobs, but our kids need to do some manual labor early in their lives. It used to be that way. I did everything from work in tobacco to wait tables to paint schools during my teenage years. It's not that I had to take on these jobs to provide for my family. My dad made good money. No, the reason I worked is because it was expected of me. Work was a bridge from carefree adolescence to responsible adulthood. In recent years that bridge has been blown up for many teens because of the influx of cheap illegal labor.

In 1978, 49.1 percent of teenagers in America between the ages of sixteen and nineteen had summer jobs. By 2007, that number had dropped to 35.1 percent. "The immigrant increase in employment is overwhelming," said Andrew Sum, who conducted a study on youth employment at Northeastern University. "Every net new job created is taken by an immigrant. I know that's shocking, but that's the truth. It happened in Massachusetts and New York in the 1990s, and now it's happening in the country as a whole."[22]

What's interesting is the stereotypical white rich kid sitting around playing video games and sponging off his rich parents instead of working is a myth. In 2006, 55.6 percent of white kids whose parents made more than seventy-five thousand dollars per year held summer jobs. That's more than twenty points above the national average. Only 17.4 percent of black kids whose parents pulled down less than twenty thousand dollars per year had summer jobs.[23] When you factor in illegal immigration, it all starts to make sense. Illegal aliens settle in the poorer neighborhoods across America. It stands to reason that the first jobs they take are the jobs closest to home. Whatever the reason for the economic discrepancies, it's certain that illegal immigration is having a deleterious effect on youth employment, which will, no doubt, translate into a poorer work ethic and lower productivity for American workers down the road. Karl Rove can protect his soft little boy from the mean outside world all he wants, but he's doing his son a great disservice. He's also teaching his son that he's above some types of work and, by association, some types of people. That's not how we should be raising the next generation of Americans.

The illegal-alien problem needs to be faced head-on. Pretending that there isn't a problem or forgiving those who break the law only places our nation in greater peril on many different levels. Needless to say, if our borders had been tighter, the September 11 terror attacks would not have happened. If we don't learn that lesson, the next one might very well be much worse.

10

JUNK SCIENCE is behind the global warming scare.

IT'S QUITE A CURIOUS thing. Each time the temperature reaches record or near-record highs, the global warming crowd comes out of the woodwork. "See? That proves it," they say. "The earth is getting warmer and we're all going to die!" But when we hit record or near-record lows, these same people are nowhere to be found. Why is that? Well, it's a sad reality that many of the global-warmers aren't at all interested in saving the planet. They exploit this issue because there's political hay to be made if the earth is heating up. It can be used, as it has been in the past, in an attempt to dismantle our capitalist society.

"Stop burning fossil fuels." "Stop spraying your underarms." "Stop using your air conditioner." All this is spewed out by the dirt people and eco-freaks, who have no credible evidence to back it up. The reason I say they have no credible evidence is because global warming, in the long scheme of things, is impossible to prove. It's impossible to prove because there simply isn't enough data available. We've only been keeping temperature records for a little more than one hundred years, hardly a blip on Earth's timeline.

One United Nations report predicted that "global temperatures could rise by as much as 10.5 degrees Fahrenheit over the next century."[1] It blamed, of course, automobiles. Its dire predictions included, "more 'freak' weather conditions like cyclones, floods, and droughts." Excuse me, but since when have we considered cyclones, floods and droughts to be "freak" weather conditions?

Like most other gloom-and-doom reports I've read from the hysterical global-warming alarmists, it predicts that global temperatures could rise by ten degrees over the next hundred years. The researchers take a relatively few years of temperature data then extrapolate that over a hundred years. That's like sampling the temperatures in May and June, then determining that it's going to be three hundred degrees by Christmas!

This is, plain and simple, junk science. Satellites, which measure the lower tropospheric mean annual air temperatures, are considered by most credible scientists to be much more reliable than spotty surface temperature samples. Certainly, with advances in technology, one cannot fully rely on the accuracy of temperatures recorded a hundred years ago. In fact, a study published in the influential journal *Geophysical Research Letters* found that the traditional measurement of global warming—using sea temperatures as has been done over the last hundred years or so—is inaccurate. Temperatures should have been taken from measurements of the air *above* the sea. With this taken into account, this distinguished international group of scientists concluded that global warming has been exaggerated by some 40 percent.[2] Whoops.

Temperatures taken from satellites tell a different story from the sea temperature findings. With the exception of 1998, which is now regarded as an anomaly, temperatures have hovered around the mean. In fact, if you track the satellite figures since 1998, you could conclude that we're actually experiencing global *cooling*, which is no more plausible than global warming. Temperatures vary greatly from region to region from year to year. The effects of El Niño and La Niña, for instance, skew data so much that making a sound scientific judgment on global temperature is impossible.

When the BBC confirmed in 2008 that we had actually cooled since 1998, it apparently came under intense fire from some global warmists. "This would mean global temperatures have not risen since 1998, prompting some to question the climate change theory," the BBC reported. Apparently this slipped by the eco-censors. In subsequent reporting, with nary a word of explanation, that sentence was changed to: "But this year's temperatures would still be way above the average—and we would soon exceed the record year of 1998 because of global warming induced by greenhouse gases." Quite a difference. The title of the piece also changed, from "Global warming 'dips this year'" to "Global temperatures 'to decrease.'"[3] Just how does temperature warm and dip at the same time?

This was a collision of the facts with those who have

espoused the global warming argument for so long who are
still at a loss as to what to do about it. The data leave no
doubt that temperatures began to dip after 1998. In fact,
temperatures in 2007 dropped by 0.75°C according to all
four major global temperature tracking outlets.[4] That may
not sound like a lot, but remember that global-warming
alarmists claim we've warmed by 0.55°C over the last one
hundred years. In other words, we cooled in the twelve
months of 2007 enough to wipe out one hundred years of
warming. That's not something the mainstream media were
eager to report. Josh Willis of NASA's Jet Propulsion Laboratory observed that the oceans are what really count when
it comes to global warming. NASA launched some three
thousand robots that can dive three thousand feet and measure ocean temperature. Guess what they found? The ocean
is not heating up. National Public Radio investigative reporters were perplexed. "That could mean global warming
has taken a breather," an NPR report acknowledged in
March 2008. No one seemed willing to suggest that the
idea of global warming might be totally bogus. No, there
must be some other explanation. Maybe it's more of that
"global warming dipping" the BBC rattled on about. Here's
the hilarious part. The piece on NPR's *Morning Edition* was
called "The Mystery of Global Warming's Missing Heat."
Hard to have warming without heat. One of the scientists
NPR interviewed was at a loss too. "It's also possible that
some of the heat has gone even deeper into the ocean," he
said.[5] Oh, that's plausible. The heat is hiding from you.

Come, heat. Come out, come out, wherever you are. And we all know that ocean water gets warmer the deeper you go, don't we? It couldn't be that you were just wrong about global warming all along. Could it? The trouble is that these scientists have fed faulty data into their computers and come up with faulty models. If they fed this cooling or plateauing temperature data into their statistical models, they would probably come up with a catastrophic ice age.

A team of international scientists met on Capitol Hill in Washington in the spring of 2002 to debunk the computer model climate projections coming out of the UN's Intergovernmental Panel on Climate Change (IPCC). Hartwig Volz, a geophysicist with the RWE Research Lab in Germany, termed the IPCC's findings "fairy tales." Fred Singer, an atmospheric physicist with the University of Virginia and the Environmental Policy Project, said the projections were "completely unrealistic."[6]

It's a given that our planet has been known to go through different stages of warming trends and cooling trends. Remember the Ice Age? To presume that we humans are the cause of it is putting a lot more stock in our abilities than we deserve. Dr. Ulrich Berner, a geologist with the Federal Institute for Geosciences in Germany, says global temperatures are unrelated to human activity. He also notes that temperatures have varied greatly in the earth's history. "The climate of the past," according to Berner, "has varied under natural conditions without the influence of humans."[7]

One volcanic eruption alone can spew more so-called greenhouse gases into the atmosphere than this country has produced in its entire history, yet Mother Nature seems to absorb them without batting an eye. The earth is amazingly resilient. Remember the *Exxon Valdez* oil spill in Alaska? The dirt people were telling us that Prince William Sound would never recover, that the ecology of the region was destroyed forever. Within a few years after the disaster, however, the ecosystem was back to normal. Just a little more than five years after the disaster, the National Marine Fisheries Service National Oceanic and Atmospheric Administration reported, "With immediate cleanup efforts and more than five years of natural healing, many of the resources of Prince William Sound are well on their way to recovery or have already recovered."[8]

A study conducted by leading environmental experts ten years after the spill concluded: "The four taxa we considered here—pink salmon, sea otters, harbor seals, and seabirds—are among those widely believed to have suffered severe impacts as a consequence of the spill. Our studies provide either no compelling evidence of initial impacts of the *Exxon Valdez* oil spill (pink salmon, roughly half of the seabird species we considered), suggestions that concerns about initial impacts may have been exaggerated (harbor seals), or indications that the resource was indeed affected by the spill but has recovered from these effects or that recovery is well under way (sea otters, half of the seabird species). These results speak to the resiliency of these species and of the larger marine ecosystem in PWS (Prince William Sound)."[9]

Massive quantities of oil seep into the ocean from the ocean floor, yet the ocean cleanses itself. Of course, I'm not an advocate of oil spills, but the point is, we don't give nature enough credit when it comes to dealing with what we would term an ecological disaster.

SUVs on Mars?

While global warming absolutists continued to feed their hysteria over anthropogenic global warming, other scientists were making interesting discoveries. According to one team of scientists, Mars was heating up at a greater rate than Earth. This group of scientists, led by Lori Fenton, a planetary scientist from NASA, published their findings in the scientific journal *Nature*. From the 1970s to the 1990s, computer models indicated that surface air temperatures on Mars increased by 0.65°C. That's more than Earth supposedly warmed up over a one-hundred-year period. Rut row. Ice on the Martian south pole has been retreating too. Could it be the Mars rovers we landed on the planet were SUVs? Of course, Fenton's colleagues were quick to draw the distinction that our heating was man-made while Mars's was not. Let's not let the facts get in the way. It's also interesting to note that the Mars atmosphere is largely made up of carbon dioxide. That's CO_2, friends. When we have CO_2 in our atmosphere, it's caused by humans; there's no chance of its occurring naturally.

Mars isn't the only planet in our solar system that's seen as warming. Benny Peiser, a social anthropologist at Liverpool's John Moores University, said, "Global warming on Neptune's moon, Triton, as well as [on] Jupiter and Pluto, and now Mars, has some [scientists] scratching their heads over what could possibly be in common with the warming of all these planets. Could there be something in common with all the planets in our solar system that might cause them all to warm at the same time?"[10] Gee, I wonder. Let's see. What do all of the planets in our solar system have in common? Hey, how about the sun? Even back in 1991, when Al Gore was first telling us Earth was in the balance, the Danish Meteorological Institute released a study using data that went back centuries showing that global temperatures were closely linked to solar activity. Early in 2008, Canadian scientists determined that solar activity was slowing down, an occurrence that comes along every couple of centuries. The Canadians predicted a coming cooling period. The last time we had such solar inactivity, from around 1650 to 1715, we had freezing winters and cooler summers that led to massive crop failures and famine in Northern Europe. R. Timothy Patterson, professor of geology and director of the Ottawa-Carleton Geoscience Center of Canada's Carleton University, observed, "CO_2 variations show little correlation with our planet's climate on long, medium and even short time scales. I and the first-class scientists I work with are consistently finding excellent correlations between the regular fluctuations of the sun and earthly climate. This is not surprising. The sun and the stars are the ultimate source of energy on this planet." A Hoover Institution study agrees. Hoover fellow Bruce Berkowitz noted, "The effects of solar activity and volcanoes are impossible to miss. Temperatures fluctuated exactly as expected, and the pattern was so clear that, statistically, the odds of the correlation existing by chance were one in 100." The Hoover study added, "Try as we might, we simply could not find any relationship between industrial activity, energy consumption and changes in global temperatures."[11]

Dr. Oleg Sorokhtin, a merited scientist of Russia and a fellow of the Russian Academy of Natural Sciences and a staff researcher of the Oceanology Institute, also warned that we might need to bundle up in the decades to come. "The real reasons for climate change are uneven solar radiation," Sorokhtin said. "Astrophysics knows two solar activity cycles, of 11 and 200 years. Both are caused by changes in the radius and area of the irradiating solar surface. Earth has passed the peak of its warmer period and a fairly cold spell will set in quite soon, by 2012. Real cold will come when solar activity reaches its minimum, by 2041, and will last for 50–60 years or even longer." Sorokhtin might be right. We may already be heading into another mini-ice age.

Global Cooling?

I bet this is one headline you didn't see in your local paper: "Animals retreat as Antarctic cools."[12] That's right—*cools!*

The well-respected science journal *Nature* reported in its January 2002 issue that much of Antarctica is actually cooling, "causing soil invertebrates to decline by more than 10 percent annually." A team of scientists headed by Dr. Peter Doran of the Department of Earth Sciences at the University of Illinois at Chicago, found that the "valleys had cooled by 0.7 degrees C per decade between 1986 and 2000, with pronounced summer and autumn trends." They said: "We believe that climate cooling has significantly impacted ecosystem properties in the valleys." Now, wait a minute. This is huge news, right? Every time a new study comes out about global warming, we see so-called experts all over the TV news. This is a significant piece of research and the networks ignored it.

Another piece of information the media ignored demonstrated how the Earth takes care of temperature changes. A team of scientists led by Richard Lindzen of the Massachusetts Institute of Technology concluded in 2001 that our planet may have a natural "vent" in its atmosphere that releases heat into space, in essence, a natural thermostat.[13] David Ridenour of the National Center for Public Policy Research points out that if Lindzen and his team are correct, this "would require global-warming theorists to significantly scale back their predictions of warming allegedly caused by the buildup of greenhouse gases."[14] By the way, Lindzen's name was attached to a National Academy of Sciences study that claimed to prove that global warming exists. Not only did Lindzen disagree with the study, he and many of the scientists named in it never even saw the darn thing before it was published—a little fact that was buried deep inside the study.[15]

Even the highly quoted and revered expert in the field Dr. James Hansen, director of NASA's Goddard Institute for Space Studies, has begun to revise his global-warming story. In his report published in *Proceedings of the National Academy of Sciences*, Hansen, who for nearly twenty years railed at countries to cut emissions of carbon dioxide and other "heat-trapping" greenhouse gases, changed his tune in the report published in 2000. He said the emphasis on carbon dioxide may be misplaced. Hansen maintained that "the burning of fossil fuels, although substantially raising carbon dioxide levels in the atmosphere, also produces a pall of particle haze that reflects as much of the sun's energy back into space as the release of carbon dioxide has trapped in the air."[16] Is that to say that carbon dioxide may actually cause global *cooling?*

To appreciate the magnitude of this about-face, you have to understand that Hansen was a principal author of one of the first papers calling attention to the links between rising atmospheric levels of carbon dioxide and rising global temperatures, back in 1981. If one of the most revered experts in the field admits that he was wrong, where does that leave all the other global-warming alarmists?

Some scientists, quite frankly, have either too much time on their hands or too much grant money, or both. Take the guys hatching a strategy for modifying planetary orbit. I'm not kidding. These three eggheads—one from the University of California–Santa Cruz, one from the University of Michigan, and the other from NASA—are working on a plan to alter Earth's orbit because, they say, the sun is getting hotter. Eventually, they claim, the earth will be too hot to sustain life. They better hurry. According to their estimates, we only have 3.5 billion years left. They want to somehow shoot a large object, like an asteroid, past the earth, gradually pulling us away from the sun![17] Now, that's got disaster written all over it, doesn't it?

Then there was the group of government scientists in 2008 that wanted to shoot microscopic particles of a specially made glass into the Earth's upper atmosphere to try to stop global warming. I wish I were kidding. Scientists at the U.S. Department of Energy's Savannah River National Laboratory developed computer models of what might happen if they shot a bunch of glass particulates into the stratosphere. I can see it now. Large sheets of glass, like windshields, forming in the atmosphere and crashing to the ground. What's wrong with these people? These folks got the idea from 1995 Nobel Prize winner Paul Crutzen. He had the bright idea of having 747s dump sulfur particles into the stratosphere to cool down the atmosphere.[18] And these are our best and brightest.

That idea sounds sane compared to the scientist who actually received a government grant from NASA to explore the possibility of launching a giant sunshade into space. Actually, he would launch trillions of small free-flying spacecraft a million miles above Earth and align them with the sun. The spacecraft would somehow hook together and form a sort of cloud about half the diameter of the earth and about ten times longer. The total mass of these sunshade spaceships would be twenty million tons.[19] At ten thousand dollars a pound to launch these things on a conventional chemical rocket . . . well, let's just say my calculator doesn't go that high. It's nice to know your tax dollars are going to such worthy causes.

Who in the world could possibly know what's going to happen in 3.5 billion years? Better yet, who cares? These are the same types of people who come up with these global-warming models. What these scientists haven't figured out is, there's no pattern. Just because the temperature has risen for the past two years, or the past hundred years, doesn't mean beans.

Al Gore: The Carbon Glutton

If anyone has made a living—and a killing—off this global-warming hysteria it's Al Gore. He left the vice presidency with little more than $2 million in assets. Seven years later he was worth more than $100 million.[20] Aside from some sweetheart deals with Apple and Google, Gore formed his own company, Generation Investment Management LLP. Gore is a founding partner and chairman of the board. The CEO is David Blood, a former chief executive of Goldman Sachs Asset Management. They affectionately nicknamed their company Blood and Gore. That may be truer than anyone realizes, given the carnage of gullibility in their wake. Generation Investment Management is cashing in on the global-warming scare. It's hard to imagine that anyone who stands to make millions from global warming would be cited as an unbiased expert on the subject. Apparently, that's the case. Gore's film, *An Inconvenient Truth*, picked up an Oscar. A story that received little attention was that Gore's movie was ruled to be a "political film" by the high court in London, and teachers in England are now required to point out the gross errors in Gore's film before showing it. Among those errors are his alarmist predictions of rising sea levels, his contention that global warming will shut down the Gulf Stream, his contention that polar bears will drown because of lack of ice, and the biggie, his assertion that there's a connection between the rise in carbon dioxide in the atmosphere and the rise in temperature over the last 650,000 years.[21] The timing of the court's inconvenient truth about Gore's film came the day before it was announced he would share a Nobel Peace Prize with the U.N. Intergovernmental Panel on Climate Change (IPCC). What global warming and peace have to do with one another is anyone's guess. All the while, Gore was sucking down electricity at just one of his homes to the tune of twenty times the average American household.

According to an investigation conducted by the Tennessee Center for Policy Research (TCPR), Gore was using more than twice the electricity in *one month* than was used by the average household in *an entire year!* That was just electricity. His natural gas bill averaged more than a thousand dollars a month.[22] The TCPR revelation came on the heels of a scathing exposé in *USA Today* by Peter Schweizer. Schweizer was the first to break the story on Gore's conspicuous consumption. He noted that Gore had a ten-thousand-square-foot residence in Nashville and a four-thousand-square-foot home in Arlington, Virginia, in addition to his family farm and home in Carthage, Tennessee. Schweizer spilled the beans that although green energy plans were available for at least two of his homes, Gore had yet to sign up.[23] Apparently, Gore wasn't too concerned about the alleged twenty-foot rise in sea level he was getting everyone so worked up over. He bought a fourth residence in 2005, a $4 million condo near Fisherman's Wharf in San Francisco, just a couple of blocks from the water.[24] That's four homes for two people. Spokesperson Kalee Kreider tried to explain away Gore's hypocrisy. On the Nashville mansion, she insisted, "They are in the midst of installing solar panels on their home, which will enable them to use less power. They also use compact fluorescent bulbs and other energy efficiency measures and then they purchase offsets for their carbon emissions to bring their carbon footprint down to zero." That still didn't change the fact that the Gores are using more electricity than some small countries. And guess from whom they were buying those "offsets." You guessed it. From Generation Investment Management, Al Gore's own company.[25]

This whole notion of carbon offsets is ridiculous. It allows people like Gore to pollute all they want and then pay somebody (in Al's case, himself) for their guilt. It's like paying a hooker three hundred dollars on Saturday night and then putting three hundred bucks in the collection plate on Sunday morning. Yep, you're good to go. It's reminiscent of the selling of indulgences during the Middle Ages, purportedly on behalf of the Roman Catholic Church. Instead of having to confess your sins to receive absolution, you were required to pay for your sins—literally. A sort of sin offset fee. That's what all this carbon offset and carbon credit business is about. It's a way for people to make money from other people's naiveté. Planting a tree on someone's behalf doesn't negate the pollution spewed on a trip to Singapore via private jet to talk to people about how global warming is ruining the planet.

Besides, carbon dioxide is not a pollutant. It's what we exhale with every breath. It's what makes soft drinks fizz and inflates self-inflating life jackets. It's used in fire extinguishers, used to decaffeinate coffee, used in lasers, and to extract oil from the earth. It's an essential part of life on Earth. It's what plants take in to make oxygen. CO_2 makes up about 0.03 percent of the atmosphere. It's measured in parts per million (ppm). Some global-warming alarmists point to an increase in parts per million like it's some huge amount. The longest running study of CO_2 is in Mauna Loa, Hawaii, dating back to the late 1950s. The Earth System Research Laboratory data show that CO_2 at that location was about 315 ppm in 1959. In 2008 it was 384 ppm. This has some dirt people freaking out, but remember, we're talking parts per *million*, so it's only gone up 69 ppm in fifty years. It still means that the atmosphere is only made up of 0.03 percent CO_2. The increase is insignificant, but everyone seems to be missing the big point that bolsters the argument against CO_2 causing global warming. Carbon dioxide levels have increased since 1959 in Hawaii, but temperatures in Hawaii have not. As the BBC noted in a rare moment of candor, "It is tempting to conclude that fluctuations in CO_2 cause temperature changes—but it could be the other way round."[26] What they mean is that the heating of the Earth and, more specifically, the ocean may cause a rise in CO_2 levels. In other words, Al Gore may very well have it backward. Carbon dioxide may not be a cause of warming; it may be the effect of it. Such talk in global-warming circles is heresy. If CO_2 is innocent of the charges against it, then that means we won't be needing those carbon offsets. Which means these shysters who are hoping to cash in on worldwide panic will have to find another ruse.

If the idea of carbon offsets weren't ridiculous enough, Al Gore organized a series of concerts around the globe to raise awareness of global warming. The irony wasn't lost on Arctic Monkeys drummer Matt Helders. "It's a bit patronizing for us 21 year olds to try to start to change the world," Helders told the French wire service AFP. "Especially when we're using enough power for 10 houses just

for [stage] lighting. It'd be a bit hypocritical." Legendary
lead singer for The Who, Roger Daltrey, agreed. "I don't
know what a rock concert's ever going to do to help," he
said. "I can't believe it. Let's burn even more fuel." Gore
promoted the Live Earth concerts by quoting Bob Dylan,
saying, "The times they are achangin'." When *Rolling
Stone* magazine asked Dylan if he was concerned about
global warming, he replied, "Where's the global warming?
It's freezing here."[27] Dylan onboard or not, Live Earth attracted rock stars in fuel-guzzling jets and legions of fans
in gas-guzzling cars and buses all around the world only to
remind us that we need to burn less fuel. Of course, they
all purchased carbon offsets, so everything was just fine.

Not only did Gore continue with the carbon-offsets
scheme, he finally turned his home "green." Of course, it
took him five years to do so *after* he was shamed into it, but
he did it. Or so he claimed. He installed solar panels, a
rainwater collection system, and geothermal heating. The
Gores even replaced all of their evil incandescent light
bulbs with compact fluorescent bulbs, just like good little
dirt people. When the dust settled, a comparison of his
electric bill showed that he had cut his energy consumption by 11 percent.[28] Wow! That means he's only using ten
times the electricity of the average household. I ran the
numbers and found he is using more than four times the
amount of electricity I was using—and there are five folks
living in my house. Over at the Gore mansion, there's only
Al and Tipper. Still, Al's villa received a nice little award

from the U.S. Green Building Council. My house received squat. It just goes to show you that talking about being green is much more important than actually doing it.

What's Really Behind the Global Warming Movement

You know the old saying: follow the money. When something stinks, like this global-warming business, there's bound to be a reason. The ultimate goal is to get at more of the American taxpayers' money. Don't believe it? Check out the Global Governance Project out of Washington, D.C. They are strong advocates of a global tax, which would hit Americans particularly hard, to pay for our sins like, you guessed it, global warming. It's a way to steal money from producer nations like ours and give it to the socialists and the communists because their economic systems are utter failures. If you feel a little uneasy about paying a global tax, Hilary French, supposedly an American who works for the Global Governance Project, says we Americans have to get over "the sovereignty thing," as she puts it.[29] These people scare me.

French joined a bunch of other leftists from around the globe at a big American-bashing confab held, ironically, at the Ronald Reagan Building in D.C. In addition to the global taxes, which would generate about $300 billion for their little "global agencies," they advocated drastic cuts in American living standards in the name of "sustainable development" for the world. They also pushed for America to adopt the creation of regional food markets, giving up our neighborhood grocery stores, along with accepting low-speed cars and low-meat diets.[30]

Emma Brindal is a climate justice campaigner coordinator for Friends of the Earth. She said, "A climate change response must have at its heart a redistribution of wealth and resources."[31]

You see, the folks at the epicenter of this global warming business are latching onto it for a reason. They don't like the American way of life, and many of them are Americans. I'm not talking about the scientists, necessarily, although many of them can be lumped into this group. I'm talking about the propagandists, who use the junk science of global warming to stir their pot of resentment for the United States. They want to change everything about the way we live, the way we consume, and the standard of living we have achieved, which is unparalleled in the world and unprecedented in the history of mankind. Many more well-meaning folks have been duped by these people into thinking that they're actually helping avert a global catastrophe by changing our way of life.

I'm all for clean air and water, but this global-warming farce goes beyond that. It's about making Americans feel guilty. These global leftists make a big deal about how much resources we consume, but they have no problem boarding a fuel-guzzling jet to stage a protest in Seattle or Washington. In their quest to destroy the American way of life, they ignore the fact that we're also the biggest producing nation on the planet. We feed the world and pollute far less than these communist and totalitarian nations they want to help with their global tax. Like it or not, these smaller countries are dependent on us, either directly or indirectly. If we followed their prescription for living, it would cripple or kill this nation. Bump us off and it's like killing the goose that laid the golden egg.

If It Ain't One Thing . . .

There's always a Plan B. The global warming crowd is ready with another set of horrific circumstances whenever we disprove their latest theory. A fad that was egged on by the 2003 movie *The Core* is the theory that the planet's poles are getting ready to flip. In an article published prior to the movie, the headline read, "Sun's rays to roast Earth as poles flip." Not too sensational, huh? The reporter stated, "Earth's magnetic field seems to be disappearing most alarmingly near the poles, a clear sign that a flip may soon take place."[32] "Soon," of course, is a relative term. Scientists predict, the article goes on to say, that this catastrophic event could happen "over the next 1,000 years."

It wasn't just the reporter working people into a frenzy. The scientists who were cited in the piece predicted the transformation of the polar flip could take anywhere from a few weeks to thousands of years. How's that for pinpoint accuracy? They claim these pole reversals happen every 250,000 years or so and we haven't had one in more than a million years (apparently they *don't* happen every 250,000 years), so we're due. When it happens, all navigational equipment will be knocked out and we'll be bombarded by "intense solar radiation bursts." Oh, my gosh! We're all gonna die! Of course, in the movie, they drill deep into the earth's surface and set off a nuclear bomb to reverse the process. Now, there's a brilliant idea. They haven't blamed your car for this one yet, but give them time.

The Bottom Line on Global Warming

If the truth be told, we have no way of knowing precisely what happened thousands of years ago, nor do we have any clue as to what the future holds. Chances are, there will be some climate changes, as there always have been. We'll either adapt or we'll be killed off. I know one thing: I'm not going to sit around and worry about it. But that's exactly what the dirt people want us to do. Why? So you'll change your evil ways.

You have to understand the mind-set of these people to understand what motivates them. Many of them hate us and everything America stands for. They see us as the big bully, the greedy fat cat exploiting the rest of the world for our own sensual pleasures. With the media as willing accomplices, it's commonly accepted that global warming is real. Those caught on the periphery of this whacked-out movement are well-meaning sorts who just want to do what's right by the planet. I understand their concern, but the science to which they entrust their beliefs is lousy.

Once you understand that the global-warming movement is purely political, it all starts to make sense. Why else would so many people buy into a theory with so little evidence to back it up? I refer to my original point about insufficient data: there just isn't enough concrete data even to begin to make an educated guess as to whether Earth's temperature is rising or falling long term. If you used the same amount of statistical sampling for a poll, Gallup would toss you out of his office on your ear.

Russ, a caller to my show, scaled it down to make it easier to understand: let's assume Earth is about sixty thousand years old. For grins, let's say we've been keeping temperature records for one hundred years. Drawing a serious conclusion on global warming based on the amount of time we've been keeping temperature records is the same as drawing a conclusion about the last 417 days based on data gathered over the last sixty seconds.[33] Scaling it down like that puts things into perspective. No legitimate scientist would accept that data as sufficient. Nor should we accept the global-warming alarmists at face value any longer.

We should strive to cut down on air pollution because it makes for a healthier life, not because some eco-freaks are telling us we're all going to roast to death within ten years. Instead, follow your common sense, something these global-warming alarmists woefully seem to lack.

11

Killing through partial-birth abortion is murder.

No matter what your opinion on abortion, reasonable people should be able to agree that partial-birth abortion is murder. Unfortunately, there are those who choose to be unreasonable. The opponents of a ban on this horrible procedure usually fall into two camps. First, there are those who deny that such a procedure even exists. Despite the evidence, the testimony, the unspeakable carnage, they refuse to accept the fact that it does happen thousands of times each year in this country.

The second group includes hard-line proabortion advocates who, when backed into a corner, will argue that a woman has a right to an abortion up until the moment of delivery. They feel that giving an inch in the partial-birth abortion battle will begin the deterioration of their cause. So, they hold their ground. They continue to defend the indefensible. However, the truth is slowly leaking out, in spite of the majority of news outlets that would rather keep this issue out of the limelight.

What Is Partial-Birth Abortion?

When I first learned of this procedure, I refused to believe that anything this gruesome was taking place in America. It sounded like something you'd see in the back-alley butcher shops of a third-world country, or some horrific punishment ordered down on the enemies of a vicious totalitarian regime.

To be clear, partial-birth abortion is a procedure in which the baby is breeched in the womb and pulled down the birth canal feet first. Once all of the baby's body, except the head, is outside the cervix, the abortionist takes surgical scissors and punctures the back of the baby's head. A catheter is inserted in the open wound and the brains are sucked out, thus collapsing the head. The birth of the baby, now dead, is completed, and it's called abortion instead of murder. Only the length of the child's head technically differentiates the two and I would submit to you that there is no difference between the two. Partial-birth abortion is, quite certainly, murder.

I remember first becoming aware of this procedure back in the mid-'90s, about the time of my second son's birth. I was horrified by what I had learned. I emotionally described the procedure to my audience. Having witnessed the birth of my sons, I could not imagine what kind of monster would purposely bring a child that close to birth and then kill it. My voice cracked that morning as I envisioned, out loud, my own tiny boys taking that same journey down the birth canal only to find, instead of a caring doctor and loving parents anxiously anticipating their arrival, an abortionist lying in wait with instruments of death with which to kill them.

Kate Michaelman and the crowd over at the National Abortion Rights Action League (NARAL) claim there's no such thing as partial-birth abortion. They claim that the anesthesia given to the mother kills the baby before it's born. Planned Parenthood says, "The fetus dies of an overdose of anesthesia given to the mother. . . . This induces brain death in a fetus in a matter of minutes."[1] (Oh, that's much more comforting.) The problem is, even that bold admission of barbarism is false.

The U.S. House of Representatives conducted a public hearing several years ago entitled "The Effects of Anesthesia During a Partial-Birth Abortion." Four leading experts in the field of anesthesiology testified that anesthesia could not kill an unborn fetus. Even if it could, would that make it any more palatable that children are being exterminated in the womb, sometimes in the third trimester of a pregnancy? Unfortunately, the truth is much more ghastly.

Brenda Pratt Shafer, a registered nurse, was assigned to an abortion clinic in 1993. She was decidedly prochoice and had no problem with the assignment, that is, until she witnessed the horror of a partial-birth abortion. The following eyewitness account from Nurse Shafer will absolutely send chills down your spine.

I stood at the doctor's side and watched him perform a partial-birth abortion on a woman who was six months pregnant. The baby's heartbeat was clearly visible on the ultrasound screen. The doctor delivered the baby's body and arms, everything but his little head. The baby's body was moving. His little fingers were clasping together. He was kicking his feet. The doctor took a pair of scissors and inserted them into the back of the baby's head, and the baby's arms jerked out in a flinch, a startle reaction, like a baby does when he thinks that he might fall. Then the doctor opened the scissors up. Then he stuck the high-powered suction tube into the hole and sucked the baby's brains out. Now the baby was completely limp. I never went back to the clinic. But I am still haunted by the face of that little boy. It was the most perfect, angelic face I have ever seen.[2]

To rebut such a horrifying story, the pro-partial-birth abortion advocates claim the procedure is necessary, either for the health of the mother or because the child is deformed. Dr. David Brown studied that very issue and found that the majority of partial-birth abortions are elective, having nothing to do with health or deformity. He said, "The 'typical' patients tend to be young, low-income women, often poorly educated or naive, whose reasons for waiting so long to end their pregnancies are rarely medical."[3]

Dr. Martin Haskell, one of the more prolific butchers of partial-birth abortions, once said that he "routinely" performed partial-birth abortions for nonmedical reasons.

This guy's performed well over 1,000 partial-birth abortions.[4] He admitted, "I'll be quite frank: most of my abortions are elective in the twenty- to twenty-four-week range. . . . In my particular case, 20 percent are for genetic reasons. And the other 80 percent are purely elective."[5]

The notorious partial-birth abortionist Dr. George Tiller of Wichita, Kansas, gave a slideshow presentation at the Feminist Majority Foundation's annual Women's Leadership Conference. He was, at the time, facing nineteen criminal charges for illegal late-term abortions in the state of Kansas. Tiller admitted to performing partial-birth abortions as late as one day before the mother's due date. One day! Oh, but it gets worse.

Tiller was reminded by a member of the Students for Life of America (SFLA) of the Born Alive Infants Protection Act signed into federal law in 2002. That law protects born children from murder. Tiller noted his objection to the law. "Let's say you have 15 or 16," the doctor said. "You had one slip out with a heartbeat; that is not a viable fetus, but that is born alive or has a heartbeat. Then you have to take that non-viable fetus and rush it directly to the hospital against the woman's wishes." You had one "slip out" with a heartbeat? One can only presume that Tiller would simply snuff out the "non-viable fetus." If a child with a heartbeat—outside the womb—is not a living child, then what is?

Eerily, Tiller's presentation evoked a standing ovation from the crowd. This was not just some assemblage of sadistic baby killers. The scary part is this presentation was given at a conference of the National Education Association.[6] That's right, the NEA, the teachers union. What killing babies and the education of your children have in common is anyone's guess, but it certainly offers a glimpse into the soul of that organization.

Another partial-birth abortionist, Dr. James McMahon, said that of the partial-birth abortions he performed, the most common reason to terminate a pregnancy was "depression." He cited other reasons, like substance abuse and non-life-threatening "fetal indications," such as Down syndrome and deformed cleft palates. Another doctor added, "We have an occasional abnormality, but it is a minuscule amount."[7]

As far as saving the life of the mother, medical experts tell me that the last thing you'd want to do if the mother's life were in danger would be to breech the child, which is done during a partial-birth abortion. The entire child is born in this procedure except for the head. It's absurd to contend that collapsing a baby's head would do anything at all to save the mother's life; therefore, the whole argument for preserving this procedure just in case a doctor needs to use it is totally untenable.

So, how many of these murders are taking place each year? It's hard to say. We know that McMahon estimated he had performed "well over 2,000" before he died in 1995.[8] An investigation and interviews with physicians in New Jersey who perform partial-birth abortions revealed that in that state alone, at least 1,500 partial-birth abortions are performed every year.[9] Just those small samples are a far cry more than the mere 450 procedures per year claimed by proabortion forces.

That brings up another curiosity: if there's nothing wrong with partial-birth abortions, why do the proabortion folks consistently lie about the number of them performed? If they truly believed these procedures were acceptable, they would have no problem confirming the actual numbers.

When Did They Come to Be?

Prior to *Roe v. Wade* in 1973, there was no such thing as a partial-birth abortion. The medical definition of abortion is the termination of a pregnancy prior to the point that the baby is strong enough to survive outside the womb. Back before *Roe*, doctors were allowed to destroy a fetus only if the mother's life was in danger. Since cesarean-section deliveries had a high maternal mortality rate before the development of antibiotics, doctors would perform what was called a "destructive operation." They used a device called a cranioclast to crush the baby's skull inside the womb. Once antibiotics were in use, C-sections took the place of destructive operations in cases where the mother's life was in danger.

After *Roe v. Wade*, abortion was more or less wide open in the first trimester, or first three months of pregnancy. After that, the state had a more compelling interest the longer the pregnancy proceeded. However, the abortion case that followed closely on the heels of *Roe* opened the door for abortion on demand, no matter what stage of pregnancy. In *Roe*'s companion case, *Doe v. Bolton*, Justice Harry Blackmun left matters concerning the mother's health to the doctor's discretion, which "may be exercised in the light of all factors—physical, emotional, psychological, familial, and the woman's age—relevant to the well-being of the patient."[10] In essence, if the doctor deemed the woman emotionally ill-prepared for the baby, even in the ninth month of pregnancy, an abortion could be performed.

In the years after *Roe*, greedy abortionists saw gold in those last two trimesters. Women who ordinarily might be turned away were "counseled" about their mental state and determined to qualify under Blackmun's language in *Doe*. Then came the ugly part. The normal procedure of sucking the fetus out of the womb became increasingly difficult the more developed the baby. Suctioning a child from the womb at seven months might produce a live, premature birth. Another procedure had to be developed.

Pulling the child down the conventional way, head first, would produce a crying baby that would have to be killed. Ah, but breeching the baby would prevent the child from crying before it was killed. Thus began a whole new industry of butchery that led to the first congressional action of the mid-'90s. The first mention of the procedure was in 1990 in a *Los Angeles Times* article in which Dr.

James McMahon described the procedure that he called "intrauterine cranial decompression."

Dr. Martin Haskell of Dayton, Ohio, introduced his paper "Second Trimester Abortion from Every Angle" at the Risk Management Seminar sponsored by the National Abortion Federation, where he presented partial-birth abortion as an alternative to D&E, or dilation and evacuation, in which the fetus is dismembered and removed in pieces. In June 1995, Republican Congressman Charles Canady of Florida introduced HR 1833, the first Partial-Birth Abortion Ban Act.

Trying to Stop the Carnage

Currently, more than thirty states have passed laws banning partial-birth abortions, but about two-thirds of those have been enjoined by federal courts either permanently or temporarily. The proabortion forces during the Clinton administration fought tooth and nail to defeat a ban while he was in office. Congress took up the issue after the Republican sweep of 1994. In 1995, both the House and the Senate passed a ban on partial-birth abortions. President Clinton vetoed the bill in April 1996. The House voted to override the veto, but the Senate fell short of the necessary votes to override.

A second attempt was made during the Clinton administration in 1997. As before, the House and Senate voted for the ban and, as before, Clinton vetoed the bill, even after the AMA had backed it. The House again voted to override, but the Senate came up short once again, this time by just three votes.

The Clintonites argued that the bills he vetoed lacked a provision taking into effect the health of the mother. This sounded reasonable on the surface, but the "health" loophole has been used to include the "emotional health" of the mother. That, in turn, has been interpreted by abortion doctors to mean that if the mother is depressed over having the baby, then they have the green light to kill it.

These two bills banning partial-birth abortion that Clinton shot down allowed the procedure's use only if the mother's life were in danger. What's interesting is that both Bill Clinton and Al Gore were against abortions of *any* kind before they started running for national office. While governor of Arkansas, Clinton wrote a letter to the Arkansas Right to Life group saying: "I am opposed to abortion and to government funding of abortions. We should not spend state funds on abortions because so many people believe abortion is wrong."[11] Al Gore wrote a similar letter, stating: "It is my deep personal conviction that abortion is wrong. I hope that some day we will see the current outrageously large number of abortions drop sharply."[12]

Yet after years of opposing abortion, the Clinton administration caved to "the ones who brung 'em," the proabortion crowd, and blew an opportunity to stop one of the most heinous crimes ever to take place in this country. It's an ugly example of selling your soul for the office.

The famous Laci Peterson murder case of 2003 best exemplifies where the radical feminists from NOW actually stand on the partial-birth abortion issue. In that case, a very pregnant Laci Peterson was murdered and her husband was charged with the crime. Morris County, New Jersey, NOW president Mavra Stark protested the fact that Scott Peterson was charged with a *double* murder, even though his wife was eight months pregnant at the time of her death. "There's something about this that bothers me a little bit," Stark told the *Daily Record* of Parsippany, New Jersey. "Was it born, or was it unborn? If it was unborn, then I can't see charging [Peterson] with a double-murder. [The boy] was wanted and expected," she added, "and [Laci] had a name for him, but if he wasn't born, he wasn't born. It sets a kind of precedent."[13] You see, all these folks care about is precedent. In their world, a child is never a child until his entire body is out of the womb. Killing him, even up until the moment of birth, is acceptable to them. Anything less and they fear their whole argument will unravel. They're willing to totally discount the life of a little baby in order to further their political agenda. That's absolutely reprehensible.

The Tide Is Turning

Finally, Congress passed the Partial-Birth Abortion Ban Act in 2003. That law deemed partial-birth abortion a "gruesome and inhumane procedure that is never medically necessary and should be prohibited."[14] Furthermore,

Congress determined that "a partial-birth abortion is never necessary to preserve the health of a woman, poses serious risks to a woman's health, and lies outside the standard of medical care."[15] However, a doctor, at his or her own discretion, can opt for the partial-birth abortion procedure if it is deemed the only way to save the life of the mother.[16] The law merely ended the legality of using the partial-birth abortion method; it did not limit when an abortion could be performed.

Of course, the law was challenged in court. It ultimately ended up in the U.S. Supreme Court. On April 18, 2007, the High Court, in a five-to-four decision, upheld the Partial-Birth Abortion Ban Act. Showing an utter misunderstanding of the role of the Supreme Court, Justice Ruth Bader Ginsburg wrote in her dissent from the majority opinion, "Today's decision is alarming." She said the ruling "refuses to take . . . seriously" previous Court rulings on abortion. She was, in all likelihood, referring to a similar case that came before the Court in 2000 that challenged a state law banning partial-birth abortion. That law was overturned by the High Court because the Court was stacked with a disproportionate number of liberal, activist judges. Ginsburg naively assumed the new configuration of more prudent justices would just rubber-stamp the old ruling. Fortunately, she was wrong.[17]

Abortion is one of the most contentious issues in American history. Like many prolifers, I was once prochoice, in my younger years. Many years ago, after thoroughly researching the issue, I decided that Ronald Reagan's position on abortion best reflected mine. He said that until we could fully determine exactly when life began, he would rather err on the side of life.[18]

Many have compared the abortion debate to the split over slavery. Although I'm extremely passionate about the subject, my feeling is that the majority of the people aren't as set in their convictions. That's a good thing, by the way. In 1992, 56 percent of Americans quizzed in a *Los Angeles Times* poll supported the *Roe v. Wade* decision. By 1996, that number was down to 46 percent. In 2000, the number had dropped to 43 percent.[19]

The polling data on partial-birth abortion is even more damaging. Seventy-two percent believe partial-birth abortions should be illegal. Only 22 percent think they should be legal.[20] That's a three-to-one margin against.

I got into an argument over abortion with Cher once on my show. She claimed that it was the woman's right to do whatever she wanted with her body. I then asserted that she must be for legalization of prostitution and drugs. "Well, no," she answered. "But I thought you just said a woman had the right to do anything she wanted with her body," I pressed. There was a long pause and then the tap-dancing started. You see, this argument that a woman has a right to do whatever she wants with her body is nonsense. And how about the rights of the child? Once you start asking for consistency in the argument, the whole thing collapses like a house of cards.

Prolifers are winning the war of the heart, which is where this fight will ultimately have to be won. Slavery was a more tangible evil. The atrocity of abortion is more covert. A hundred years after its abolition, we will look back on the argument of a woman's right to choose with as much scorn as we view the contention that slavery was a property rights issue. The proabortion forces, through their partial-birth abortion support, have unwittingly unleashed the dogs of truth, and they have consumed every morsel of their pro-partial-birth abortion argument. Now they look hungrily at the main course—the abortion issue itself.

12

LIBERALISM is an ideology doomed to failure.

PEOPLE OFTEN ASK ME what the difference is between conservatism and liberalism. The answer isn't too complicated. I think it's best summed up by the old Chinese proverb that says, "Give a man a fish and you feed him for a day. Teach a man to fish and you feed him for a lifetime."[1] Sometimes liberalism and conservatism have the same goal, but they just have different ways of getting there.

Liberalism is oftentimes a quick fix, while conservatism takes a little longer. This is a partial explanation for why the news media tilt to the Left. Let's face it, good news just ain't news. Journalists, by the nature of their jobs, focus disproportionately on what's *wrong* with the world. Day in and day out, they wallow in the pain and misery that they witness in their reporting. Theirs is also a fast-paced business, moving rapidly from one story to the next. They don't have time to focus on one problem for very long, so, from their standpoint, each story needs a quick fix. Unfortunately, as the Chinese proverb illustrates, it takes time to solve a problem long term. Politicians oftentimes fall into the same trap.

The Great Society is a perfect example. Black people were treated so badly in this country for so long that the cumulative effect had left many black Americans disenfranchised and locked out of our nation's prosperity. There's no doubt there was a problem. The disagreement centered on how to solve it. Lyndon B. Johnson's administration decided on a course of action that would incorporate its efforts to rectify the situation into its broader-based War on Poverty. Conservatives, who had a different approach, were castigated as mean-spirited and cold-hearted. They advocated teaching the disenfranchised to fish. The liberals pushed for *giving* them the fish instead, which only staved off the inevitable.

As we look back over the past few decades, we can see that the Great Society, which was designed to lift people out of poverty, had merely trapped them in it for generations by making them dependent on the government. I'm convinced that most of the people who advocated the Great Society at its inception had good intentions, but they didn't think through the long-term effects of their actions. It was a quick fix, which led to even bigger problems down the road, problems that a liberal mind-set could not have foreseen.

The Real Civil Rights Story

Another issue that has become conjoined with the Great Society is the 1964 Civil Rights Act. However, the two must be disentangled to fully understand and appreciate conservatism. The truth is, one has little to do with the other. In fact, the Great Society did more to impede civil rights than to broaden them. It stigmatized a whole segment of our society, leading to more prejudice. The mistake many make is trying to attach the liberal label to the civil rights movement. It may have been liberal in that it was changing the status quo, but the whole concept of everyone being treated equally under the law is quite conservative.

In his book *A Coach's Life*, legendary University of North Carolina basketball coach Dean Smith recounts his part in the civil rights effort of the 1960s. "I'm not sure how liberal I truly am," Smith writes. "I think we should be free and tolerant as a society. Does that make me liberal? Maybe so. Mainly, I hope I'm sensible."[2] Coach Smith obviously struggles with labels, and rightfully so. Liberals and Democrats did not, by any means, corner the civil rights market.

Contrary to what most people have grown up to believe, the truth behind the 1964 Civil Rights Act is this: a greater percentage of Republicans than Democrats in the U.S. House and Senate voted *for* civil rights legislation (see the appendix for the full roll-call vote). That's right. More Democrats voted *against* the 1964 Civil Rights Act than Republicans. In the House of Representatives, 80 percent of Republicans voted for the act while just 63 percent of Democrats did.[3] To put it another way, ninety-one Democrats voted against the Civil Rights Act compared to only thirty-five Republicans.

In the Senate, Richard Russell (D-GA) ran the opposition to the bill and spearheaded a filibuster to try and stop it. Only one Republican joined him. When the votes were counted, twenty-one of the twenty-seven votes against the Civil Rights Act were Democrat. Only six were Republican. That's 82 percent of Senate Republicans who voted for the bill as opposed to just 69 percent of Senate Democrats. In other words, Democrats made up 78 percent of the no vote.[4]

Such noted Democrats as Al Gore Sr. voted against the measure, yet the Democratic Party somehow hijacked the issue. His son has even claimed a family history of civil rights support that is just not true. Other Democratic luminaries who voted against the 1964 Civil Rights Act were Bill Clinton's "mentor," then-Senator William Fulbright, and "the Conscience of the Senate," Robert "KKK" Byrd. Robert Byrd has tried to hide behind the excuse that he really wanted to vote for the Civil Rights Act but he had to vote as his constituents wanted him to vote. It's funny, but Byrd was the only one of the West Virginia delegation—House or Senate—to vote *against* the Civil Rights Act.

With such Democrat luminaries siding with racists, it's hard to imagine how Democrats have come out smelling like a rose on this issue.

I suspect having LBJ sign the act into law, surrounded by the civil rights leaders of the day, had much to do with Democrats getting the credit, but that credit is undeserved. Republican Senator Everett Dirksen deserved a lot of the credit. He hammered out a compromise bill in his office that was able to attract enough votes to kill a filibuster. The civil rights issue was more a battle between regions rather than ideology. Remember that George Wallace, who stood in the schoolhouse door in an attempt to prevent integration, was a Democrat. Most of the bigots of the 1940s, '50s, and '60s were Democrats, because the Republican Party of the South was virtually nonexistent back then.

In reality, Republicans and civil rights have a long history. Since 1933, when the first civil rights legislation began to surface, Republicans have had a much better record on civil rights than Democrats. There were twenty-six major civil rights votes between 1933 and 1964, and in 80 percent of those, a majority of Democrats opposed the legislation. By stark contrast, a majority of Republicans voted in favor of civil rights more than 96 percent of the time.[5]

Despite the history revisionists, John F. Kennedy was in no hurry to advance the civil rights agenda either. As a senator from Massachusetts, Kennedy had the chance to vote for the 1957 Civil Rights Act. Instead, he voted to send it to the Senate Judiciary Committee where it was certain to languish.[6] When he ran for president in 1960, Kennedy avoided the civil rights issue like the plague, hoping not to pit the views of his native Northeast against those of the Democrat-controlled South, which he desperately needed to win the election. Kennedy was more focused on his domestic and foreign policy agenda and didn't want to jeopardize either by hacking off the folks in Congress. That's why he made no move on the civil rights front for the first two years of his administration.

By 1963, he could avoid the issue no longer and was pressured into proposing a civil rights act. He would not see it to fruition as later that year an assassin's (or assassins') bullets ended his life. Civil rights supporters in Congress, primarily led by Republican Everett Dirksen, the Senate minority leader, and Democrat Mike Mansfield, the Senate majority leader, pushed the bill through. Also keep in mind that Dirksen was no "Northern Republican Liberal." When asked what his greatest legislative achievement was, Dirksen replied by quoting historian Edward Gibbon. "Progress is made not so much by what goes on the statute book," he said, "but rather what is kept off."[7] Certainly a statement of true conservatism.

Something else most Americans don't realize, and many liberals try to hide, is that the Ku Klux Klan was a militant offshoot of the Democratic Party. Klansmen organized in the South primarily to keep blacks away from the polls, in defiance of Republicans in the North. West Virginia Senator Robert Byrd was once a member of the Klan. He explained later that he joined in order to get elected to office. Oh, well, that explains it, then. For a moment I thought he was just some sleazy political opportunist! Look, if that's the only way you can get elected to office, you're better off not running. Can you imagine the outcry if a Republican senator carried those credentials? Senator Byrd has tried to explain away his vote against the Civil Rights Act as acquiescing to the wishes of his West Virginia constituents. Funny, isn't it, how his West Virginia colleague, Senator Randolph, managed to muster the courage to vote for the Civil Rights Act?

I belabor this point on civil rights only to deflate the holier-than-thou liberals who try to paint conservatives as racists. It's time the record was set straight regarding this issue. Supporting civil rights for blacks was neither conservative nor liberal—it was just right.

Labels Are Relative

"The American Republic will endure, until politicians realize they can bribe the people with their own money." Those words are attributed to Alexis de Tocqueville, a great French student of American democracy. Although Tocqueville spent just nine months in the United States, he was a much more insightful prognosticator than many who lived here. He understood that there was a thin line between democracy and mob rule. He foresaw the pitfalls that awaited a society that allowed its government to overshadow the governed. It's interesting to note that Tocqueville is regarded as a liberal in early to mid-nineteenth-century France. The reason was that the *conservative establishment* of his time was the constitutional monarchy of King Louis Philippe. All the more reason to be constantly cognizant of the changing dynamics of interpretive labels.

The liberalism to which I attach the dismal future of failure is American liberalism of the late twentieth and early twenty-first centuries. It's a basic philosophy that the government knows better how to run your life than you do. That's quite condescending, when you get right down to it. It supposes that the people, excluding the ruling class, have neither the intellect nor the resources to fend for themselves. It supposes that we're like a child with a pair of scissors—if we're left to run free, we will surely hurt ourselves.

This is best illustrated in our government's wholesale warehousing of the poorest Americans in housing projects. We have congregated the most desperate of society in one, convenient location, making them easy prey for the hucksters, swindlers, pimps, and drug dealers. How compassionate is that? As Tocqueville forecast, the politicians have learned to bribe the people with their own money, enslaving a substantial enough segment that they can use the voting bloc of the government-dependent to confiscate sufficient money from the rest of the population to keep the Ponzi scheme alive. Eventually, you run out of productive citizens to bilk, and the whole thing implodes. Thus is the fate awaiting runaway liberalism.

Another reason liberalism is doomed to failure is because it's based largely on emotion instead of facts. It's what I refer to as *liberal logic*. I'll give you a couple of examples: in order to stop kids from having sex, liberals hand out condoms at school. Or, to stop innocent citizens from being gunned down, they take away their guns. Starting to get the picture? Liberal logic is a purely emotional approach to solving a problem. Liberal logic is, in essence, an oxymoron because it is completely devoid of logic.

A few years back, I was invited to be a panelist on a discussion of hate crimes at the American Bar Association's annual meeting in Atlanta. I discovered when I arrived that I was the token conservative. The panel included such noted liberals as civil rights veteran Joseph Lowery and the Clinton Justice Department's Bill Lann Lee. (Bill turned out to be a very nice guy, by the way. Just misguided.) We all met one another at a luncheon held for the panelists before the discussion. The only other panelist whom I determined was, perhaps, conservative was Guy James Gray, the district attorney from Jasper, Texas, who prosecuted the killers in the infamous dragging death of James Byrd. I couldn't say for sure that he was on my side, but I decided from our private conversations at the lunch table that he probably was. However, his capacity there was to provide insight into the Byrd case. As I was to learn later, he was none too eager to enter into the political fray. No one on the panel knew very much about me because I was a late addition after the ABA got a complaint that the panel was heavily tilted to the Left. I used my anonymity to listen and learn from the table discussion.

The conversation began lightheartedly but inevitably turned to the subject at hand. They talked extensively about the dire need for hate-crime legislation but this room, filled mostly with attorneys, failed to come up with one logical reason that would justify treating one victim better than another.

When we arrived at the World Congress Center, we each took our places on the panel. The victim mentality began, with one panelist after another describing hate crime after hate crime. Most of the panelists were from specific groups that would enjoy special protection under hate-crime laws, and they offered some very heart-rending stories from their own personal experiences to make their case. I, of course, could not deny that there was hate in America, nor could I deny that people were singled out for crimes just because of who they are.

My argument centered on a simple phrase, one that is literally etched in stone on the front of the Supreme Court Building in Washington. It states, simply, *Equal Justice Under Law*. That means that if a person hates me because of what I say on the radio and kills me, he should be dealt with just as severely as one who hates a homosexual and kills him because of his sexuality. Setting up a list of protected citizens runs counter to the basic principles of justice. Hate-crime laws are, plain and simple, discriminatory.

The other panelists became incensed at my remarks and began to ratchet up the emotional reasons for more hate-crime legislation, still avoiding any logical reason for it. A woman at the far end of the panel, in a move to evoke sympathy from the crowd and the C-SPAN audience, began to heap praise on Guy James Gray. She spoke of his courage in his vigorous prosecution of James Byrd's killers and how, thanks to him, these killers would pay for their crimes. His case was exalted as an example to the world of how we should deal with hate crimes. I had been waiting for just such a moment.

I agreed that Guy James Gray did indeed have courage. He had tenaciously pursued justice in a racially charged atmosphere under the glare of the national spotlight. He had made his case with passion and conviction, determined to send a message to the world that Jasper, Texas, would not tolerate such a barbarous and contemptible crime. I then pointed out a bit of information that I had learned at the luncheon from Gray himself during our private conversation: Texas hate-crime legislation does not apply to capital crimes. In other words, the very case that the other panelists had used as a centerpiece for their whole argument was actually prosecuted successfully *without* the killers having ever been charged with a hate crime!

A hush fell over the room as spectators looked on in astonishment. How could this be? There was no denying that justice had been served in Jasper, Texas. They had all said so. How could it be that it was served *without* the aid of hate-crime laws?

One of the other panelists suggested that we need hate-crime legislation much like we need affirmative action, to level the playing field. I noted that affirmative action, although its intentions were honorable, had become a quota system, and hate-crime legislation discriminated in much the same way. "You don't right the wrongs of the past by wronging the people of the present," I told them.

The discussion then deteriorated into emotional jabs at me, with Reverend Joseph Lowery leading the charge. He adamantly insisted that there was no such thing as quotas. In the face of several well-known examples that I cited for him, he angrily lashed out, calling me a hate monger. It was the verbal equivalent of running out of ammunition then—out of desperation, he just threw his gun at me. It was rather disappointing to see a man of Reverend Lowery's stature resort to name calling, but that's what happens when you base your whole argument on emotion instead of facts and logic. I have learned from years of debate that it is one of the hallmarks of liberalism.

Where Was the Outrage?

Another disturbing aspect of the whole hate-crime movement is its hypocrisy. Other than the Byrd dragging death, probably the highest-profile hate crime in America has been the tragic death of Matthew Shepherd, a homosexual, in Wyoming. On October 6, 1998, two men lured Shepherd from a bar and drove him to the outskirts of town where they tied him to a fence, pistol-whipped him and left him for dead. Shepherd died six days later. This sparked outrage across the country. Americans, no matter their sexual orientation, were shocked by the story. Like the James Byrd killing, it was another senseless act of violence.

The media played up the crime and the subsequent call from the Left for federal hate-crime legislation to protect gays. Countless hours of news time and endless barrels of ink were devoted to this story. Yet, less than a year later, another murder took place in Arkansas and was completely ignored by the national media. In fact, you may very well be learning of this crime here for the first time.

On September 26, 1999, thirteen-year-old Jesse Dirkhising was lured to the apartment of two gay men where he was repeatedly raped and then strangled to death, some reports say with his own underwear. Where was the national outrage? Here was a *child* who was sodomized and murdered by two adult men and the mainstream media ignored it. Sure, the story made the local papers in Bentonville, Arkansas, but where was the national media outcry?

Unfortunately for little Jesse Dirkhising and his family, he doesn't fall into any protected group. The crime against him wasn't based on race or religion or sexual orientation. It was merely two deranged, perverted monsters who preyed upon an innocent little boy. Was he any less dead than Matthew Shepherd? There's no question that his death was more tragic—a young boy, repeatedly raped then killed. Why did the media ignore it? Because it didn't fit their definition of a politically correct story.

In another case, on December 14, 2000, in Wichita, Kansas, five young people were gathered at a home when two assailants burst into the house and held the group at gunpoint. Among the items the pair found while rifling through the house was an engagement ring. One of the young men admitted to his girlfriend, as the group huddled together in terror, that he had planned to ask her later that evening to marry him. The youngsters were taken to an ATM where they were forced to withdraw money. Then they were driven to a soccer field and the women were raped while the men were forced to watch. After that, the women were forced to perform sex acts on each other, then the men were forced to have sex with the women while the attackers watched. In the end, the five friends, one of whom had planned to enter the priesthood, were made to kneel and were shot execution-style.

Unbeknownst to the assailants, one of the women lived and was able to trudge more than a mile across the snow in the middle of the night, naked and bleeding, until she found help. The two animals were arrested the next day and charged with the murders.[8] In this particular case, the assailants were black and the victims were white. Why was there no cry for hate-crime prosecution? Why did the national media never pick this up? Four people were brutally murdered, yet you probably never heard a word about it. Stop and think for a moment. If the victims were black and the assailants were white, do you think you would've heard about this case? Let me put it to you another way: do you think you'd ever *stop* hearing about this case?

But would a racial role reversal have made these murders any more brutal? I ran a search on the Yahoo! search engine for each of the victims' names in the Wichita slaying. I came up with zero hits. Then I ran a search for Matthew Shepherd and got 43,800 hits. For James Byrd I got 80,400. It is unconscionable that the murderers involved in the Wichita mass killing and the case of little Jesse Dirkhising in Arkansas should be punished *less* than the killers in the Shepherd case, but in a land where hate-crime legislation protects the chosen few, that's liberal logic.

Liberals and AIDS

AIDS has a cure, it's called abstinence. As provocative and implacable a statement as that might be, you know in your heart it's true. Liberals love to blame conservatives like Ronald Reagan for the AIDS virus. They claim it's spread by lack of federal funding. Actually, it's spread by lack of common sense. To understand the race to find a cure, you must also understand how long a cure for *any* virus has eluded researchers. Almost since the dawn of medicine, man has been looking for cures for viruses. An Egyptian carving dating back to around 1500 BC depicts a priest with a shriveled leg, a characteristic of recovery from paralysis caused by the polio virus.[9] It wasn't until the 1950s that a vaccine was developed.[10] Mind you, that wasn't—and isn't—a cure. It's an inoculation; a way of preventing the disease before it strikes.

Scientists know that if you can develop something that will prevent a viral disease, that's about the best you can hope for. If you don't have a vaccine, containment is the name of the game. When a certain virus breaks out, you isolate those with the disease in order to keep it from spreading, allowing it to die out. Why, then, do you think they would treat AIDS any differently? The truth is, one of the most preventable deadly diseases in the history of this country is, without a doubt, AIDS. We know *exactly* how it's transmitted. We know *exactly* who is most a risk. We know *exactly* how to prevent it. You don't need a vaccine. It's almost wholly the result of reckless behavior. There are, indeed, horror stories of people contracting AIDS as the result of blood transfusions, but those cases are extremely rare. That's not to say that we shouldn't have compassion for people afflicted with this disease. We most certainly should. People find themselves with all sorts of ailments because of bad choices, and kicking them when they're down serves no purpose. We should treat them with compassion, just like anyone else who is dying, but it only serves to perpetuate the problem if we continue to condone the behavior that causes it. But that's what liberals do. Instead of facing the facts of why we have AIDS to start with, they insist on spending hard-earned taxpayer money to find a cure. That's the liberal way of solving problems.

Our country's approach to the AIDS problem (it's not an epidemic, by the way) has been to throw good money after bad at an elusive cure while failing to condemn the very behavior that's at the root of the problem. Passing out condoms at school in an effort to stop the spread of AIDS is like handing out low-nicotine cigarettes as a means of stamping out smoking. Both send the wrong message; that the behavior is okay as long as you're "safe." Cities across the country do the same with needle exchange programs instead of attacking the basic problem of intravenous drug use. Come exchange your dirty needle for a shiny, new, clean one, they beg. It's easy to cry that our need to save lives is immediate, thus justifying programs like needle exchange, but short-term solutions have long-term consequences. You don't patch a roof with cardboard. It may get you through one rainy day, but it doesn't solve the problem. Nor does the patchwork approach solve the AIDS problem.

Contrary to the publicity campaign launched by the AIDS lobby, this disease will never be a problem for the vast majority of us. Let's look at the real numbers. The latest data show that only about three-tenths of 1 percent of the American population has AIDS. The fact remains that, by far, the highest risk categories are gay men and intravenous drug users. Those two categories make up at least 66 percent of AIDS cases. Another 33 percent are those engaged in "high-rise heterosexual contact." The Centers for Disease Control and Prevention (CDC) defines "high-risk heterosexual contact" as "heterosexual contact with a person known to have, or to be at high risk for, HIV infection." In other word, these people are having sexual contact with people who are either gay, bisexual, or intravenous drug users.[11]

So it's clear where the risk lies, but the AIDS lobby would have you think that everyone is at peril of contracting AIDS. They have perpetuated a myth that AIDS is infecting the heterosexual community at alarming rates in order to galvanize support in the federal government for more and more funding for AIDS research. In his book *The Myth of Heterosexual AIDS*, Michael Fumento points out that heterosexuals are in less danger of contracting AIDS than they are of dying from shark attacks, being hit by lightning, or accidentally drowning in the bathtub. We know what causes AIDS. More important, we know that the most effective way to rid our country of AIDS is to stop the risky behavior. Instead, those at greatest risk want the government to spend every dime it takes to find a cure. That's akin to someone with lung cancer continuing to smoke while admonishing the government for not spending enough on cancer research.

Some gay activists are finally coming around to rational thinking in order to save gays from themselves. Matt Foreman, executive director of the National Gay and Lesbian Task Force, made a startling admission to the NGLTF in February 2008. "Folks, with 70% of the people in this country living with HIV being gay or bi[sexual]," Foreman told the group, "we cannot deny that HIV is a gay disease. We have to own that and face up to that."[12]

With all the hysteria surrounding AIDS, you would think it would be the number-one killer in America. Not even close. According to the latest data from the CDC,

HIV/AIDS is number seventeen on the list of the leading causes of death in America. *Seventeen!* To put it into perspective, almost five times more people die from diabetes each year. The same goes for pneumonia and influenza. Almost forty times more people die of cancer each year. Fifty times more die from heart disease.[13] Yet the National Institutes of Health (NIH) spends more on AIDS research than any other disease, including all cancers *combined*.[14] That's not a misprint. We spend more money on AIDS research than all cancers put together.

If relatively so few people die of AIDS in this country, how did we come to pour so much money into AIDS research? Quite simply, it's the squeaky-wheel syndrome. This disease has such an active and tenacious lobby that Congress has found it easier to give in than to fight. The AIDS lobby has also manipulated the data to make the problem look worse than it actually is. A good example of that was the buzz that the disease was spreading like wildfire among women. Nonintravenous drug-using women with AIDS make up about two-hundredths of 1 percent of the population. Since that number is so small, any shift will seem drastic when shown in percentages. For instance, if two women have AIDS and two more contract it, that's a 100 percent increase. It's easy to see how they've managed to create a panic with women and AIDS, but women are not, nor have they ever been, at great risk of contracting AIDS. The odds of a woman contracting AIDS in this country are infinitesimal. The odds of a woman who doesn't engage in risky behavior contracting AIDS are nearly incalculable.

The only way we're ever going to rid American society of this disease is through abstinence and by insisting that individuals take responsibility for their actions, not through liberal pandering to special interests. This will save not only billions of dollars but thousands of lives. And, after all, isn't that everyone's ultimate goal?

What Liberals Really Believe

To better understand liberalism, one need only read some of the liberals' beliefs. Steve Kangas, a devoted liberal, was a political journalist for the Internet site Votelink out of Boulder, Colorado. He wrote extensively on his Web site about liberalism. Some of his writings better illustrate than I ever could the differences between liberalism and conservatism. Kangas wrote that liberalism believes in collectivism (read: communism), while conservatism believes in individualism. Liberals are for democracy, while conservatives are for constitutionalism. (Never mind that America is not a democracy but a constitutional republic.) He says liberals believe in pacifism, while conservatives believe in armed deterrence.[15] I plead guilty on all counts.

Kangas goes on to explain that liberals believe in "progressive taxes, anti-poverty spending, and other forms of regulation." He says they view "the runaway profits of the rich—especially in the later stages of wealth accumulation—as undeserved, so redistributing them among the workers who produced them is necessary to prevent exploitation."[16] Undeserved? Who is Kangas or any other liberal to determine who makes what? This, of course, is an admission to waging class warfare, something most liberals aren't willing to admit. At least Kangas was honest enough to have stated it.

Kangas writes extensively about the evils of guns and how society should ban them. "The gun lobby has perpetrated a widespread myth," he writes, "that an individual's right to own a gun is protected by the U.S. Constitution." Tragically and ironically, shortly after compiling his extensive dissertation on liberalism, including his attack on the Second Amendment, Kangas took his own life . . . with a gun.

Ultimately, it's the obsession with class warfare that marks liberalism's failure. George Bernard Shaw reportedly once said, "A government with the policy to rob Peter to pay Paul can be assured of the support of Paul." The have-nots will always outnumber the haves. The producers are always going to make more money than the nonproducers or underproducers because they either work harder, are smarter, or are more tenacious. This notion that the producers' accumulation of wealth is, as Kangas put it, undeserved, stokes the fires of resentment. Eventually, those fires burn so hot that the nonproducers try to vote away the wealth via graduated and punitive income taxes.

To paraphrase Tocqueville, once the nonproducers realize they can vote the producers' money into their pockets, the jig's up. Don't misunderstand. Capitalism is fueled by a certain degree of envy too. The difference is, under capitalism, that envy is translated into more productivity from the one who's envious, which is beneficial to everyone. With capitalism, the producer is prone to produce even more to keep up, and the nonproducer is enticed to become a producer. Liberalism gives the nonproducer no incentive to get off his duff.

Also, the currency of liberalism is fear. Fear of global warming. Fear that the mean old Republicans will take away your Social Security. Practically everything deals in fear. They tell us we're one paycheck away from being homeless. This fear leads to envy, which is where liberalism lives.

To use an environmentally incorrect analogy, capitalism is like cutting more firewood to make your fire as big or bigger than the other guy's. Liberalism, on the other hand, is like taking the wood that the other guy has spent all day chopping because he doesn't deserve that much wood. Under the liberal scenario, eventually the guy who's been working to amass his pile of firewood, only to have most of it taken from him, is going to stop cutting wood. At that point, both fires will go out. If the fire is our economy, then capitalism is kerosene. Conversely, liberalism is water, which will eventually extinguish the flames of capitalism.

13

MILITARY STRENGTH
deters aggression.

IT SEEMS TO BE an age-old recurring problem, a lesson we just can't seem to learn. After riding high on a victory, we inevitably downsize the military after the perceived threat is extinguished, with little or no regard to future adversaries. I'm reminded of the famous quote from George Santayana, the American poet and philosopher, whose words are often mangled and misquoted. However you remember the quote, its meaning is essentially the same. Santayana simply said, "Those who cannot remember the past are condemned to repeat it."

The annals of history are filled with those who did not learn from their own mistakes, let alone those of others, and, predictably, they repeated those mistakes. The unflappable confidence of Americans leads us to believe that we're somehow immune from the frailties of other nations. That overconfidence could very well prove to be our undoing.

Peace Through Strength

After the fall of the Soviet Union, the mood shifted dramatically in America. At least it did in our political body.

Those who fought loudest, longest, and hardest for disarmament during the cold war were also those who declared a moral victory over the Soviet Union and then demanded that the military, which had brought the Soviets to their knees, be drastically scaled back. It's as if all our enemies, large and small, had suddenly vanished, leading to the downsizing of all facets of our military.

Our focus was certainly different after the break-up of the Soviet Union, but the threats were still there. You could argue that our not knowing where in the world all of the former Soviet Union's nukes were posed a larger problem than we had faced before. That's not to diminish the importance of the fall of the Evil Empire but merely to highlight the fact that when you're number one, everybody's gunnin' for you. Instead of focusing on one country, we were suddenly faced with several breakaway republics that had the potential for nuclear weaponry, not to mention the rogue nations eager to employ those newly unemployed nuclear scientists. Despite the new threat, the same nuclear-freeze crowd was bragging about the "peace dividend." Remember that? Their point was that we had all sorts of cash that previously had been devoted to defense that could now be rerouted to social programs. Bad move.

No sooner had we begun to scrap a large portion of our military might than we started building up for a campaign in the Persian Gulf. Another despot had been emboldened by our downsizing to invade his neighbor, an American ally. Before we knew it, we were pulling our military from all parts of the globe to ready ourselves for battle with Saddam Hussein. The showdown in the sand would be a test of, and a testament to, our military might. But imagine if the Gulf War had taken place a decade earlier. In 1980, we were prepared neither militarily nor mentally for the challenge of taking on "the world's fourth-largest standing army," as the press would bill the Iraqi military, fronted by the famed Republican Guard.

Those reports of the fourth-largest standing army were meant to put things in perspective, that such a tiny country had amassed an enormous military machine. What was assumed by most Americans was that *our* standing army was either first, second or third in terms of size. The press reports didn't mention that we sported only the world's seventh-largest standing army.[1] Even with all of the buildup during the Reagan years, we still had a long way to go.

The Gulf War should have been the generational wake-up call that downsizing the military was a lousy idea. Instead, we rejected the commander in chief who prosecuted that war, casting him aside in favor of our latest sensory whim, our immediate demand for a perfect economy. Americans discarded sanity—and a fine man in the process—as we demonstrated our complete ineptitude in understanding Santayana's words. We placed in power an opportunist who took full advantage of his dumb luck; a sacrificial lamb the Democrats had offered up to the gods of war, not foreseeing that the masses would fall back to that old standby, the golden calf.

George H. W. Bush's successor began anew the task of dismantling the military. After sitting at 95 percent readiness in 1989, the U.S. Air Force had slipped to only 65 percent readiness by 2000.[2] The lessons of the Gulf War were lost on the Clinton administration, which sought to castrate the military machine, the very institution Student Clinton wrote that he "loathed." In light of that loathing and subsequent starvation of the military, it's ironic that Bill Clinton used that military in more separate conflicts around the globe than any other president in recent memory. As it turned out in Mogadishu, we were unable, perhaps just unwilling, to bring down a common street thug. That's not to take anything away from the men who fought and died for the cause. The soldiers there overcame unbelievable odds, facing thousands of angry citizen soldiers—gang members, to be more accurate—who were hell-bent on their destruction.

The sad reality is, the Clinton administration cut our soldiers off at the knees, never allowing them the strength or the authority to do the job properly. He had taken the proud military of Reagan and Bush and returned it to near Carteresque levels of readiness. The lessons of Somalia and Bosnia were ignored by the Clinton administration. By 2000, the air force alone had been downsized by an astonishing 40 percent from where it was when Reagan left office![3]

As the George W. Bush administration prepared to do battle with Saddam Hussein once again, the value of having a top-notch military came back into clear focus. North Korea's threats of nuclear weapon development seemed to coincide with our buildup in the Middle East. Sensing that our military was spread too thin, the brutal regime in Pyongyang flexed its muscles again.

North Korea was on the ropes in the early '90s. Thanks to a deal brokered for the Clinton administration by former President Jimmy Carter, we resuscitated this dying, despotic regime by supplying it with much-needed light-water nuclear power plants under the 1994 Agreed Framework plan.[4] Once again, we were faced with war on the Korean Peninsula. Once again, we had failed to learn from history. No wonder, though, since Carter had never embraced Reagan's "peace through strength" philosophy, despite its overwhelming success, and the fact that Carter's own appeasement policies had been a colossal failure.

Apparently emboldened by a perceived lack of military might or, perhaps a perceived lack of resolve on the part of the Americans, North Korea refused to dismantle its nuclear program, calling our bluff.[5] Thanks to the Clinton administration, George W. Bush had to prosecute a war with Iraq while dealing with the distraction of a potential nuclear war with North Korea. That's not the type of fix you relish as commander in chief. There W was, trying to rebuild the military, fight the war on terrorism, and fight off critics who somehow blamed him for the bad economy—just the kind of situation that invites rogue nations to probe your underbelly to see how soft it is.

No one on the left ever expected the U.S. military to cut through Iraq like a hot knife through butter. North Korea had taken the occasion of our diverted attention to threaten a first attack against America. It jumped back when allied troops marched into Baghdad. Kim Jong Il, North Korea's nutcase dictator, suddenly offered to scrap his country's entire nuclear program.[6] Of course, he wanted some concessions from the United States, like much-needed materials to prop up his dying regime, but the fact that he was suddenly in a negotiating mood spoke volumes.

Libyan leader Col. Muammar Gaddafi suddenly decided to allow weapons inspectors in and to scrap his weapons of mass destruction after he saw what the United States did to Iraq. Years of defiance and foot dragging suddenly turned to eager cooperation once Gaddafi had an up-close look at what might be in store for him. Once the Libyans opened their country to inspections, we found their capabilities far exceeded what anyone had ever dreamed. They had all the necessary ingredients to make a nuclear weapon and admitted that was their goal.[7] Had the United States not gone into Iraq, it's doubtful Libya would have ever come to the table.

Despotic, rogue nations like North Korea understand only one thing: force. If you're weak, they'll attempt to exploit that weakness. If you're strong, they'll back down.

The only thing that deters aggression by your enemies is a strong military. Churchill and Reagan understood that. Chamberlain and Clinton didn't.

Our Founding Fathers on Strength

It should be noted that many of our Founding Fathers, particularly Thomas Jefferson, detested maintaining a standing army in time of peace. They feared such an army could be used against its own citizens, as the standing army of England had been used against them. Rather than standing armies, the Founding Fathers preferred militias, private citizens armed and ready to fight for their country against foreign aggressors or against tyranny within their own nation.

George Washington, however, had a change of heart after the Whiskey Rebellion broke out in western Pennsylvania during his presidency in 1794. He sent in 12,950 troops to suppress the rebellion. After the disturbance had been quelled, Washington understood that merely having a pool of armed men from which to draw was not enough in times of crisis, and he then saw the need for a standing army. That's not to say that he traded armed citizens for an army. He knew, as did the other founders, that an armed citizenry would help keep the military—and the politicians—honest.

Still, Washington was always a proponent of a strong defense, whether in the form of militias or standing armies. As commander of the Continental army, he had taken on the mightiest military machine in the world and won. Instead of leaving his country vulnerable to another invasion, newly elected President Washington understood all too well the dangers of appearing weak. "To be prepared for War," he said, " is one of the most effectual means of preserving peace"[8] In his second term, his resolve only grew stronger: "If we desire to avoid insult, we must be able to repel it; if we desire to secure peace, one of the most powerful instruments of our rising prosperity, it must be known, that we are at all times ready for War."[9]

Washington knew very well the danger of letting down your guard. As the leader of a new nation, he fully understood the fragility of freedom and the deep desire of others to take it away. Having lived under the tyranny of the king of England, he and his countrymen were determined to keep their newly won freedom, even if it meant fighting another bloody war. The most certain path to war, he knew, was weakness.

Thomas Paine, another staunch supporter of strength as a deterrent, wrote: "The balance of power is the scale of peace. The same balance would be preserved were all the world not destitute of arms, for all would be alike; but since some will not, others dare not lay them aside. . . . Horrid mischief would ensue were one half the world deprived of the use of them . . . the weak will become a prey to the strong."[10]

It's all too easy for us to become complacent and lackadaisical when it comes to protecting our freedom. Our Founding Fathers didn't have the luxury of basking in freedom; instead, they set about the task of first winning it and then protecting it with their lives. The liberties we all take for granted these days were gained by strong military might, not by disarmament and pacifism.

The Great Appeasers

The year was 1935. Adolf Hitler had become chancellor of Germany just two years prior, and upon the death of President Paul von Hindenburg in 1934, had seized complete control of the country. Now he was boldly announcing that Germany would begin rearmament, in direct violation of the Treaty of Versailles. France and England did nothing. The following year, 1936, Hitler waltzed into the Rhineland, an area set aside as a demilitarized zone under the Treaty of Versailles. France and England did nothing. When Germany annexed Austria in 1938, France and England protested but, again, ultimately did nothing.

A meeting between British prime minister Neville Chamberlain and Hitler, along with representatives of France and Italy, was arranged in Munich, September 29–30, 1938, to discuss Hitler's designs on territory inside Czechoslovakia called the Sudetenland. In spite of Hitler's aggression and continual lies, Chamberlain went into the meeting in Munich commenting that Hitler appears to be "a man who could be relied upon when he had given his word." In the wee hours of September 30, Chamberlain signed on with France and Italy to allow Hitler to take the Sudetenland. He went back to England and proclaimed that he had achieved "peace with honour," adding, "I believe it is peace in our time." Within five months, the whole of Czechoslovakia had fallen to the Nazis.

In September 1939, Hitler rolled into Poland, and England finally declared war. Chamberlain would meet his political demise after his country's military defeat in Norway some months later and be replaced by a man who had no plans to appease anyone—not even British public opinion—Winston Churchill.

Geographically, the United States didn't have as much at stake as our European friends, and we were not signatories to the Treaty of Versailles. But instead of standing up for what was right and enforcing it when Hitler first starting rearming, we passed the Neutrality Act, in retrospect a cowardly piece of legislation that prevented us from carrying out our duties abroad. No doubt, had we forced Hitler's hand at his first breach of the treaty, we very well could have avoided World War II.

How soon we forget these lessons of war and aggression. After World War II we weren't quite sure how to deal with our old ally, the Soviet Union. Joseph Stalin had vowed to hold free elections in Poland but reneged. In 1946, Churchill, who by that time was out of office, coined the term "iron curtain." The following year, President Truman requested $400 million for the Truman Doctrine that pledged to provide American economic and military assistance to any nation threatened by communism. That's an interesting piece of history when you consider how far to the left today's Democratic Party has drifted. On January 12, 1955, U.S. Secretary of State John Foster Dulles announced the doctrine of massive retaliation. What that essentially said was that we would use nuclear weapons against any Soviet aggression anywhere in the world.

The Soviets put that doctrine to a serious test in 1979 when the Americans, under President Jimmy Carter, stood by and watched as one hundred thousand Soviet troops invaded Afghanistan. Although we gave some aid to the Muslims fighting the Soviets, our doctrine of massive retaliation proved to have no teeth. The Soviets were astute judges of presidential backbone and saw that Jimmy Carter, although a very decent man, had none. That's not to say that diplomacy doesn't have its place. Carter did an admirable job getting Egypt and Israel together at Camp David. Still, the mark of a true leader is one who understands when to stand up to aggression, and apparently Carter was lost when it came to dealing with the Soviets.

The same could be said about Richard Nixon to a lesser degree. It wasn't until Ronald Reagan took office that we began to slap the Soviets back and play hardball. As you'll see in a later chapter, Reagan hatched a definitive plan to defeat Soviet communism, and he followed that plan to the letter. No more appeasement. No more compromise. Reagan had grown tired of the SALT treaties because his intelligence agencies were telling him that the Soviets weren't living up to their end of the bargain. When Gorbachev asked him, "You don't trust us?" Reagan replied with a Russian proverb: *"Doveryai no Proveryai"* (Trust but verify). The moment the appeasement stopped, the clock began winding down for the Soviet Union.

The American Neville Chamberlain Society

As President Reagan began a massive nuclear buildup in 1981, an NBC–Associated Press poll showed that 76 percent of Americans feared a nuclear war with the Soviets was "likely" in the next five years.[11] A left-wing group called the Union of Concerned Scientists and dozens of other groups sponsored what they called "nuclear war teach-ins," which spread to 151 campuses in 41 states. In 1982, Democratic Senator Ted Kennedy and Republican Senator Mark Hatfield introduced a nuclear freeze resolution that drew the backing of 122 representatives and 17 senators. In November of that year, voters in eight states passed referenda calling for a mutual and verifiable freeze on the testing, production, and deployment of nuclear weapons.

News reports were abuzz with Armageddon-style hysteria over Reagan's seemingly total disregard for sanity. They were convinced he was itching to get into a nuclear war with the Soviets. As all of this swirled around him, Reagan went about the business of actually winning the arms race, thus averting war and running the Soviets over the edge of the cliff into the abyss. Nuclear-freeze loudmouths like Kennedy, Ted Danson, Ed Asner, and Barbra Streisand were made out to be fools. In researching this book I visited the Web site of the Coalition for Peace Action. They list highlights from their history, but there is absolutely no mention of one of the most important events of the twentieth century—the fall of the Soviet Union. Had these folks gotten their way, we would still be dealing with the Soviet Union and living under the omnipresent cloud of global nuclear war.

Some of you reading this may not remember what it was like living under that cloud, but I sure do. I remember watching the TV movie *The Day After*, which depicted the effects of a nuclear war. I remember what I felt as I watched Jason Robards walking around amid the total devastation at the end of the film. I know the filmmakers hoped that I, as a viewer, would join Danson and Streisand in their protest, but it had just the opposite effect on me. It strengthened my resolve that we should not sleep until the Soviet Union was gone.

Now we live in a new era of appeasers. Some are the same tired faces. The Hollywood kooks are still out there warning us that we should appease the dictators lest we be forced into war. Formerly respected organizations like the NAACP have joined the American Neville Chamberlain Society. They staged protests around the nation and formally declared their opposition to the war with Iraq. What peace protests have to do with the advancement of black causes is anyone's guess.

Shortly after the outbreak of the Iraq War, a pattern began to emerge among the so-called peace protesters. We learned that many of the antiwar protests were being organized by agents and sympathizers of the Communist Party. When similar protests started popping up in Nashville, I began looking into the events' organizer—the Nashville Peace and Justice Center (NPJC). What I learned was shocking but not really surprising. The NPJC listed, among its members, the Communist Party USA (CPUSA) and the Democratic Socialist Party. Not only was the CPUSA a member of the NPJC, the national CPUSA Web site listed the Middle Tennessee CPUSA chapter at the *very same address* as the NPJC. What was even more shocking was the fact that organizations like the Board of Church and Society of the Tennessee Conference of the United Methodist Church and the Community Relations Committee of the Jewish Federation were also members.

When I brought this to the public's attention, I got a call from the Jewish Federation. The spokesperson first denied that the CPUSA was a member of the NPJC. When I provided concrete proof, she admitted that the CPUSA was in fact a member, but that both groups shared a common goal and she didn't see anything wrong with the CPUSA being a member. I asked if she would give the same answer if the co-member happened to be the American Nazi Party. That was different, according to her. The only difference I saw was that the communists worldwide had killed *hundreds* of millions of people, while the Nazis had merely slaughtered *tens* of millions. Still, the Jewish Federation refused to disassociate itself from the NPJC.

The head of the Nashville Peace and Justice Center claimed the Web site I was viewing was outdated, that the CPUSA had been a member organization but no longer was. When I checked the new Web site, both the CPUSA and the Democratic Socialists of America were listed. By the next day, both of those groups had been deleted from the new Web site, and the national CPUSA Web site no longer listed the Middle Tennessee chapter's address. Quite interesting, I thought. It was only after their exposure on the radio that these changes were made—I suspect more for show than anything else.

I spoke with someone who had actually attended an NPJC meeting just before the start of the Iraq War. Those on hand were trying to organize a group called Veterans for Peace. When it was suggested that a picture of the American flag be used on the group's literature, my source claims the head of the NPJC said that the American flag was as offensive to some of its members as the Confederate flag is to blacks. The NPJC denied the charge, but my source was very specific and quite reliable.

The Methodist Church experienced such a backlash among its members that it reluctantly severed its ties with the NPJC. The church did, however, reserve the right to fund the NPJC for special projects that shared their mutual interests. To me, that was merely a public relations move designed to appease the disgruntled members among them. The Methodist Board of Church and Society routinely supports a left-wing agenda, and most of its members have no idea their tithes are going to fund such efforts. The board supports, among other things, a ban on oil drilling in Alaska, campaign finance reform, and the radical Kyoto Protocol on greenhouse gases—global warming. It also opposed President Bush's national missile defense, supported gun control, advocated the release of drug offenders from prison, and asked the Washington Redskins to change the team's name. What this has to do with the work of Jesus Christ is beyond me. I know a lot of Methodists, and most would be appalled to learn that church officials were supporting such an agenda in their name.

The American Neville Chamberlain Society has members in some of the most unlikely places. We, as citizens, need to be aware of this and stay alert to the dangers these appeasers pose. Upfront discussion about important issues like national defense are important. I don't, in any way, mean to cast aspersions on anyone who questions a particular military action. Questioning authority is healthy. But it's important to look at the motivation behind such stands. Clearly, the NPJC is influenced by the Far Left. I know the group has had communist ties in the past, and I question whether those influences have been completely cleansed from that organization. I do know that those who hate this country with a passion have been behind many of the antiwar protests, and those who join them need to understand who they're crawling in bed with.

War is certainly not my first choice as the way to solve problems with errant nations and despots. Even those of us who have never been to war understand that it is a tragic and horrible thing. But even more tragic and horrible is the prospect of losing our way of life, of losing our freedom. Sometimes, especially when our core American values are threatened, there's no alternative but war. The question remains: at what point are you willing to go to war to protect those things that are most precious to you? I suspect that many on the left, if they answered from their hearts, would say "never." If they can look at the rubble that was the World Trade Center and not be moved to war, then nothing will move them.

The rest of us need to understand where they're coming from when they spew the "guilt-ridden American" rhetoric in hopes of changing our minds. They hate our military might. They're embarrassed by our blatant display of military technology and hardware, but it's this display that deters rogue nations from putting it to the test.

The peaceniks look upon our military as a war machine. I look upon it as a peace machine. As long as I can see it, I know we're safe. As long as there are men and women willing to give their time and, if need be, their lives to protect this nation, then we're safe. It's only when we're not strong, when the appeasers win, that we all lose.

14

NATIONAL SECURITY is the first responsibility of the federal government.

IF OUR MILITARY IS the deterrent to aggression, national security is the by-product. Let's face it, if our country is not secure, nothing else really matters, now does it? If September 11 proved one thing to us, it's that our security and our economy are joined at the hip. We can't have economic security without national security, and that is the primary responsibility of our federal government.

It's one thing to argue over foreign wars on distant shores, but domestic tranquility is our birthright. It's laid out in the preamble of the Constitution. Even after the 2001 terrorist attacks, we Americans can't comprehend widespread war within the confines of our borders. We've been relatively blessed in that regard. Still, the imminent threat exists and we must be proactive in combating that threat. First and foremost, we *must* secure our borders.

The Wrong Kind of Tolerance

Not only do we tolerate illegal aliens in this country, we encourage them. My state of Tennessee passed a driver's license law in 2001 that allowed illegal aliens to obtain a driver's license without presenting a valid Social Security number. Driver's license stations across the state were swamped with illegals from all over the country. Meanwhile, legal residents waited in lines for hours just to renew their own licenses. The bill's sponsor told me that he had requested the Department of Safety set up two lines; one for citizens and one for illegals, but he was informed that couldn't be done because it would be discriminatory!

After September 11, what was merely an annoyance turned into a security risk. The ringleader of a group of Arab men from New York who were involved in obtaining driver's licenses for illegal aliens told the FBI that they chose Tennessee, in part, because the state did not require applicants to have a Social Security number.[1] This same group of men was also believed to be connected to the death of a driver's license examiner who had helped countless Arab illegals obtain Tennessee driver's licenses.

How hard do you think it would be to move around the country once you secured legal documentation? A terrorist could easily use it to board a plane. If a check were run on the license, it would only show that he was who he claimed to be. If there were no Social Security number associated with the license, it couldn't be determined whether the person had obtained it legally. Look, I certainly don't advocate requiring each license holder to display his Social Security number on his license. I've requested that my number not appear on my license just so I don't oblige someone prone to identity theft. However, my Social Security number is in the system and will help identify me if there's ever a question about who I am.

The sad part is, at the time, these guys could've gotten the same licenses legally just by walking into any Tennessee driver's license testing facility. My best guess as to why they didn't is that they didn't want to call attention to themselves waiting in line. Even in the wake of September 11 and the arrest of these Arab illegals, the governor and General Assembly stubbornly refused to repeal the law. Those of us who vehemently argued to repeal it were labeled as racists. It's hard to have an intelligent discussion of an issue when that's their first line of defense.

Although the governor and the General Assembly showed little concern, obviously someone in charge of the investigation became suspicious when Katherine Smith, the license examiner, was released on her own recognizance but the Middle Eastern men were being held in virtually round-the-clock lockdown. It doesn't sound like the FBI thought they were merely routine tourists.

The politically correct defended the illegal-alien driver's license law and the men in jail. The mainstream media in Nashville all but ignored the case, that is, until Katherine Smith turned up dead. She was burned to death in a 1992 Acura Legend she was in the process of buying from codefendant Khaled Odtllah (the car was still registered in his name)[2] when the vehicle ran off the road and hit a pole in the middle of the night—conveniently, the evening before she was to appear in court.[3] By the way, according to eyewitness accounts, she was on fire *before* the car hit the pole. Still, little was said about the incident in the Nashville press.

I believe the story was spiked on purpose. What purpose, I'm not really sure. I don't think the Nashville media were covering up for terrorists, but I do believe some refrained from reporting the story out of fear that the illegal-alien driver's license law would be repealed, thus killing an idea near and dear to their hearts. They were overly anxious not to profile, and they missed a huge story in the process.

Several weeks after the death of Katherine Smith, several bombs were found in the Memphis forensics lab that was conducting an investigation into her death. Officials stated that they couldn't see why anyone would want to blow up the lab and wrote it off as a case of someone planting the explosives at the wrong target. Less than three months later, the county medical examiner was found wrapped in barbed wire with a bomb strapped to his chest in the stairwell outside his office. After being freed by a security guard, the examiner managed to come away with only minor injuries, despite having some kind of acid thrown in his face.[4] No link was drawn between the bombs, the death of Katherine Smith, and the mysterious disappearance of a world-renowned scientist who vanished from the bridge over the Mississippi River while attending a conference in Memphis. Dr. Don Wiley was an expert on dangerous viruses, including Ebola, and some experts have speculated that bioterrorists may have been responsible for his disappearance. His body was found about a month later, some 320 miles downriver from Memphis. The body and the case were turned over to, you guessed it, the county medical examiner.[5]

Perhaps a terrorist cell working out of Memphis was taking advantage of Tennessee's lax driver's license laws. That would certainly explain the death of Katherine Smith. Tennessee hasn't been alone in allowing illegals to obtain legal documents from the state government. Several other states have done the same thing. Before September 11, these driver's licenses for illegal aliens were just a pain in the neck for citizens renewing their own licenses, as well as being a magnet for illegals coming up from Central and South America. They had become a potential national security risk, yet the authorities did not seem to take the threat seriously. Once again, political correctness overshadowed common sense. Once again, it could prove to be fatal.

Even after September 11, even after the murder of driver's license examiner Katherine Smith, and even after other states repealed their own illegal-alien driver's license laws, Tennessee stubbornly refused to change. The new governor, Phil Bredesen, in an effort to fix the budget problems he inherited, "tagged," or refused to fund, any new legislation that would cost money. The driver's license reform legislation was tagged because it would cost $150,000 per year. That's the amount of money the state figured it was getting from the eight thousand illegal aliens who pay for driver's licenses each year. I thought the figure was low but beside the point. The issue was not money but security and common sense. With that logic, why didn't they just ask the illegal aliens to step to the next window and sell them gun carry permits, for crying out loud? Here was a matter of national security and the politicians were quibbling over $150,000 out of a $20 billion budget! It was insane.

Governor Bredesen compromised and set up "driving certificates" for illegal aliens, but only because of pressure from the Department of Homeland Security and the risk that Tennessee licenses would not be approved to board planes if they didn't. Ultimately, in 2007, Tennessee came to its senses, and the state legislature voted to abandon driving certificates for illegals altogether. The shortsightedness on the part of two governors and countless state lawmakers was mind-boggling. Our national security was at risk, but they chose instead to pander to business interests and the politically correct crowd.

Costing American Lives

The gross ineptness of the Immigration and Naturalization Service (now Immigration and Customs Enforcement) before and after September 11 has become legendary. I could regale you with some of the more interesting stories, but I'll limit my point to just one. John Lee Malvo, the young accomplice in the D.C. Sniper murders, was a Jamaican national stowaway on a cargo ship. Under U.S. law, stowaways are to be immediately deported without a hearing.[6] Malvo was arrested on December 19, 2001, three months after the terrorist attacks in New York, Pennsylvania, and Washington. Common sense would tell you that he should be deported immediately. However, despite being unable to provide any documentation, Malvo was turned loose on his own recognizance—in clear violation of the law and standard operating procedure—and he then hooked up with John Allen Muhammed, the infamous D.C. Sniper.[7] The rest, as they say, is history. That's one of the benefits of screening applicants for visas into this country. Hopefully, you screen out cold-blooded killers.

Rich Pierce, executive vice president of the Border Patrol Council, the union representing agents, was incredulous. "They should hold on to all of them," he said, "they" being the INS. "These were two illegals (Malvo and his mother were arrested as stowaways). They were both illegally here, and they let them both go."[8] The rest of us stand there with mouths agape wondering, as Pierce does, how such a thing could happen, but it happens far more often than any of us suspects. Despite the wake-up call on September 11, 2001, there are still many within our government who continue to hit the snooze button. It's not clear what, if anything, will wake them from their slumber.

Steps need to be taken to secure our borders. Since the September 11 attacks, that task has risen to the top of our priority list. After all, if we're not safe within our own borders, we simply aren't free. The sensible thing to do would be to use our military to enforce our border laws. I know. Every single time I suggest such a thing, I hear a chorus of caterwauling from folks who claim that it would violate the Posse Comitatus Act—the act that prevents U.S. military forces from engaging in most domestic law enforcement activities.[9]

First of all, repelling foreign invaders, armed or unarmed, does not constitute an engagement in domestic law enforcement. The primary difference is, the guns are pointed outward, not inward. Second, the Posse Comitatus Act dates back not to the founding of our country but to the post–Civil War era, when Union forces were found to be overbearing, and sometimes brutal, when it came to keeping the peace in the South.[10] Our military is designed to defend and protect us, and we face no greater threat than that of illegal immigration. It's time we stop making excuses and start protecting ourselves.

Nukes, Nukes, Who Has the Nukes?

Think of how far we've come since the inception of our country, when the largest weapon of mass destruction was the cannonball. Now we have to contend with nuclear, chemical, and biological weapons that can wipe out large segments of our population in mere moments. The apparatus to contend with such threats is massive. Still, determining where the nuclear weapons are and who exactly is in control is a challenge, even to our large intelligence operation.

Some of the obvious threats on that level are China and North Korea. Kim Jong Il, the madman with his finger on the button in North Korea, was enabled by the inept policies of the Clinton administration. The Central Intelligence Agency stated in February 2003 that North Korea had the capability to strike the West Coast of the United States, something unthinkable just a few short years ago.[11] John McCain responded to former President Bill Clinton's suggestion that we begin an "intense, exceedingly high-level engagement" with North Korea with this retort: "My reaction is that the greatest failure of the Clinton administration was the agreement they made with North Korea, which allowed them to reach the stage where they are today, where they have nuclear weapons. We supported their regime with over a billion dollars and fuel while two million of their citizens starved to death (and) 200,000 of their people are in gulags reminiscent of Joseph Stalin."[12]

Former Defense Secretary Caspar Weinberger and noted author Peter Schweizer made some chilling predictions regarding North Korea in their 1996 novel *The Next War*. Based on geopolitical conditions as they stood in the mid-1990s, Weinberger and Schweizer laid out five different war scenarios. In the section on North Korea, they describe Kim Jong Il as an egomaniac who obtains enough technology and enough gumption to launch an attack across the demilitarized zone into South Korea, culminating with the dropping of a nuclear weapon on U.S.

troops.[13] That story line, incredible as it sounded in '96, was given credence in February 2003 when North Korea threatened a "first strike" against the United States.[14]

Thanks in large part to the appeasement policies of the Clinton administration, North Korea has become a real threat to stability in the Korean Peninsula area as well as to the United States. Instead of starving a rabid regime that had barely more than spitballs to hurl at us, we chose to nourish Kim and company back to health and provide them with the technology with which to inflict horrible damage on us and their neighbors. When will we learn to let these brutal terrorist regimes collapse?

The Delicate Balance

Too much national security power in the wrong hands can spell trouble for Americans' liberty and freedom. It can also turn a protector and defender of allies into a despotic bully. We, the people, need to be constantly vigilant to make sure those in charge don't overstep their boundaries. National security should be our government's first and foremost responsibility, but we must continually remind our leaders that it's *our* freedoms and rights they're protecting. As the government seeks to safeguard us from outside aggressors, we must be careful that it does not become what we so vehemently decry.

An erosion—some say an outright usurpation—of our rights has already happened. In post-9/11 America it was felt by some that our open society had been used too readily against us. The USA Patriot Act allows federal agents to, in essence, write their own search warrants and conduct all sorts of intrusive searches without your knowledge. Where the Patriot Act differs from its predecessors, namely the 1977 Foreign Intelligence Surveillance Act (FISA), is that it, for the first time, allows seized evidence to be used against individuals in court. FISA is a tool intended to ferret out enemies of the state, and it unashamedly violates the Fourth Amendment's protection against illegal search and seizure, but it has no teeth when it comes to prosecution. In other words, if a court issues a FISA search warrant simply based on suspicions about the company a suspect may work for, and that leads to evidence that he has committed a crime, he cannot be prosecuted. He's merely deported. FISA is specifically aimed at foreign nationals. The Patriot Act is different in several ways. Most notably, there is no court-issued warrant. Like its predecessor, the 1978 Right to Financial Privacy Act, the Patriot Act allows federal agents to write their own warrants. But even with the Right to Financial Privacy Act, no evidence gathered is admissible in court. The Patriot Act changed that, and it was a huge jump. Now warrants can be written by federal agents, they can snoop into all facets of your life without telling you, and they can prosecute you with whatever evidence they find.[15] This is a huge violation of our constitutional rights, but most people are willing to give up a little freedom for more safety and security.

It's a balancing act to maintain national security without making us prisoners within our own borders. It's even harder to know when to get involved abroad to thwart perceived threats. A good rule of thumb is not to be penny wise and pound foolish. History teaches us that getting involved too late can cost a lot more in terms of lives and money. In the words of that great philosopher, Barney Fife, sometimes you have to "nip it in the bud." But "nipping it" needs to be done with caution and common sense. One way for us to ensure that delicate balance is to stay informed and stay involved.

15

OPPRESSION should not be fueled by American capitalism.

ASK MANY ON THE left what brought about the collapse of the Soviet Union and you'll get an interesting response: capitalism. It's interesting because these darlings of liberalism generally are quick to point to greedy capitalists as the source of most of the world's problems. Yet, in the case of the Soviet Union, they note that Mikhail Gorbachev's introduction of capitalism gave the Russian people such an appetite for the free market that communism was overrun by it. As much as I'd like to agree with them on this one instance of capitalistic exaltation, I can't. Capitalism was not the silver bullet that killed communism. In fact, it was the life-support system that kept it alive past the point when it should have died.

Why this odd admiration for capitalism from the classic capitalist bashers? It's an attempt to rob Ronald Reagan of his just credit for killing the Evil Empire and place that crown upon the head of their hero, the so-called great reformer Gorbachev. But history will tell the true story of the Soviet demise. The Soviet Union's eleventh-hour infusion of capitalism was too little too late to enable it to keep up with the arms race embarked upon by President Reagan when he vowed to relegate the Evil Empire to the ash heap of history. It's true that communism is destined to failure from its beginning. The question is, how long will it take?

The Soviet Union lasted about seventy years, and its appetite for real estate kept it alive for nearly thirty-five of those. But once the Reagan administration stopped Soviet expansion, it marked the beginning of the end. Gorbachev attempted to expand the small vestiges of capitalism his nation allowed, but it was not enough to save his precious communist state. The Soviet Union, in all its paranoia, was consumed with military superiority. Even as its citizens starved, it was bound and determined to outclass the American military machine. It was that very obsession, that weakness, that Ronald Reagan chose to exploit. As you will learn later in this book, Reagan knew exactly what he was doing, and his plan brought the great Bear to its knees.

The Soviets Redux

We have a golden opportunity for history to repeat itself. This time the oppressive regime destined to fall is Communist China. Again, it's only a matter of time before that brutal regime implodes, but there are outside stimuli that can nurture it back to health. One of the most brutal and barbaric totalitarian regimes of terror teeters on the brink of collapse, yet we continue to fuel its sinister fires with capital. Democrats and Republicans alike have continued to place profit before principle in a quest to accumulate more wealth. We may one day choke on our own gold as we help build an adversary too powerful to overcome.

It was back in May 2000 that Chinese dissident Wei Jingsheng (pronounced: Way Gin-shun), known as the father of China's democracy movement, said that China's unemployment rate was at a thirty-year high and its economy was on the verge of collapse.[1] This was exactly what the oppressed people of China needed to oust this freedom-hating, tyrannical regime, but America stepped in to prolong the agony indefinitely. Shortly after this stark reality check on China, the United States granted it *permanent* normal trade status, thus ending the annual review in place since 1974 that forced the Senate to face China's human rights atrocities every single year before deciding on trade status. Of course, the annual review has always been a farce, since we perpetually turn a blind eye to China's human rights violations and give it the nod for trade.

The communist government in China has killed more than 35 million of its own citizens. An estimated 27 million more died from the famine resulting from Chairman Mao's economic policies.[2] As horrific as Hitler's Nazism was, its brutality pales in comparison to the carnage that has occurred in Red China. The granting of permanent normal trade status by America also paved the way for China to join the World Trade Organization, thus providing the communist government with enough capital to continue its brutality.

Feeding the Beast

Congressman Dana Rohrabacher (R-CA) scolded Congress on the House floor in April 2001 for continuing to aid Red China's despotic regime. "Our massive investment in China," he admonished, "pushed and promoted by American billionaires and multinational corporations, has created not a more peaceful, democratic China, but an aggressive nuclear-armed bully that now threatens the world with its hostile acts and proliferation." China had, not one month before, forced down a U.S. surveillance plane flying over international waters. "Large financial interests in our country whose only goal is exploiting the cheap, near-slave labor of China have been leading our country down the path to catastrophe," Congressman Rohrabacher pointed out. "How much more proof do we need that the so-called engagement theory is a total failure?"[3]

It has always troubled me that we ban trade with a small, insignificant country like Cuba because it's communist, yet we fall all over ourselves to trade with a far more sadistic bunch like the Red Chinese. We displayed a similarly schizophrenic trade policy by approving sanctions against the system of apartheid in South Africa but not against China. On the one hand, we condemned state-sponsored racism by bringing economic pressure to bear, but we now openly ignore state-sponsored murder and religious persecution, among other blatant human rights violations, by granting China permanent normal trade status.

The reason is, of course, the sheer size of the Chinese market. We drool at the prospect of getting our products in front of more than a billion people. It reminds me of the old joke about the guy who asks the girl if she'd sleep with him, just once, for a million dollars. She answers, "Absolutely." He then says, "What about for fifty dollars?" "Of course not," she answers, indignantly. "What do you think I am?" He replies, "We've established what you are. Now we're just haggling over the price." I think it's obvious exactly what the United States is too, when it comes to trading partners. We are more than willing to compromise our most sacred beliefs and turn a blind eye to wickedness that surpasses even the Nazis—all for money. Mark my words. That policy will come back to haunt us.

As we're busy counting our coins, the Red Chinese continue to spin their web. They now control both ends of the Panama Canal and have formed "strategic partnerships" with Venezuela and Cuba. They've also built the world's largest port just sixty miles from the United States, in Freeport, Bahamas, through, according to published reports, one of their front companies.[4] Now that they have what they want from America, they virtually laugh in our face when we request they stop shipments to countries that sponsor terrorism. The CIA has warned that matters will get decidedly worse by 2015, when China will be in a position to subject us to nuclear blackmail.[5]

The Chinese Satellite Scandal

You have to go back to 1998 to untangle the web weaved with the Chinese, satellites, and U.S. business interests. While the Monica Lewinsky scandal occupied the front pages, there was a far more serious scandal going virtually unnoticed, one that involved potentially secret missile technology falling into Chinese hands.

It all started when Loral Space and Communications Ltd. received a waiver from the Clinton administration to launch a satellite from China in 1996. The reason Loral wanted to launch from China was because the cost was considerably less than launching from the United States. But something went wrong with the Chinese launch, and the satellite was destroyed. In the postaccident report, Loral engineers supplied the Chinese with technological data the air force said could aid the Chinese in future missile launches and could be detrimental to the United States. The State Department viewed the Loral incident as having the potential to provide technological assistance for future Chinese ballistic missile guidance systems. One source told the *Washington Post*, "[The Chinese] were given some stuff, but there is a question of whether they have used it or will use it."[6] We'll get to whether or not they used it in a moment.

The largest contributor to Democrats in the 1996 election cycle was Bernie Schwartz, president of Loral Space and Communications. There also was a campaign contribution of one hundred thousand dollars that reportedly originated with a Chinese general's daughter. This Chinese general, ironically, formerly operated a satellite-launching business. Then there was the cloud of the Chinagate scandal that hung over the White House. Guys like Johnny Chung, Charlie Trie, and John Huang paraded all sorts of nefarious characters in and out of the White House dozens of times while hundreds of thousands of dollars in shady campaign contributions tied to China dropped into the coffers of Democrats. The Clinton administration was hauled before Congress to explain the Loral affair, but the White House maintained that Bernie Schwartz's contributions and his waiver to launch satellites in China were simply coincidence. Congress held hearings to determine if political considerations had had any effect on the Clinton administration's judgment. They also sought to determine if Loral had disclosed missile guidance secrets to the Chinese. Richard C. Shelby (R-AL), chairman of the Senate Intelligence Committee, stated that CIA testimony in closed hearings showed that China tried to influence the outcome of the 1996 U.S. elections. Whether China succeeded was unclear.[7]

Although China had been spying and stealing secrets long before Bill Clinton took office, a congressional inquiry found that sixteen of seventeen major technology breaches were discovered after 1994. Among them, according to Senator James Inhofe (R-OK), were all sorts of sensitive nuclear technology but also something potentially even more dangerous. In 1999, Inhofe cited a major breach that included the "compromise of advanced electromagnetic weapons technology useful in the development of anti-satellite and anti-missile systems."[8] This may not sound nearly as menacing as nuclear technology, but flash forward to 2005. A report from the Hudson Institute noted that China had shifted its emphasis from conventional warfare to "space warfare." Their objective was to dominate their enemies by dominating space. The Hudson report on "China's New Great Leap Forward" noted the "principal forms of space information warfare are: (1) conducting space electronic and space network warfare to inflict 'soft' strikes on enemy space platforms, thereby disrupting and destroying their electronic equipment and computer systems; and (2) employing all types of anti-satellite weapons to inflict 'hard' strikes on enemy platforms, thereby fundamentally destroying his space information system."[9] Reagan's Star Wars plan all of a sudden wasn't looking so far-fetched.

Planning is one thing, implementing is another. In January 2007, China launched a missile and made a direct hit on one of their weather satellites 537 miles above the Earth. This test sent shockwaves around the world. Suddenly the rules of engagement had changed. What if China decided to simultaneously take down all of our satellites, military and civilian? It would be like gouging out our eyes. We depend on satellite communication to coordinate counterattacks and track our ships at sea and to talk with our troops on the ground around the world. In the civilian world there would be a virtual communication shutdown. Radio and television depend on satellites to deliver news and other programming. Some could be rerouted to land lines but not all. The resulting mayhem and destruction wrought upon this country if we were blinded by a crippling of our satellites is unimaginable. Yet despite this threat, we were in Beijing a year later, kissing up to the Chinese at the 2008 Summer Olympics.

The damage the Clinton administration did through either deliberate transfers of sensitive technology or simply being asleep at the switch is incalculable. No doubt, blind eyes were turned toward China because of the colossal sums of money to be made by working with them as well as our growing dependence on the cheap goods they sell us. But Bill Clinton wasn't the last president to miscalculate China. His successor continued the appeasement despite their complicity in a whole new threat to the United States—terrorism.

The Unholy Alliance

CIA director George Tenet gave a chilling assessment of threats against America in February 2001, a full seven months *before* the September 11 terrorist attacks. "Osama bin Laden and his global network of lieutenants and associates remain the most immediate and serious threat," he told the Senate Select Committee on Intelligence. "His organization is continuing to place emphasis on developing surrogates to carry out attacks in an effort to avoid detection, blame, and retaliation. As a result, it is often difficult to attribute terrorist incidents to his group, al-Qaida."[10] How right he was. But just who was supplying these terrorists with weapons?

In the early months of the War on Terrorism, the Pentagon confirmed that "large quantities of Chinese-manufactured ammunition were discovered in the Tora Bora cave hideouts of Osama bin Laden."[11] Secretary of Defense Donald Rumsfeld revealed just that during an in-flight press conference, but very little about this incendiary fact was mentioned in the mainstream press. Furthermore, Chinese "advisors" were found among the dead, alongside Taliban forces, after the October 2001 bombing of Afghanistan.[12] That's something that didn't go widely reported either. The *Hindustan Times* reported that same month that "China is still assisting the Taliban in the war against the United States."[13]

Chinese dealings with Osama bin Laden date back to 1998, when U.S. forces bombed an al-Qaida network camp in retaliation for the U.S. embassy bombings in Africa. A few of the cruise missiles fired were found unexploded. China bought them from bin Laden for several million dollars, thus setting up a relationship that apparently continued beyond September 11.[14] Still, the United States maintained its trade relationship with these brutal killers despite President Bush's promise that we would retaliate against anyone who aided or harbored terrorists.

His words were drowned out by the shrill cry of greed and the deafening silence of the mainstream press.

Taiwan—Where Will We Stand?

China's first major test of American resolve will be Taiwan. Like Hitler in Czechoslovakia, the Red Chinese will calculate our appeasement level with each new act of aggression. The question will be whether the United States will draw the line at Taiwan.

To understand the significance of an invasion of Taiwan by the Red Chinese, you must first understand the history of Taiwan as it relates to China. In 1949, when the brutal communists in China took over the country, the Chinese Nationalists, led by Chiang Kai-shek, fled the mainland to Taiwan. Understand that, although Chairman Mao was a ruthless dictator, Chiang Kai-shek was no day at the beach either. He ordered the murder of countless Chinese, primarily communists, in order to hang on to power.

The bloody civil war between Chiang's Nationalists and Mao's Communists began in earnest in 1946. By 1949, Chiang realized the jig was up and headed for Taiwan with what was left of his military and set up shop there. In Taiwan, Chiang continued to rule with an iron fist, insisting that he would one day retake mainland China. That day never came. The United States built a relationship with Taiwan over the years, primarily because China had taken sides against us in the Korean War. In those days, communism, whether the Chinese or the Soviet variety, was the enemy.

After Nixon went to China, Sino-American relations thawed a bit. Many thought it prudent to make friends with the Red Chinese to thwart any plans they might have to make war against us. The United States officially recognized the communist People's Republic of China in 1979. In order to clarify our position regarding Taiwan and not leave her twisting in the wind, the United States passed the Taiwan Relations Act. This legislation spells out the U.S. position, "to make clear that the United States' decision to establish diplomatic relations with the People's Republic of China rests upon the expectation that the future of Taiwan will be determined by peaceful means."[15] It also states that it is the policy of the United States "to consider any effort to determine the future of Taiwan by other than peaceful means, including by boycotts or embargoes, a threat to the peace and security of the Western Pacific area and of grave concern to the United States."[16] We also reserve the right to defend Taiwan from foreign aggression and pledge to provide her the necessary arms to defend herself.[17]

This promise to support Taiwan was seriously damaged during the Clinton administration, which sought to placate the Red Chinese, who were determined to bring Taiwan into the fold—by force, if necessary. Clinton and his appeasers backed off our commitment to defend Taiwan by trying to short-circuit any arms sales to the island. Susan Shirk, Clinton's deputy assistant secretary of state for Asia and Pacific affairs, told Congress that plans to expand arms sales to Taiwan "will be seen as an effort to reverse our commitment to an unofficial relationship and to recreate in its place a formal military relationship with Taiwan."[18] *What?!*

Our commitment to provide Taiwan with a necessary defense and defend her ourselves, if need be, is clearly stated in the Taiwan Relations Act, yet Clinton's people appeared totally oblivious to it. Later revelations of Chinese money given illegally to the Democratic National Committee and the Clinton-Gore campaign and special waivers allowing Clinton contributors to sell high-tech equipment to Beijing would bring prior acts of appeasement to China by the Clinton administration into sharp focus.

A month after Shirk's remarks to Congress, the former CIA director under Clinton, James Woolsey, said Clinton's affirmation of a "strategic relationship" with China and his adoption of a one-China approach regarding the dispute between China and Taiwan had only encouraged hard-line factions in Beijing.[19]

After taking office, President Bush reversed the unlawful policy of the Clinton administration when he stated, "We'll help Taiwan defend herself. And people have got to understand, that's the spirit and they can surmise what they want to. They've just got to understand our country will stand steadfast by them."[20] Despite that stern stand, the Bush administration sent enough mixed messages to Beijing to tempt its testing of his resolve.

I believe it's not a matter of *if* China invades Taiwan; it's a matter of *when*. We certainly can't say we didn't see it coming. The Chinese have made their designs on invading Taiwan crystal clear. "Battling Taiwan independence has been listed as the PLA's (People's Liberation Army, China's military) main task, while crossing the strait and landing have become the focus of troops' training," news sources in the region reported in September 1999. "One expert said history showed the PLA always undertook military action against its enemies once an objective was set."[21]

The same month of that news report, Chinese President Jiang Zemin opened a world business forum by referencing Taiwan. "No country will allow its own territory to be split off," he said, "nor will it allow any foreign force to create or support such a split." By November, the rhetoric was ratcheted up a notch in Singapore by Chinese Prime Minister Zhu Rongji, who warned that China would use force, if necessary, to establish its claim of sovereignty over Taiwan.[22]

When the invasion comes, the United States must stick to its original commitment to Taiwan. That commitment, coupled with ample evidence of terrorist funding, should give us enough reason to stop the Red Chinese in their tracks, provided their development of nuclear weapons technology hasn't made them unstoppable. The longer we feed the beast with much-needed capital, the harder it will be to defeat that beast in what I see as an inevitable showdown between the United States and China.

Capitalism's Mortal Enemy

But it doesn't have to be. The only reason China hasn't challenged us before is because it hasn't had the resources. You must understand that, unlike capitalism, communism is not self-sustaining. By its very nature it chokes off production. Therefore, it has to expand to survive, just as the Soviet Union did. Communist nations must either depend on other communist nations for survival or gobble up nations with resources they need.

The Red Chinese hate capitalism as much as we hate communism. It goes against everything they believe in. They tolerate it only because it is a means to an end. They see capitalism as a corrupting force, one that will spell its own demise. As soon as they see an opportunity to rid themselves of it, they will do so. They will continue to use near-slave labor to produce cheap goods and sell them to the United States as long as they can turn that cash into weapons. When they have enough weapons to take what they want, there will no longer be a need to trade.

We only fuel their oppression—their slave-labor camps, their children's sweatshops—by continuing to trade with them. The next time you buy a Happy Meal for your precious little child strapped into the car seat, take a look at where the toy was made. Chances are, someone else's precious little child halfway around the world made it while chained to a dingy desk in a dark, damp factory. Instead of affecting change, we are merely perpetuating misery. The more Chinese goods we buy, the more Chinese people are forced into low-paying factories to make them. You don't seriously think anyone other than the communist hierarchy is getting rich off America, do you?

As Congressman Rohrabacher stated, the so-called engagement theory is indeed a total failure. We've not made the lives of the Chinese people any better. We've made them worse. U.S. capitalism should not be used to fuel Chinese oppression, or any other oppression, for that matter. It is morally wrong to contribute to such a tyrannical regime, but the stakes for America are even greater. The longer we engage in such foolhardy activity, the closer we inch toward the point of no return.

Like opium addicts, we have become hooked on these cheap products and the access to millions of new consumers. Check the labels on some of your favorite products sometime. In many instances, especially with the cheaper plastic products, you'll see the words *Made in China*. The flip side of the coin is the lure of a lucrative new market, one that enticed us to sell precious military and computer secrets to the Chinese, catapulting them decades ahead of where they had been, technologically. This has become a clear threat to the security of our nation.

Wretched Human Rights Record

Ironically, the Chinese government has managed to do what the old Soviet Union never could. They've made us dependent upon them financially. Now our foreign policy decisions are clouded by the financial ramifications. That can be fatal to a country. When we place profit above principle, we have lost the ability to act in our best self-interest, therefore exposing our nation to danger. Money can dull an otherwise rational human being's senses.

Here's some of what our "Buy China" policy is supporting, according to Amnesty International: thousands of political prisoners sentenced by unfair trials or no trial at all; "endemic" torture, including severe beatings, the use of electric batons, and suspending victims by their arms; re-education through labor camps; imprisonment of unauthorized religious groups; forced abortion and sterilization; the harvesting of body organs from executed political prisoners without their consent; and mass execution[23] (China executes more prisoners each year than the rest of the nations of the world combined). These are just the human rights violations we know about. I imagine that in a country with more than a billion people, it's hard to keep track of all the brutality. Dissidents have managed to make it out of China and their tales make Josef Mengele look like a choirboy.

As early as 1999, former Soviet Col. Stanislav Lunev warned that "by strengthening . . . its relations with Cuba, China intends to penetrate Latin America and take charge of supply lines and resources crucial to the US."[24] No one seems a bit concerned that now China reportedly is moving into our hemisphere.

Famous dissident Harry Wu joined the Communist Party as a young man. At a local party meeting he asked if some of the riches being hoarded by the local leaders might be distributed to some of those in his community who needed help. For that he was labeled a subversive.

Wu was one of the million or so weeded out during the so-called One Hundred Flowers Movement of 1957. This was when young Chinese were supposed to "blossom" into full-fledged communists. Wu was a college student at the time and was actually attracted to communism. His father had been a banker before the communist takeover. He believed the status his family enjoyed wasn't fair when so many other people were poor. Ironically, it was because he came from a nice family that he was suspected from the beginning. He made the mistake of condemning the 1956 Soviet invasion of Hungary when asked his opinion at a Communist Party meeting. He became a marked man because of that and the fact he dared question the local communist leaders. Eventually his family and friends were forced to denounce him publicly. He struggled with the unfair label for several years until he couldn't take it any longer. He and a small group of dissidents decided to escape from China. Their plans were found out, and Wu was sentenced to life imprisonment. "Of course there was no trial, court or paperwork. I was sent to a slave-labor camp," Wu told WorldNetDaily years later. That was April 27, 1960. He was only twenty-three.

Wu was forced to work in chemical plants, brick factories, iron mines, and steel factories. "We worked seven days per week and thirty days per month," he said. "Each worker had to fulfill a quota. If you did not meet the quota, they would reduce your food or send you to solitary confinement. For our political performance, we had to make a confession for our crimes. A prisoner could not practice his religion. You have to betray yourself." He had his freedom stripped from him by the communist Chinese government all because he simply had a couple of minor disagreements. He never saw his family during that time. His mother died shortly after he left for the slave-labor camp. Wu wasted away to nothing. His weight dropped to eighty pounds. "I almost died," he said. "I was like a skeleton."

After the death of Mao, the communist government decided to release some of the "old counterrevolutionaries." Wu was among them. He was set free on February 21, 1979, at the age of forty-two, after spending nineteen years of his life in a slave-labor camp. Upon his release he kept a low profile, studying hard and staying away from politics. He became a lecturer at China Geoscience University. Then a chance of a lifetime presented itself. Wu was offered an opportunity to go to America as a visiting scholar in civil engineering at the University of California at Berkeley. "I remember the day I arrived at the airport in San Francisco. I said, 'God, I am free now!' I got on my knees and kissed the ground. I remember that day. It was November 20, 1985." Wu knew he was in America to stay.

Poking a stick at the communist regime in China was the last thing on his mind. He was simply interested in working hard to establish his life in America, but then he was convinced by Senators Alan Cranston (D-CA) and Jesse Helms (R-NC) to testify before the Senate about China's slave-labor camps. That was the beginning of a new life dedicated to bringing the truth about China to the American people. Wu bravely returned to China several times to secretly videotape the conditions in the camps and smuggle the images out of China. He led a *60 Minutes* film crew into China's slave-labor camps. "I said at that time, 'People tirelessly talk about the Nazi Holocaust. In the Soviet gulags, 25 million have been killed, and now that is over. It is common knowledge that all totalitarian regimes—Stalin, Pol Pot in Cambodia—use such camps. Where are the American academics, experts and Sinologists on this issue? I will tell you exactly where. They identify with Marxism themselves, but moreover, America needs the Chinese market. Free enterprise needs markets."

By 1992 Wu was back on the Chinese government's radar. Still, he braved going back to China to expose the brutal communist regime. He was arrested in 1995 and charged with stealing state secrets. The difference now was that he had become a U.S. citizen. Because of his high profile as a Chinese dissident, he was merely detained for a short time then deported. He had hoped for more from the Clinton administration in the way of condemning the Chinese government. Instead, the president visited China on a goodwill tour. "When [Bill] Clinton came back from China in 1998, he was like [Neville] Chamberlain returning from Munich before World War

II," Wu said. Instead of standing up to the Chinese, the U.S. government simply waded deeper into its economic partnership with China. "Take Sandy Berger for example," Wu told WorldNetDaily in 2001. "Before he worked in the White House, do you know what he did? He worked at a law firm that was hired by the Chinese as lobbyists. Could an American lawyer working as a lobbyist for the Soviets get a job in the White House?" Wu asked. "In 1992, Clinton spoke to the National Geographic Society. He said, 'We want to see a prosperous and peaceful and stable China.' What does he mean by 'stable'? Cuba, the Soviet Union, North Korea and the Soviet bloc, Iraq—we don't want to use the word 'stable' in relation to these states. America didn't and doesn't want them stable," Wu commented. "There is chaos and starvation in some of these places. Clinton meant that he wanted a stable investment climate in China for American businesses. Under the communist system, the government controls labor and resources. If chaos would result, the Western investors would lose their money they have invested in communist China."[25]

Like the arguments for turning a blind eye to the wave of illegal immigrants, the appeasers warn that our entire economy will collapse if we cut off trade with China. That is the desperate cry of someone either blinded by greed or by ignorance. It is ridiculous to assume that no other country can make toys for Happy Meals. It is ridiculous to think that if we suddenly cut off the supply of computer components from China that no one else would step in to sell them to Americans.

Then there are those who claim that we're actually helping the Chinese people by trading with China. They argue that further opening of trade with a communist country will spark change. That's simply not true. The Soviet Union, to which they so readily point, is a prime example. The Soviet Union became weaker and weaker and was left with only limited established trade with the United States and other countries to sustain it. Many in this country, including now-known Soviet agent Armand Hammer, insisted that trading with the Soviets would more rapidly bring about change. We have learned since the demise of the Evil Empire, through FBI and KGB records, that Hammer and others were doing the bidding of the Soviet government in order to keep it afloat via an infusion of American money. In fact, Hammer was good friends with Russian tyrants Lenin and (later) Stalin and was doing their bidding starting in the 1920s.

The FBI was very well aware of Hammer's ties to the Soviet Union but could not act because the shrewd Hammer had made himself well connected in Washington.[26] According to one declassified 1961 memo between J. Edgar Hoover and William Sullivan, head of domestic counterintelligence at the FBI, Hammer could not be pursued because he was "protected" by Senator Albert Gore Sr. Some deridingly referred to the senior Gore as "the distinguished senator from Occidental," referring to Hammer's multibillion-dollar oil company.

History is against those who make the claim that trade with a nation will bring about desired change. The Soviet Union enjoyed sixty years of trade but ultimately collapsed under the weight of trying to keep up with Ronald Reagan's arms race. Conversely, change in South Africa came about relatively quickly after trade with that nation was cut off.

It appears that we haven't learned the lessons of history. The sad truth is, we've become dependent upon cheap Chinese products and would rather make a buck, or save one, than stand up for what is right. It's becoming increasingly hard to do, but I try very hard not to buy anything from China. I know that every pair of sneakers I buy means another pair is being stitched together by some unfortunate laborer, very likely a child, in wretched, inhumane conditions. The faster we wean ourselves from these cheap products, the faster we'll see real change in China.

Capitalism is a wonderful thing. It enables so many people to reach their goals, to touch their dreams. It feeds, it clothes, it houses, it betters so many lives. We Americans are the masters at using it to its fullest potential. However, capitalism without a conscience soon loses its way. Ambition gives way to greed. Instead of building dreams, it perpetuates nightmares. Whether that nightmare is China or North Korea or any modern-day incarnation of totalitarianism, oppression should never be fueled by American capitalism. Those who must live under such brutal regimes deserve a fighting chance at change without our keeping the monster alive.

16

POLITICAL CORRECTNESS is the liberal version of fascism.

JUST WHERE DID ALL this political correctness garbage come from, anyway? Many theories abound. I had never heard the term until the 1990s, but apparently it's been around for quite some time. Whether it went by its current title is hard to determine. William Lind of the Free Congress Foundation insists that it got its start back in the 1920s with a bunch of Marxists who were adamant about dismantling democracy.[1] Whatever its origins, the political correctness movement professes openness and diversity while defining what's open and diverse by its narrow-minded left-wing lexicon. No matter who dreamt it up, they understood that controlling the language to fit your agenda ranks right up there with controlling the currency. If left unabated, you soon control the entire society.

Frank Sinatra, Chairperson of the Board

It started off innocuously enough. *Chairman* became *chairperson*. Okay. If a woman holds that position it's understandable that she might not like being referred to as a man. (I never understood why they didn't change *woman* to *wo-person* if they were that offended.) *Stewardess* became *flight attendant*. *Fireman* became *firefighter*. Then came the next phase. *Handicapped* became *physically challenged*, and *Indian* became *Native American*. Then we were into the whole hyphenated thing: *African-American*, *Mexican-American*, etc. We began feeling self-conscious every time we spoke. Who were we going to offend? What phrase that I had always used was now taboo? We literally became afraid to utter the wrong thing.

Once the PC crowd got us used to the new language, they started to dismantle time-honored American traditions. Musical chairs was an early victim. It was cruel and destroyed self-esteem. It caused antisocial and violent behavior and was probably dangerous to the ozone. It must be banned! It was only then that we began to question this new indoctrination. Musical chairs? Could they be serious? Why, when I was growing up, no kid's birthday party was complete without a good round of musical chairs. Speaking of birthday parties, it became politically incorrect to open presents at birthdays lest we make the birthday child feel superior at the expense of the poor little guests or embarrass a guest because his of her gift was not as nice as another. We at the Valentine house always ignore that idiotic new rule and dive right in with paper tearing and ribbons flying.

Then the left-wingers lunged from the ridiculous to the frightening. They wanted to ban dodge ball. *Dodge ball!* That game we all played on the playground at school with a soft rubber ball that could not be found in any store. It was one of those things you could only find at school, like the gallon-sized cans of beets and that peculiar smelling cleaner the janitor used after somebody threw up. According to folks like Judith Young of the National Association for Sport and Physical Education, "The object 'to throw things at the kids, to hit the kids, and then thereby eliminate them from participation' is not consistent with wanting them to be participating."[2] Many schools have banned or are considering banning dodge ball. It is no longer politically correct.

Gentlemen, Start Your Native Americans

The problem with the PC crowd is they tried to move the herd along too quickly. We were coming along just fine with hyphens and the gender-neutral terms. We had begun to let go of our so-called sexist stereotypes. Then they came after dodge ball. That was a kid's game too far. Then they began attacking innocuous expressions like *chink in the armor*, not because those expressions were actually offensive but because they *sounded* offensive. This exposed the utter ignorance and stupidity of the PC crowd.

Who can forget the brouhaha over the word *niggardly*. The first case of oversensitivity occurred back in the summer of 2000, when the word first gained national attention. It means *stingy* or *miserly* and is used several times in the works of Shakespeare. In September 2002, a fourth-grade teacher in Wilmington, North Carolina, decided to teach the word to her students, knowing that it would come up in their reading and subsequent discussion of literary characters. One supposes that she sought to defuse a potential bomb by explaining the word's true meaning to her students. Instead, the bomb blew up in her face after one of the kids complained to her mother. The parent complained to the principal that she was offended because the word *sounded* similar to a racial slur. Forget that it wasn't a racial slur and that the word is used in classic literature, it *sounded* like a racial slur.

It gets worse. You'd think that the principal would come to the teacher's defense, but he instead made her write a letter of apology to the parents. Not only that, the teacher was forced to undergo sensitivity training in order to fend off further action. The president of the North Carolina Parent-Teacher Association piled on, saying, "Many of us know that it is offensive, and we choose not to use words that may offend other people." She added that the *niggardly* incident demonstrated the need for effective diversity and sensitivity training. "Incidents such as this," she said, "can polarize the community. We can't allow that to happen. This can be captured as a teachable moment, and we can learn from it."[3] The ignorance is exasperating, isn't it?

It was a teachable moment, all right. They missed a golden opportunity to teach the kids, and the parents, that words really do have meanings and they should learn them before they go berserk just because something *sounds* offensive. Not only did the parent show her ignorance, the school establishment opted to perpetuate it by condemning the teacher for teaching a legitimate literary word. You see, all you need to do these days is *sound* politically incorrect and you're ostracized and subjected to sensitivity training by the idiots in charge. I suppose *Homo sapiens* will have to be stricken from use since it *sounds* offensive. That's all these people deal in anyway—perception rather than reality.

Although exasperating, it's almost comical, this political correctness. In Eugene, Oregon, the city manager banned Christmas trees in public buildings.[4] Citing the fallacious argument of "separation of church and state," he thought it was his duty to cleanse the city of anything religious. In reality, it's anything *Christian*, the only politically incorrect religion. When it comes to other religions, the PC zealots conveniently forget their "separation" tirade. For example, in the wake of September 11, many California schools initiated Islam sensitivity training classes in which students dressed in robes, assumed Arab names, and memorized verses from the Koran.[5] Ultimately, in an attempt to keep from offending a few, they've managed to offend everyone else.

Political correctness can sometimes come back to bite the politically correct. In the 2008 presidential campaign, a Barack Obama delegate from Illinois found herself in hot water over a comment she made to some children. Apparently, some kids were playing in a tree next to her house, and Linda Ramirez-Sliwinski told them to "quit playing in the tree like little monkeys." Now we've all heard the term "yard apes" applied to children, but if the children happen to be black, well, you've got yourself a snoot full of trouble. The children in this case were indeed black, and Ramirez-Sliwinski was actually ticketed. I'm not kidding. Ticketed for calling some kids monkeys. The Obama camp forced her to resign her seat as a delegate, saying her remarks were "divisive and unacceptable"—even though they weren't. It doesn't matter what she meant by them. All that matters is they *sounded* offensive. Ready for the ironic part? Ramirez-Sliwinski is the only Hispanic on her town's board of trustees, and she had opposed attempts at passing an English-only proposition and an ordinance to crack down on illegal immigrants.[6] I guess all these years of being a lefty paid off for you, Linda. At the first opportunity, your compatriots threw you under the bus.

PC, B.S.

Political correctness has gone beyond being fodder for late-night comedians. It has made medicine downright dangerous. In her book *PC, M.D.*, Yale psychiatrist Sally Satel points to a number of disturbing politically correct measures in medicine. In one instance she cites Sally Zierler of the Department of Community Health at Brown University. Zierler calls AIDS a "biological expression of social inequality." Here's what Zierler proposes we do to cure AIDS: "Limit the power of corporations, cap salaries of CEOs, eliminate corporate subsidies, prohibit corporate

contributions to politicians, and strengthen labor unions."[7]
Oh, yeah. That'll cure AIDS, all right.

On the faculty of the psychology department at
Wayne State University sits one Rodney Clark. This brain
trust maintains that emphasizing personal responsibility
for good health (such as advising a patient to quit smoking) is a "form of racism."[8] Is that not exactly what's wrong
with modern liberalism, a de-emphasizing of personal
responsibility? More and more pediatricians are now as-
sessing a child's vulnerability to violence by asking if
there's a gun in the house.[9] Pretty soon, parents with guns
will be arrested for contributing to the delinquency of a
minor. It's not that far-fetched.

In Carrollton, Texas, a town outside of Dallas, they
banned toy guns in public.[10] "You want to play with them,
fine. Play with them in a contained situation, in your house
or in your back yard," said Carrollton Police Chief David
James, the one who proposed the change. "But don't take
those things out and brandish them in public," he added.
The truth is, using a toy gun in a threatening manner is already against the law. Banning them from public won't stop
anyone from using them in a threatening manner, if that's
the intention. Likewise, real guns will be used in an illegal
manner despite gun bans. The only reason to ban toy guns
is because they've become politically incorrect.

In San Francisco, where nothing would surprise me, a
loony group of animal rights folks pushed to have the
wording changed in city ordinances from *pet owners* to *pet*

guardians. They said the word *owner* encouraged people to treat pets like disposable property and likened their movement to the abolition of slavery and the women's suffrage movements.[11] (Pardon me while I roll my eyes.) This is also the same city with a $7 million SPCA shelter that sets stray cats and dogs up in private "condos" complete with wicker furniture, fluffy pillows, framed prints, and TVs that play nature programs and cartoons. The shelter staff boasts six behaviorists.

Another growing movement of the politically correct set is protecting and excusing graffiti. Vandals who spray-paint buildings and overpasses and public walls are hailed as "artists" who should be allowed to "express themselves." When I once told Jesse Jackson in a radio interview that I thought the first real sign of a declining neighborhood was graffiti, he shot back that graffiti was "the hieroglyphics of oppression." The hieroglyphics of oppression? Gimme a break. We have pandered to these people for far too long. It's time we started holding vandals responsible for their actions instead of making excuses for their conduct.

Politically Incorrect: The Ultimate Sin

We can laugh at all these idiotic examples of political correctness, but the frightening part is, these PC people are actually serious. Many of them are also in positions of power and are changing laws, or bending them, to suit their agenda. Once political correctness is entrenched, it begins to take over all rational thinking. For instance, you'd think that if someone's wife were being accosted by another man that the assault would overshadow anything her husband may have said to the assailant *after* the assault. I mean, if someone attacks your wife, that's more important than anything you may have said to the guy in the heat of the moment, right? Not so in the case of Kimberly and Lonny Rae.

She was covering a high school football game for a small-town newspaper in Idaho when she decided to photograph one of the referees. Apparently that didn't sit too well with the ref and he grabbed her from behind, attempting to snatch the camera. Because the strap was hung around her neck, he couldn't wrestle the camera from her but left her with bruises and a neck injury in the process. Her husband heard her screams and came to her aid. Rae shoved the ref away from his wife and a school official whisked the ref into a locker room.

Rae stood outside the locker room and shouted, "Tell that nigger to get out here, 'cuz I'm a gonna kick his butt!" When the ref failed to emerge, Rae went to the police and demanded his arrest. But instead of charging the ref with assault and battery, they charged Rae with a hate crime for using "the *N* word"![12] Certainly Rae was wrong for using such a word, but that didn't negate the ref's crime—at least it shouldn't have. Because of political correctness, the assault and battery were completely overlooked in favor of prosecuting a man for his words. Rae was acquitted of the hate crime but, get this, he was found guilty of assault for using the forbidden word. The ref, who actually committed the assault, was never charged.

The politically correct have infiltrated some of our most beloved institutions, like our schools, where we charge them with shaping our children. I remember when one of my boys was in kindergarten, they spent weeks and weeks studying the rain forest. This wasn't something the teacher dreamed up, this was done school-wide, even statewide, for all I know. I know it wasn't the teacher's idea, because this teacher, whom we dearly loved, was very conservative and listened to my show.

Apparently there was a lesson plan for kindergarten that required teaching about the rain forest. The kids learned all about the animals and the plants. They learned about how the rain forest was being destroyed by evil developers. It all culminated in their making T-shirts that said "Save the Rain Forest." It looked like my kid had been to a Sting concert! I have no problem with learning about the rain forest. Maybe spending a day or two on it would be reasonable, but to put that much time into it smacked of some politically correct agenda. All the while, news reports were crying that our state's reading test scores were lagging behind and the governor wanted to spend $100 million more per year to teach children how to read. Imagine if all that energy expended on the rain forest had been spent on making sure each child could read.

Even at church, political correctness can sneak in. A gentleman who was hired to speak to the youth at our church asked the kids to raise their hand if one of their parents smoked. My oldest son raised his because his dad likes a cigar every now and then. When interrogated, he told the speaker that I smoked the occasional cigar, and the speaker instructed him to tell me that I needed to seek professional help. I would suspect that *he* was the one who actually needed professional help. Fortunately, my son, even at the tender age of nine, was savvy enough to realize this guy was out to lunch and laughed about it when he told us.

Imitation Is the Most Sincere Form of . . . Racism?

Who's the most impersonated figure in the history of the world? That's right, Elvis. You have people all over the planet impersonating him, people from all cultures and races. There are Hawaiian Elvises, Japanese Elvises, black Elvises. Nobody takes offense. Most people are amused by it. I'm sure even the King himself would be flattered that so many people from so many countries take the time to dress up like him. Innocent fun, right? Well, that all depends. It depends on where you are. If you're on one of our nation's college campuses, you'd better beware.

At the University of Tennessee in Knoxville, a group of five fraternity brothers were going to a battle-of-the-bands party where pledges dressed up as famous singers and pantomimed their hit songs. These five guys decided to go as the Jackson Five. You'd have thought they'd shot Abbie Hoffman. The headline in the paper screamed "Complaints about blackface episode bring action."[13] Blackface? School officials were horrified that these frat boys had ignored their sensitivity training. The national office of the fraternity suspended them and UT officials indicated that the university might choose not to recognize the fraternity even if the national office reinstated them.

Ironically, Michael Jackson dressed up as a white guy in one of his videos, poking fun at right-wingers. Where was the outcry? Was anyone upset when Billy Crystal used to do Sammy Davis Jr. on *Saturday Night Live*? How about Gene Wilder in the movie *Silver Streak*? Richard Pryor instructs him on how to apply shoe polish to his face and act black to get past police. Perhaps these were moments of hilarity that belong to another age. Or, perhaps, the politically correct have corrupted the psyche of America to the point of absurdity.

Shortly after that UT–Jackson Five story broke, I was at the mall and saw a young black girl dressed as a clown. I couldn't help but chuckle to myself. She was in "whiteface." Was I supposed to be offended?

Contrast the UT incident with a seriously offensive situation at Auburn University in 2001. In that particular case, frat boys dressed up for Halloween in KKK robes and blackface, one with a noose around his neck, their idea of humor.[14] This is a great lesson in distinguishing what is acceptable and what is not. Demeaning black people, in general, in this manner is totally reprehensible and conjures up ugly images of snotty little white boys looking down their redneck noses at anyone who happens to be black. Universities should never tolerate such conduct. Where we have to differentiate is between mean-spirited, negative stereotyping and legitimate parody, as was the case at UT.

Perpetuating negative stereotypical images of black people is certainly in bad taste. However, a caricature of a particular performer or movie character should never be off-limits. But I would go further. Stereotypical humor, when not meant to humiliate and inflict pain, is funny. Sure, you have to be careful not to go too far, but you can't tell me Eddie Murphy wasn't funny in the movies impersonating an old Jewish guy. He was hilarious as "the white guy" in the *Saturday Night Live* bit. Most stereotypes are rooted in truth. That's what makes them so funny.

Have we reached a point in our country where we can't chuckle at our differences and peculiarities? I certainly hope not, but the PC police are out to eradicate all vestiges of stereotypical humor. They will be the arbiters of what's funny. They will be the deciders of what is socially acceptable and what is not. Ultimately, they will strip us of our sense of humor but, worse, our safety in the process.

Political Correctness: The Profile of a Killer

Fascism is defined, in part, as *oppressive, dictatorial control*. That is exactly what political correctness is. In the name of tolerance, practitioners are totally *intolerant* of anyone who disagrees with them. Political correctness is not about broadening opinion. It's about restricting what is allowable conduct to that deemed appropriate by the politically correct.

One form of conduct heavily targeted has been racial profiling. Before we go any further, I want it understood that pulling over a black guy because he happens to be in a so-called white neighborhood is not profiling. That's called harassment, and it's totally unacceptable and unlawful. What's generally deemed profiling is using a particular profile to aid in solving or preventing crimes. For example, after September 11, Americans looked at people of Arab descent more suspiciously. Is that racist? Of course not. That's not to say that people of Arab descent should've been harassed, only that we should exercise caution. The terrorists were Arabs. It's not unreasonable, then, that other Arabs are looked at a bit more closely. Let me put it this way: not all Arab Muslims are terrorists, but all of the September 11 terrorists were Arab Muslims.

One of my brothers spent his honeymoon in London back in the early 1980s. He has red hair. When he went through security, and at various times during his visit, he was closely examined and questioned. Why? Because he fit the profile of an IRA terrorist. Was he offended? Certainly not. He understood and appreciated that authorities were doing their jobs in keeping the public safe.

Had airport screeners been employing these same techniques on September 11, 2001, they possibly could have saved three thousand lives and the Twin Towers might still be standing. Instead, a computerized system that was used by airlines to screen for suspicious passengers failed on September 11. Why? It was specifically set up *not* to screen passengers based on national origin. It turns out that during the 1990s, the Gore Commission on aviation security prohibited such profiling. Profiling at airports is, according to at least one Federal Aviation Administration official, "the single biggest deterrent against terrorism in aviation industry."[15] Political correctness, in its effort not to offend anyone, may very well have caused the bloodiest attacks by foreigners against Americans on U.S. soil in the entire history of the country.

In the wake of the terrorist attacks, I and other concerned citizens called on the president to ask all noncitizens who were from a country we deemed to be sympathetic to terrorists to leave until we sorted everything out. It was my belief then, and is my belief now, that our need to ensure the safety of our citizens precludes any perceived rights anyone has to stay in the United States if he or she is not a citizen. I compared it on my show to someone poo-pooing in the pool. It doesn't matter who did it, everyone has to get out of the pool until things are cleaned up.

By not insisting that noncitizens from terrorist nations leave immediately, we missed a window of opportunity to secure our country. Even worse, we continued to allow visitors from these terrorist-sponsoring nations to gain entry to our country. There were even Arab students who came here after September 11 to attend flight school![16]

If anyone directly has blood on their hands for 9/11—

aside from the terrorists themselves and their supporters—it's Norman Mineta. As transportation secretary under George W. Bush, it was Mineta who vehemently banned any kind of profiling in airports. Despite the overwhelming intelligence that Arab terrorists were up to something that might very well involve airplanes, Mineta stood his ground and made sure airport screeners didn't profile. It was that atmosphere of mandated political correctness that completely blocked the common sense of Michael Tuohey, a ticket agent for U.S. Air on the morning of September 11. He was suspicious of two passengers hurrying to catch a flight from Portland, Maine, to Boston. He had a bad feeling about them. They looked angry. They looked suspicious. "I looked in this guy's eyes, and he just looked angry," Tuohey recalled. "I just got an uncomfortable feeling. It just sent chills through you." But Tuohey had been trained to override his instincts. "I said to myself, 'If this guy doesn't look like an Arab terrorist, then nothing does.' Then I gave myself a mental slap, because in this day and age, it's not nice to say things like this. You've checked in hundreds of Arabs and Hindus and Sikhs, and you've never done that. I felt kind of embarrassed." The two were Abdulaziz Alomari and Mohamed Atta—two of the 9/11 hijackers.[17] Tuohey later felt responsible for allowing them on the plane, but it wasn't his fault. It was Mineta's fault. Mineta created the atmosphere that allowed 9/11 to happen.

Yet instead of learning his lesson from 9/11, Mineta turned up political correctness a few notches. Just eight months after 9/11, Mineta instituted an affirmative-action program for Arabs interested in pursuing careers in aviation. I kid you not! He said, "Surrendering to discrimination makes us no different than the terrorists."[18] And failing to learn the lessons of 9/11 made Mineta nothing more than an idiot.

Mineta wasn't alone in his naiveté. Voices of reason were drowned out by the din of political correctness.

In order to better secure our country, Attorney General John Ashcroft ordered the questioning of five thousand Arab men. The cry went out from the politically correct that we couldn't profile like that; it was a violation of their rights. Our country was under attack from Arab extremists, and still the politically correct tried to stand in the way of common sense. Their compatriots in the press continue to do their bidding by publishing biased stories or, in some cases, no story at all.

Political correctness is dangerous to America on so many different levels. It has become a way to limit free speech and label those who disagree with you as not being worthy of consideration. It's frightening that a large segment of our society just goes along to get along instead of challenging political correctness as the threat that it is. Until Americans stand up to it, political correctness will be allowed to shape the debate in this country. Its labels of what is correct and what isn't will choke off democracy. Left unabated, free speech as we know it will cease to exist.

17

QUOTAS are wrong.

THE TERMS QUOTAS AND *affirmative action* are often used interchangeably these days. However, at one point in time, the two had very different meanings. In order to fully understand those differences it's important that we go back to the origins of affirmative action to learn what it meant in the context of the day. The intentions were certainly honorable: take a segment of the population that had been relegated to the back of the bus, blocked from higher education in historically white universities, and generally locked out of the American dream, and break down those racial barriers. There has never been any question that, before the Civil Rights Act of 1964, blacks were treated as second-class citizens in many parts of America. The debate was over what to do about it.

Where Did Quotas Come From?

The term *affirmative action*, as it applies to racial equality, first appeared in JFK's Executive Order 10925, signed March 6, 1961. This order set up the Committee on

Equal Employment Opportunity, which was charged with the task of assuring that projects financed by federal funds "take affirmative action" to ensure that hiring and employment practices are free of racial bias.[1] Note that Kennedy did not intend to set quotas. He never meant to set aside jobs for any particular race. His intent, as clearly stated in his executive order, was to tear down the walls of discrimination, to level the playing field. His intention certainly was not to give anyone an advantage.

That notion began to take shape several years later under President Lyndon B. Johnson. President Johnson argued that fairness required more than just tearing down the walls of discrimination. In his 1965 commencement address at Howard University, he said: "You do not take a person who for years has been hobbled by chains and liberate him, bring him up to the starting line of a race and then say, 'you're free to compete with all the others,' and still justly believe that you have been completely fair. Thus it is not enough just to open the gates of opportunity. All our citizens must have the ability to walk through those gates. . . . We seek not . . . just equality as a right and a theory but equality as a fact and equality as a result."[2]

President Johnson put his words into action with Executive Order 11246, which stated, in part: "It is the policy of the Government of the United States to provide equal opportunity in federal employment for all qualified persons, to prohibit discrimination in employment because of race, creed, color, or national origin, and to promote the full realization of equal employment opportunity through a positive, continuing program in each department and agency." He abolished the Committee on Equal Employment Opportunity that Kennedy had established and moved its responsibilities under the Secretary of Labor. In doing so, he authorized the secretary to "adopt such rules and regulations and issue such orders as he deems necessary and appropriate to achieve the purposes thereof."[3] Rather ambiguous on the surface, but those inside the Labor Department took it to mean: take any steps necessary to make sure government hiring reflects the population. More specifically—quotas.

Interestingly enough, it was Richard Nixon, a Republican, who turned up the heat on quotas with the "Philadelphia Order" in 1969. The Nixon administration was eager to guarantee fair hiring practices in construction and chose Philadelphia as a test site. In the words of Nixon's assistant labor secretary, Arthur Fletcher, "The craft unions and the construction industry are among the most egregious offenders against equal opportunity laws . . . openly hostile toward letting blacks into their closed circle."[4] Nixon instituted a set of goals and timetables. Thus began the pressure to set quotas to achieve those goals.

The brakes were put on quotas in the Supreme Court's 1978 ruling in *Regents of the University of California v. Bakke.* Allan Bakke was a white student who was twice denied acceptance to medical school despite the fact that he had a higher grade-point average than several minority students who were admitted. The University of California–Davis had a policy of maintaining a 16 percent minority quota. The Court ruled that the university could use race as a factor but could not establish quotas. Bakke was admitted and graduated.

The schizophrenic High Court would dismantle most of *Bakke* two years later through *Fullilove v. Klutznick*. In *Fullilove*, the justices decided that modest quotas *were* constitutional. The inconsistency of the Supreme Court demonstrated what a difficult issue this was. There was no disputing the problem. The devil was in the details of the solution. Just as soon as it looked like quotas were necessary, some egregious case would pop up and the Court would swing back the other way.

Backward, redneck segregationists, hanging onto the last vestiges of institutionalized racism in Alabama, attracted the wrath of the Supreme Court in 1987. In *United States v. Paradise*, the Alabama State Department of Public Safety had thumbed its nose at a 1970 federal court ruling ordering an end to its systematic discrimination against black state troopers. At the time of that ruling, there was not a single black on the force. Twelve years after the federal court ruling, no black state trooper had been advanced beyond entry level. In response, the federal court ordered racial quotas to end the "pervasive, systematic, and obstinate discriminatory exclusion of blacks."[5]

The court ordered that each time the department hired or promoted a white, one black would also be hired or promoted until at least 25 percent of its upper ranks were filled by blacks. The state challenged the use of numerical quotas all the way to the Supreme Court. The High Court upheld the use of strict quotas in this particular case as the only means of combating the department's defiant racism.

In my opinion, the federal court erred in its remedy. No doubt there was a problem and something needed to be done. But what the court should have done was prosecute those racist SOBs who perpetuated the discrimination and defied the court order. Penalizing innocent white officers in an effort to rectify the situation certainly didn't change any hearts. It may have been an immediate fix to the problem, but there are better ways to deal with discrimination that don't drive a wedge between the races.

Two years after the *Paradise* decision, the Supreme Court made it clear that its fix for the Alabama Department of Public Safety was an isolated case. In the *City of Richmond v. Croson*, the Court called the use of quotas a "highly suspect tool."[6] Richmond had been setting aside 30 percent of city construction money for black-owned firms. The Court ruled that such set-asides were unconstitutional unless there was demonstrative industry-wide discrimination.

In spite of the myriad examples of quotas, and the court rulings surrounding them, there are those who still refuse to admit they even exist. As if acknowledgment will somehow erase the progress made in the area of civil rights, they cling to the fantasy that no black person has ever been placed ahead of anyone else simply based on skin color. Martin Luther King Jr. had a dream that one day his children would be judged not by the color of their skin but by the content of their character. You have to wonder if he would approve of children being passed over for admittance to universities simply because the color of their skin happens to be white.

In Quota Denial

Dr. Joseph Lowery, one of the founders of the Southern Christian Leadership Conference and my co-panelist at an American Bar Association discussion a few years ago in Atlanta, quite nearly came unhinged when I mentioned quotas. He fumed that there was no such thing as quotas. As I looked back at him in utter incredulity, I couldn't help but notice that "Mr. Quota" himself, Bill Lann Lee, former *acting* assistant attorney general for civil rights in the Clinton administration and a fellow panelist, sat conspicuously quiet. And with good reason. Although he had told a Senate confirmation committee that he was opposed to quotas, his life's work told a different story.

Lee's advocacy of racial quotas is quite extensive, so I won't bore you with all of the cases here. One in particular illustrates his warped sense of justice. This quote from the *Washington Times* says it all: "As counsel for the NAACP Legal Defense Fund, Lee supports a court challenge arguing that graduate and professional schools in California violated federal law when they began admitting between 50 and 75 percent of the students based on merit."[7] Can you believe that? He believes California violated federal law because it was actually admitting students based on merit. He also called California's Proposition 209, which passed in November 1996 and eliminated quotas, "unconstitutional" and said the Constitution not only permits, it requires preferences.[8] Requires preferences? Where in the Constitution does it *require* preferences? Now you know why Lee sat quietly when Reverend Lowery claimed there was no such thing as quotas.

His official biography from his *acting* assistant attorney general days read, in part: "Mr. Lee was born and raised in New York City where his parents owned a small laundry. He credits his late father, who experienced bigotry despite his proud military service to his country, with providing the inspiration for a career in civil rights law. After graduating from the Bronx High School of Science, Mr. Lee won a scholarship to Yale University, where he benefited from an affirmative action program to include minority students." As it turns out, Yale's first attempt at affirmative action happened in 1973. The curiosity is that by then, Lee had already won the scholarship, graduated magna cum laude, been elected to Phi Beta Kappa, and was a year away from receiving his doctorate at Columbia University Law School.[9] The ugly and ironic truth is that he achieved all that without affirmative action!

By the way, just to give you an idea of where Bill Lann

Lee is coming from, his claim to fame during his time as *acting* assistant attorney general was investigating schools that used Indian team names and mascots.[10] Very nice guy, I might add. I enjoyed getting to know him before, during, and after our panel discussion in Atlanta—but, boy, what a screwed-up view on racial preferences.

Here's another piece of irony for you. Before Proposition 209, which Lee assailed as unconstitutional, the University of California at Berkeley, right there in his home state, routinely admitted black students with lower grades and SAT scores two hundred points lower than students of Chinese heritage. Other examples of so-called reverse discrimination (I prefer to call it just plain discrimination) include a white firefighter in Birmingham, Alabama, who finished eleventh in his class of fellow firefighters taking a promotion exam for lieutenant. He was passed over in favor of a black who finished ninety-fifth. The U.S. Department of Defense requested bids for a road construction project to be built at the White Sands missile range. The department told white bidders that the contract was "sheltered" and reserved for racial minorities.[11] Lowery is in denial when it comes to quotas, but the woods are full of such stories. It bears repeating: you don't right the wrongs of the past by wronging the people of the present.

Who's Harmed by Quotas

Aside from the white folks who are displaced by quotas, there's a segment of society that has heretofore not been associated with its destruction—blacks themselves. If you're scratching your head, allow me to explain. I would venture to say that there's scarcely a white male alive who hasn't, at some point in his life, wondered whether a particular black person he's encountered on the job or in higher education didn't get where he or she was because of quotas.

Who does that hurt? It doesn't hurt the white guy. It hurts the black person by creating a stigma that far outreaches the confines of merely those who actually benefited from quotas. An entire race is stigmatized and has to work that much harder to overcome the doubt in many minds. You may say it doesn't matter, but in reality it does. Blacks still only make up about 12 to 14 percent of the population. Their success is ultimately determined, in part, by nonblacks. As much as blacks have gone through over the years in this country, the last thing they need is someone wondering about their abilities and qualifications.

Quotas do that. They put doubt in people's minds, where none would exist if a white were doing the same job. That's certainly not to say that every black in America is looked upon with suspicion. It simply means that quotas have allowed us to keep prejudice alive.

Have you ever worked with the boss' son and wondered about his qualifications? In your mind, you knew exactly how he got the job. That's exactly the kind of suspicion and doubt I'm talking about. That son may be perfectly capable, but because he's working for dad, every move he makes will be examined under a microscope by the other workers. Everyone feels that the son got a leg up, and they resent it, even if it's not true.

Let's use a sports analogy. What if, during the NCAA basketball tournament, a certain team were allowed two losses instead of having to abide by the usual single-elimination rule? What if they went all the way to the Final Four and then won the tournament? How many folks do you think would be crying foul? The quota folks would tell you that it isn't fair for a small school like, say, Creighton University in Omaha, Nebraska, to have to play against the big boys like Michigan State and the University of North Carolina without receiving some sort of help. Yet little ol' Creighton has been known to top these traditionally strong teams in the weekly Top 20 polls. How can that be? How can a team from such a small school outshine some of the nation's best basketball programs without receiving special treatment? They can do it because there's nobody propping them up or putting them ahead of anyone else. They have to work hard for everything they get, and that makes them a better team. It also earns them the respect of their peers instead of disdain for being treated differently.

Color-Blind Is Not the Goal

You often hear quota activists yearning for a color-blind society. This is where they really begin to expose themselves as hypocrites. You'd think that when Ward Connerly, a member of the University of California board of regents, brought forth his Racial Privacy Initiative (RPI) to end the practice of filling in one's race on government documents, it would have been the ultimate in color-blindness. You'd also think that the so-called civil rights groups would have applauded such a move. You'd be wrong. The American Association for Affirmative Action (AAAA), which touts itself as being for "equality in employment, economic and educational opportunities," sailed on Connerly's RPI like white on rice.[12]

This was a golden opportunity for the AAAA and others to put their money where their mouths are and get on board something that would truly make the state color-blind. The truth is, they don't want a color-blind society. They want race data so they can promote their agenda of quotas. They claim they were against the RPI because it would allow companies to cover up their discriminatory ways.

See, you have to try to understand that mentality. These so-called civil rights advocates look at raw numbers to determine if a company is racist or discriminatory. If a business is 40 percent white, 50 percent Asian, and only 10 percent black, that doesn't demonstrate anything about discrimination. Each situation is different. Maybe there weren't enough qualified blacks, or maybe blacks had no interest in that particular company. The reasons could be endless, but organizations like the AAAA simply look at numbers and jump to conclusions. Take away the numbers and they have to actually go out and find someone who's been discriminated against.

If the AAAA were true to its own philosophy, there would be plenty of black-dominated businesses that should be forced to hire white folks. What would you guess is the percentage of blacks working at the Black Entertainment Television network? How about the NBA or the NFL? Start talking that talk and these quota folks start to hem and haw and flail about.

Speaking of the National Football League, the late attorney Johnnie Cochran had the gall to issue a bogus study that said black coaches were held to a different standard than white coaches. He cited that black coaches, on average, had won 1.1 more games per season than white coaches. What kind of proof is that? He threatened a lawsuit if the teams didn't start rewarding teams coached by blacks with an additional draft pick![13] I'm not making this up.

What's the primary goal of an NFL team owner? To win the Super Bowl, right? Up until the Colts and the Bears played in 2007, there had been no black head coaches in the Super Bowl. Suddenly there were two in the same game. This was done without quotas and without Cochran's harebrained draft pick scheme. You don't think these team owners would hire the Man in the Moon if he'd take them to the Super Bowl? Of course, the big moneymakers in the NFL are the players, and the majority of them are black, a little stat Johnnie chose to ignore.

Sports is probably the best example of an institution that allows people to be all they can be. You can make or break your own career with your talent, your attitude, and your determination to win. No quotas. No set-asides. No propping up nor holding down. It's all about competition. Isn't that what the rest of America should be like too?

End It, Don't Mend It

Affirmative Action, as envisioned by JFK, was good and necessary. Opening up American society to everyone, regardless of race, was and is the right thing to do. Even university admissions policies that take into consideration the adversity one has had to overcome are probably wise. But assuming that only blacks have faced adversity is in itself racist.

For instance, take the example of two students with identical SAT scores and grade-point averages applying to a college. One is a white boy, the oldest of six kids from a very poor family. With no father in the house, he not only had to study hard and stay in school, but he also had to help his mother raise his siblings. The other applicant is a black girl whose father is a lawyer and mother is a doctor. Nobody can tell me with a straight face that she should get the nod over the boy.

Many proquota folks like to point to Republican Colin Powell as someone who not only benefited from quotas but also supports them. I've heard Secretary Powell speak to this issue on a number of occasions, but even some conservatives still misconstrue his position. He said it best in his autobiography, *My American Journey*: "If affirmative action means programs that provide equal opportunity, then I am all for it. If it leads to preferential treatment or helps those who no longer need help, I am opposed. I benefited from equal opportunity and affirmative action in the army, but I was not shown preference. The army, as a matter of fairness, made sure that performance would be the only measure of advancement. Affirmative action in the best sense promotes equal consideration, not reverse discrimination. Discrimination 'for' one group means, inevitably, discrimination 'against' another; and all discrimination is offensive."[14]

Secretary Powell fully understands the difference between affirmative action and quotas. He understands the need to help everyone who needs help, but he's aware that not everyone who needs help happens to be black.

I'd like to coin a term, if I may, at the risk of adding another psychobabble phrase to the American lexicon: *socioeconomic consideration*. One word of caution. I do not envision, nor do I see it feasible, to use socioeconomic consideration as a factor in hiring. Businesses are in business to make money, and they want the most qualified employees for the job. However, when it comes to admissions policies at colleges and universities, socioeconomic consideration could be made *if*—and that's a big if—all other criteria, like grades, SAT scores, etc., are equal. That goes back to my earlier example of the boy who came from an impoverished background. If we're going to lift people up and help prepare them for life, let's lift up those who actually need lifting, not those who may be of a certain race or ethnic background.

While the Supreme Court continues to fluctuate between embracing quotas and rejecting them, the justices seem oblivious to the obvious solution: strict enforcement of existing antidiscrimination laws. As with gun control, prosecuting the offenders, not passing more laws, is the best way to rectify the disparities in hiring and education. Making innocent people pay for the sins of previous generations runs counter to our fundamental principles as a nation. Quotas, without question, are wrong—and it's time we ended them once and for all.

18

REAGAN was right.

THEY SAY A PRESIDENT will ultimately be judged by one yardstick: history. No matter his popularity, or unpopularity, when he leaves office, only time will tell how his presidency will be regarded by generations down the road. If history were ever kind to a former president, it has to be Ronald Reagan. Although he was held in high esteem when he stepped down in 1989, his popularity among Americans has continued to grow.

With each passing year, we come to appreciate more and more the wisdom of President Reagan. He was a man who was comfortable in his own skin and comfortable in the presidency. He wore the office like a tailor-made suit of clothes. What made him so well-suited for this particular job were his undying faith in America and his optimism for her future. His unapologetic patriotism was reviled as hokey by some, but he came along at a time when the political landscape was littered with bitterness and despair. The American people were demoralized and searching for hope, and they found that hope in Ronald Reagan.

That Vision Thing

Reagan had a two-pronged vision for America when he ran for president in 1980. He wanted to bring this country back by restoring people's optimism and her flagging economy. He also wanted to defeat the Soviet Union. How he managed to do both is an interesting piece of American history because he forever changed the course of the world in the process. His detractors have maintained that he was a bumbling, disconnected leader who got lucky. You will learn in this chapter that Reagan's vision was very pronounced, his path very calculated.

The accusation by some that he was a useful idiot of the right wing was totally destroyed with the publication of *Reagan In His Own Hand.* One of the editors of the book, Kiron Skinner, happened upon more than six hundred radio addresses Reagan had written between 1975 and 1979. The speeches, written on yellow legal pads, complete with edits and revisions, showed the depth of his intellect and the thought process he used in writing. These weren't the shallow ramblings of a mental midget. What she found, and subsequently published, were reasoned, articulate positions on everything from communism to marijuana.

Reagan was indeed his own man. He formulated his own positions based on his life experiences and his vast knowledge of world affairs through voracious reading. His basic philosophy could be boiled down to his fundamental belief that communism was the natural enemy of capitalism. He fully understood the broader implications of such a philosophy and his role in spreading it. He had a basic vision for the world, and he carried that vision forward from his radio speeches to the White House.

The Shaping of Reaganism

Unlike many politicians who seek office first and then decide where they stand once they get there, Ronald Reagan spent years developing his ideals before he ever ran for office. He came of age at the dawning of Franklin D. Roosevelt's presidency. He loved Roosevelt. Not so much because of his political philosophy, although the Works Progress Administration (WPA) did put his father back to work, but because of Roosevelt's optimism. Reagan classified himself as "a New Dealer to the core" in his own autobiography.[1] He saw the same greatness in FDR that he had admired in the Founding Fathers. Even during his presidency, he defended the New Deal as a necessary step to get the country through difficult times.

The New Deal created an alphabet soup of federal agencies, everything from the AAA (Agricultural Adjustment Agency) to the TVA. Many viewed these new entities not as government on steroids but as a way of getting people involved in their government. To Reagan, and millions of other Americans, the New Deal was a safety net, not a way of life. As we've learned from history, though, government has a bad habit of slowly creeping, virtually unnoticed, until it takes over our lives. Like beautiful ivy planted to accent the front wall, before you know it, you can no longer see the wall.

The real line of demarcation for many, perhaps even Reagan, was drawn on January 11, 1944. On that day, FDR outlined what he called a "second Bill of Rights" that would guarantee each citizen "the right to a useful and re-munerative job"; "the right of every family to a decent home"; and the right of every businessman "to trade in an atmosphere of freedom from unfair competition"—just to name a few.[2] The Declaration of Independence main-tained that we had a right to the *pursuit* of happiness. Now FDR was declaring our right to happiness itself. It was the blueprint for modern liberalism.

Within eight years, the self-proclaimed "near hopeless hemophilic liberal"[3] was a "Democrat for Eisenhower" in the 1952 presidential campaign. In 1960, he was ready to make the switch and support Richard Nixon, but Nixon's people insisted that he'd be much more effective support-ing their man as a Democrat. By 1962, Reagan could deny his allegiance no longer. He changed parties and joined the Republicans.

The increasing government intrusion troubled Rea-gan. He commented to wife Nancy that the very Demo-crats for whom he'd campaigned several years before were responsible for the problems he now railed against on his speaking tours for General Electric.[4] Reagan didn't like the direction in which the country was heading. He saw the massive expansion of government as a direct threat to

America's freedom. At the same time, he recognized another threat, which he had been following very closely
since witnessing its influence in Hollywood. The threat of
communism, specifically Soviet communism, represented
a clear and present danger to the United States, and Reagan never missed an opportunity to spread the word.

Reagan's defining political moment came in 1964 as
he actively campaigned for Barry Goldwater. Goldwater's
people had heard Reagan's stump speech, which he'd made
countless times for General Electric. They convinced
Goldwater to air a version of that speech on his behalf in a
nationally televised fund-raiser. Not even Reagan's brilliant address could save the Goldwater candidacy, but it
was the launching pad for his own political career. Reagan
told the American people, "I suggest to you that there is
no left or right, only an up or down. Up to the maximum
of individual freedom consistent with law and order, or
down to the ant heap of totalitarianism, and regardless of
their humanitarian purpose, those who would sacrifice
freedom for security have, whether they know it or not,
chosen this downward path."[5]

It's easy to see the wisdom of his comments now, but
remember, this was 1964, the year in which the Great Society was born. There were certainly others who questioned the rate at which the government was growing, but
Reagan went far beyond that. He dared to question the
role of government as the solution to all of society's ills, a
notion that had become ingrained in the American psy-

che. But it would be sixteen more years before Americans had their fill of bloated government and would, finally, turn to Reagan for relief.

His message, however, had hit a chord with a group of California businessmen who liked what they heard and convinced Reagan to make a run for the governor's office. Sticking to his ideals and bedrock beliefs, Reagan ran and upset incumbent Pat Brown, who had virtually laughed at Reagan throughout the campaign. In fact, Brown's people had aided Reagan during the Republican primary by leaking some damaging information about his opponent, thinking that going up against a political novice would be a cakewalk. They were wrong. Reagan thumped Brown in '66, winning by more than a million votes. It would not be the last time Reagan was underestimated by his enemies.

Reagan Governs

Reagan stuck to his principles even in the face of an ever-changing political climate. While other California politicians tried to play to the emerging '60s counterculture springing up in places like Berkeley, Reagan clearly abhorred it. He saw them as spoiled little children who wanted to enjoy the fruits of the land of opportunity but were willing to risk nothing to preserve them. As governor, Reagan met with some of the activists to hear their complaints. In one exchange, a student lectured Reagan that he couldn't possibly understand the issues of the day because he had grown up in a different world. "Today we have television, jet planes, space travel, nuclear energy, computers," the young student informed him. Reagan responded, "You're right. It's true that we didn't have those things when we were young. We *invented* them."[6]

There was a weak attempt at promoting Reagan for president in 1968, though Reagan always insisted he never ran that year. He did make a serious effort in 1976, giving Gerald Ford a scare, but Americans still were not ready for him. We hadn't become fed-up enough yet. We weren't angry enough at how far astray the country was going. It would take four more years, four years of probably the most decent man we've seen in the White House, but Jimmy Carter lacked the vision to take America where it needed to go. Nineteen eighty, at long last, was the year that Americans became tired of appeasement abroad and rudderless leadership at home—and they turned their lonely eyes to Ronald Reagan.

The Reagan Legacy

Historians will argue about the Reagan years for decades. Those historians ideologically opposed to Reagan find it difficult, if not impossible, to record his presidency in a good light. As long as they are writing the history books, the truth will be hidden. But as the years wear on and the truth begins to harden, we're finding more and more books coming closer and closer to the truth. I'm confident that history will be kind to the Reagan legacy. As younger historians with no political stake in Reagan begin to revisit his presidency, they will find that the facts are indisputable and, in the end, impossible to deny.

Some of today's historians make the Reagan legacy out to be more complicated than it actually is. It's not complicated at all, really. Reagan had a domestic agenda to roll back government intrusion and taxes, lower interest rates and inflation, and put America back to work. His foreign agenda was to rebuild the military to ensure peace through strength while putting an end to the Soviet Union. That was basically the plan, and in 1981 Reagan set out to achieve it.

Ronald Reagan campaigned on a pledge to push Congress to give Americans a 30 percent across-the-board tax cut. Once elected, he set out to fulfill that promise, but the left wing of the Democratic Party tried to thwart his efforts. In spite of the stiff opposition, Reagan was able to push through a tax-cut plan at a reduced rate of 25 percent. Since the cuts would be phased in over three years, the effective rate cut was 23 percent. In 1981, income tax rates were cut 5 percent. Over the next two years, taxes were cut again, by 10 percent each year. Much to the dismay of the doom-and-gloomers who said cutting tax rates would further wreck the economy, they had just the opposite effect. In the 1980s, federal revenues *doubled*, from $517 billion to $1.031 trillion![7]

Instead of wrecking the economy, the tax cuts spurred the longest peacetime expansion America had ever seen up until that point. The annual inflation rate, which stood at

13.3 percent in 1979, had been slashed to 4.4 percent by the time Reagan left office.[8] Interest rates fell from 21 percent in 1980 to just 8 percent.[9]

Ah, but Reagan gave us those big budget deficits, right? No, in fact, he did not. The revisionists would have you think that Reagan spent money like a drunken sailor. The fact is, Reagan's budgets were rejected by the Democrat-controlled Congress. I remember seeing news reports of Democrats walking Reagan's budget up the Capitol steps in a mock coffin, calling it "Dead On Arrival." If you go back and look at the budgets Reagan proposed and the budgets that were actually passed, you'll see that Reagan wanted to spend far less than Congress, even in the years of rebuilding our military.

Each of the eight budgets Reagan submitted to Congress proposed spending less money than was eventually spent except one, the 1984 budget, which proposed spending 1.2 percent more. Pay attention to this part, because it's real important: if Congress had passed Reagan's budgets instead of its own, even the 1984 budget, we would have seen a surplus in 1989.[10] You see, as revenue increased by about 100 percent in the '80s, spending increased by about 112 percent, thus there was an increase in deficits.[11]

Another promise Reagan made on the domestic front in 1980 was to give our military the tools it needed. Our military was spread too thinly, ill-prepared with substandard machinery, and suffering from low morale. I remember vividly leaving high school in the late '70s and learning about classmates' career plans. Many were going to college, others to work, but the conventional wisdom was, if you could do neither, you joined the military. That's not to say that everyone in the military was of a lower caliber than your average person, but at that point in our history, it seemed to be the choice of last resort rather than proud young men and women setting out to make a career in the military. Reagan saw all that and was determined to change the situation.

Interestingly enough, the stronger the Soviet Union became prior to the Reagan administration, the less we spent on our military. Part of the reason was the endless parade of treaties through which we compromised our readiness in order to appease the communist thugs in Moscow. During the Kennedy administration, the military budget constituted 49 percent of our discretionary budget. By 1980, that figure had dropped to an anemic 22.8 percent.

Historical revisionists would have you think that Reagan spent 90 percent of the budget on defense and that's why we accumulated the large deficits. You now know the reason for the deficits was that Congress outspent the prosperity of the '80s. You should also know that by the time Reagan left office, the military portion of the budget was up to 26.6 percent. That was an increase from the Carter years, no doubt, but a far cry from the nearly 50 percent of the discretionary budget of the Kennedy years.[12]

This rebuilding of the military allowed Reagan to realize the second part of his two-pronged vision—bringing the Soviet Union to its knees.

The Bear Takes a Direct Hit

It's easy to look back at the now-defunct Soviet regime and say its demise was inevitable. Newspaper articles are replete with journalists and pundits today who claim they knew the USSR's days were numbered. But where were they back in the '80s? None of the so-called experts of the time thought the Soviets were on the ropes. Not a word was written about the Soviet empire being on the brink of collapse. In fact, just the opposite was true.

Harvard economist John Kenneth Galbraith wrote in 1984: "That the Soviet system has made great material progress in recent years is evident both from the statistics and from the general urban scene. . . . One sees it in the appearance of well-being of the people on the streets. [T]he Russian system succeeds because, in contrast with the Western industrial economies, it makes full use of its manpower."[13]

This was the conventional wisdom of the time in the mainstream media. Journalists like one-world-government proponent and former Clinton official Strobe Talbott, who as a senior correspondent for *Time*, sneered incredulously, "Reagan is counting on American technological and economic predominance to prevail in the end."[14] The eggheads scoffed at the notion that Reagan could destroy the Evil

Empire. Yet when the Soviet Union crumbled, they all proclaimed that it was such a surprise that no one could have
predicted it. Someone, in fact, *did* predict it. More than
that, he *engineered* it. That man was Ronald Reagan.

Former Reagan Domestic Policy Analyst Dinesh D'-
Souza relays a story in his wonderful book on Reagan,
How an Ordinary Man Became an Extraordinary Leader,[15]
of reporter Lou Cannon setting up a meeting between
Reagan and the editorial board of the *Washington Post* in
June 1980. The editors expressed to Reagan their concerns
that his rhetoric would escalate the arms race. Reagan assured them there was nothing to worry about. "The Soviets can't compete with us," he told them. The editors were
shocked. None of them believed that the Soviet economy
was vulnerable. Reagan reassured them, "I'll get the Soviets to the negotiating table."

D'Souza also recalls a speech Reagan made in 1981 to
the students and faculty at the University of Notre Dame.
He told them, "The West won't contain communism. It
will transcend communism. It will dismiss it as some
bizarre chapter in human history whose last pages are,
even now, being written." Remember Reagan's famous
speech to the British Parliament? That's the one in which
he declared that the march of freedom and democracy
would "leave Marxism-Leninism on the ash heap of history." Do the experts who never saw the downfall of the
Soviet Union coming remember that speech? It was made
on June 8, 1982.

Underestimate Him at Your Peril

In the six years before he ascended to the presidency, Reagan researched and wrote extensively. During what D'-Souza calls Reagan's "wilderness years," he not only scoured the latest publications looking for ammunition, he also read periodicals like *World Marxist Review* to find out as much as he could about the other side. The image of Reagan as shallow and of limited intellect, which was manufactured by his enemies with the willing accomplices of the national media, was dreadfully off the mark. He was a voracious reader who did thorough research for his speeches, newspaper column, and daily radio commentary.

Lee Edwards, an early Reagan biographer, told D'-Souza that he once spent hours perusing the books in Reagan's study. He learned that Reagan had gone through most of them, underlining parts he wanted to remember and jotting notes in the margins. Reagan would also surprise his aides by occasionally citing the Roman Emperor Diocletian's policy of wage and price controls or Islamic historian Ibn Khaldun's views on taxation and government revenues.[16]

The fact that so many of his opponents perceived him as shallow became one of Reagan's strongest weapons. Throughout his career, both as a politician and as president of the Screen Actors Guild, adversaries were lulled into a false sense of superiority only to find themselves blind-sided. Reagan biographer Lou Cannon tells of one such instance in May 1967. Senator Bobby Kennedy and Reagan were debating the Vietnam War in an informal town meeting–type format that was broadcast to the nation. A crowd of left-wing student radicals were quite vocal in their support of North Vietnam. Kennedy tried to pacify the brood by trying to find some common ground. Reagan, on the other hand, would have no part in giving one inch of ground to them. He dealt with them firmly and decisively. As a result, Kennedy was overwhelmed with angry letters, while Reagan was thanked and congratulated for standing up for America. Kennedy would later confide in his younger brother, Teddy, that Reagan was the toughest debate opponent he ever had.[17]

Although the political landscape was littered with competitors who had underestimated Reagan's intelligence, like Pat Brown and Jimmy Carter, others who chose to take him on continued to repeat the same mistake. Walter Mondale thought him vulnerable enough to take on in 1984. He was constantly frustrated during the campaign by a man who was supposed to be too stupid to find his way back home. Reagan seemed to have a comeback retort to everything Mondale threw at him. Exasperated, the Democrats began a whisper campaign that Reagan was too old to be president for another term. The idea seemed to be gaining traction, thanks, again, to the willing accomplices in the press.

One such accomplice asked Reagan the question outright at the crescendo of the campaign, a debate leading up to the election. Thinking on his feet, Reagan responded, "I will not make age an issue in this campaign. I am not going to exploit, for political purposes, my opponent's youth and inexperience." Mondale's only retort was a hideous, Mr. Ed–like grin. Reagan dusted him in the election, in one of the worst political thrashings in American history.

Still, the opponents didn't learn. They kept on underestimating him and he kept on showing them up. When the Washington press corps would twist and mangle his message, Reagan would bypass them and go straight to the American people. Thus, they labeled him the Great Communicator, a title meant as obloquy but one that caught on in a positive way. And that he was. Like no other president before or since, Reagan was able to articulate his vision so that everyone could understand. Once they understood it, they were on board and the liberal press machine had been short-circuited once more.

They still continued to take potshots at him after he left the presidency, but far less so once he announced he had Alzheimer's disease. Although a tragic way to spend the twilight of one's life, Alzheimer's gave Reagan the opportunity few conservative presidents have been afforded by the press—to be honored in life for his achievements. His birthdays are marked by interviews with friends and acquaintances who laud his achievements. Television biographies of his life aren't nearly as biting as they might be had he not died such a slow death. All of these are made softer because of his disease. In the end, Reagan had the last laugh on the media. I just wish he were cognizant enough near the end of his life to see them fawning all over him.

Whether it was tax cuts or fighting the Soviet menace, Reagan was right and history has proven him so. His life's record speaks for itself. Except for a slight glitch in the early '90s, the Reagan economy lasted well into 2001, almost twenty years of prosperity this country had never before seen. He's the only president in the modern age to have his name incorporated into a form of economics—Reaganomics. Although the term Reaganomics, like Great Communicator, was first used as a term of derision, it has come to symbolize successful economic policy. The vast void that was once filled by the angst and tension known as the Soviet Union stands as another testament to Reagan's legacy. He devised a means by which we would defeat Soviet communism, and he took his concepts from the radio studio to the bargaining table at Reykjavik.

Ronald Reagan restored America's prosperity, defeated our mortal enemy, and rejuvenated our sense of patriotism. He led by example and showed us what it means to be an American. He was indeed an American original.

19

SCHOOLS are best run by local people on the local level.

To FULLY APPRECIATE OUR public school system today, it is essential to look at its history. Universal education was not always the norm in the United States. In many sections of the country, education was reserved for the landed gentry and our society's aristocracy. Free public education in America traces its roots to the Massachusetts Bay Colony in 1647. The colony's general court required every town numbering at least fifty families to have an elementary school. Towns of one hundred or more families were required to provide Latin schools. Contrary to our present obsession with keeping religion out of schools, the express purpose of these early schools was to teach kids how to read the Bible and learn about their religion.[1]

The next big leap in public education occurred in Pennsylvania in 1790. At that time, the state's constitution called for free education—but for poor children only. Parents with the means to pay were required to do so.[2] The first high school in America opened in Boston in 1820, three years after a petition was presented in a Boston town meeting calling for free public primary schools. It was believed that a free public education was essential to produce good workers, not so much for the knowledge they would acquire but for the discipline the schools instilled.

In 1827, Massachusetts passed a law that opened public education to all pupils, thus creating the first public school system in the country. Ten years later, the Massachusetts State Board of Education was formed. By 1854, public education was not only available but mandatory in the state.[3] Compulsory education would not spread throughout America until many years later. In Tennessee, for example, compulsory education laws weren't enacted until 1913.[4]

Why do you suppose states like Tennessee took more than sixty years to do what Massachusetts did? There are those who would say that Tennessee was backward, but I would argue that the evolution of public schools there and elsewhere was a direct response to those states' immediate needs. In other words, since Massachusetts was more industrialized, it had a greater need for skilled workers than did states in the largely agrarian South. Farm laborers learned on the job, and schools were seen by many in those days as a distraction from the work at hand.

The point is that the educational needs of Massachusetts were quite different from the educational needs of Tennessee. Today, in our homogenized educational system, we tend to forget the particular needs of different regions. Sure, we're a more mobile society these days, and there should be a certain degree of consistency from state to state to reduce culture shock among those who move around the country. However, that same mobility also affords us the opportunity to relocate if a particular school system is not meeting our needs. For those who can't, or simply don't want to move, the viable option is school choice, which we'll jump into with both feet later in this chapter.

Homogenization is good only up to a certain point. The basic skills of reading, language, and mathematics are essential no matter where you go. But *how* you teach those skills should be left to the individual school systems. As I've learned in radio, what works in one part of the nation doesn't always work in another. I once worked for a radio company based in San Francisco. The corporate program director tried to program our station in Nashville just like the company's station in San Francisco. It was a disaster. Nashville and San Francisco are two totally different markets with two totally different sets of needs.

Schools are the same way. They're best run by local people on the local level. Whole language may work in one school system, for example, while phonics may work in another, although I'm convinced phonics is the only way to learn to read. Too many times, a system of learning is developed (oftentimes in California), then force-fed to local school systems with dismal results. The reasons we have so many failing public schools today are complicated and varied, but lack of local control is a large part of that equation.

Are Public Schools Really That Bad?

Most of us hear the horror stories about public schools, and the impression we most often get is that it's impossible to get a quality education there. I've had parents insinuate that sending kids to public school is tantamount to child abuse. Let's look at the facts:

- SAT scores have risen in the verbal and mathematical sections since 1980.[5]
- Public school scores on the National Assessment of Educational Progress (NAEP) test is at an all-time high for all ethnic groups.
- The proportion of students scoring above the 92nd percentile on the SAT mathematics section is at a record level.
- Seventy-eight thousand students took advanced placement tests in 1978. Today that number is more than one million.[6]

In the mid-1990s, *Money* magazine compared suburban private schools to suburban public schools. The editors went into the study expecting to find private schools superior. They were "shocked" when they didn't. They said, "The best news to come out of *Money's* survey of public and private schools across America was that, by and large, public schools are not lacking in experienced top-notch teachers, challenging courses, or an environment that is conducive to learning."[7] Admittedly, there are students who require more personalized attention in order to succeed, and those kids may benefit from a private school. The fact is, on average, your child can get an education in a public school that is as equal, if not superior, to the one he or she can obtain in a private school. For the most part, the resources are there, if our children will only take advantage of them.

But let's not ignore the fact that some schools *are* failing, and failing very badly. These tend to be in urban areas with high crime and low income. That's largely a product of our society warehousing people in public housing projects, making a difficult situation worse. The federal government has already screwed up their lives with a broken welfare system, and over the past twenty years or so, it has rubbed salt into the wound by trying to run their schools from Washington.

The U.S. Department of Education works best when it acts as a clearinghouse for good ideas. Its tempestuous past relationship with the states has more resembled that of an overbearing boss looking over their shoulder and forcing them to adopt its edicts, dangling federal money in front of them as both the carrot and the stick. And just like that radio program director I had from San Francisco, it has found the cookie-cutter approach doesn't always work.

Just Throw More Money

The general consensus, when schools are failing, is to throw more money at the problem. I equate this to driving down the road and having a flat tire, limping into the nearest gas station, topping off the gas tank, and then limping back out onto the highway. You've spent money, but you haven't fixed the problem.

You see, when schools are failing, it's rarely because of a lack of money. If that were the case, it would have been impossible for our ancestors to obtain a proper education in a one-room schoolhouse. Sure, fancy computers and televisions in every room look nice, but if a school is failing, it's most likely because the educational model being used is broken.

Finally, school administrators are bucking the trend of moving great principals up to the administrative office and are now keeping them where they're doing the most good. Don Nielson, chairman of the school board in Seattle, Washington, says, "You can walk into unbelievable schools in Seattle or in Nashville, and what you will find is an unbelievable principal."[8] Principals are the general managers of the school. They set the pace. They inspire, if they're doing their jobs, and they have a tremendous amount of influence as to the direction the school takes. These managers should be given more authority to control discipline problems—with spanking, if necessary—and to adapt their school in a manner that will best serve its students. After all, the students and their parents are the "customers," and they should be happy with the results.

Having had my kids in a big-city public school system, I know that results vary from school to school. Some schools have taller hurdles, but there's no excuse why any school should be failing. One teacher in our school system took a failing school in a disadvantaged area—its students were so poor that virtually all of them qualified for a free lunch program—and turned it into a winner. She began flashing math problems on the lunchroom wall, incorporating students' names in them to capture their attention. She also invited a chess club to come in and help the kids with their reasoning skills.

These were ideas that cost little or nothing to implement, and the results were astounding. Reading scores were raised above the national average and math scores went through the roof. The key here is this: the farther away the controlling authority of a school is, the less accountability its administrators and teachers will have. Put somebody's job on the line and you'll see some results.

Unfortunately, teachers unions are doing everything they can to protect mediocre teachers. (We'll deal more with unions in a later chapter.) Teaching is one of the few professions in which employees are not measured by results but merely by how long they've been there. If you've ever had kids in school—or can remember when you were in school—you know there are great teachers, good teachers, and bad teachers. All the teachers know who's who. The ones just marking time hate the great teachers for making them look bad. The great teachers would love to see the bad ones tossed out on their ears, but the union protects them.

I know of one case in which a principal continually received complaints from parents about a particular teacher. Instead of firing her, the school moved her from grade to grade. In the real world, she'd be told to hit the bricks, but that's not allowed because of the teachers unions. Their stranglehold on our educational system must be broken if public schools are going to survive. And I believe they must survive.

I certainly have nothing against those who choose to send their kids to private school or home school, but whether you use them or not, public schools are a necessity. Most parents can't afford to send their kids to private school, nor do they have the time to home school their children. Public schools are their only alternative, and if those schools continue to deteriorate, there will come a point where they will ultimately produce the dregs of society. We're a long way from that right now, but some schools and school systems are a lot closer than you might think. The difference lies in who controls the school and who's responsible for its success or failure. Controlling a school system from Washington cannot be done without horrendous results. Making local schools answerable to local people will get the results those local people demand.

President George W. Bush had the best intentions when he pushed his No Child Left Behind (NCLB) initiative on the states. It's a good idea that schools should be accountable for their work. To whom they're accountable, however, is what makes all the difference. NCLB's cookie-cutter approach meant that principals were strapped with foolish requirements that made no sense for their particular schools. For instance, one middle school in our county had test scores through the roof. Parents were involved in the school and their children's education. They were blowing the doors off NCLB except in one area. Many of the parents liked to take their kids on ski vacations in January and February. The principal had to clamp down on unexcused absences or the school risked being placed on probation—despite the fact that the kids were doing everything they were supposed to do scholastically. It was silly, but that's what happens when schools are controlled from Washington instead of their own county. The results of NCLB have been as mixed and varied as the many school districts across America, which should tell our friends in Washington a little something about what works and what doesn't. Setting standards is great, but state and local authorities, not the federal government, should set those standards. There's nothing in the Constitution about education, therefore it is under the authority of the states.

Does Size Matter?

Many in Washington have placed a great deal of emphasis on reducing class size. At first blush, that seems to make sense. Give a child more one-on-one time with the teacher and he'll perform better, right? Not so fast. The danger lies in reducing class size just to meet goals and ratios. What if the teacher hired for that classroom is not as good as the teacher the kids just had? Since many states are facing a teacher shortage, once all the best teachers have been hired, school systems will have to lower their standards a bit to hire more.

Amy Wilkins of the Education Trust, a group that works with local schools and parents to promote high academic achievement for students, agrees. "The difference between a well-prepared teacher and an under-prepared teacher can be a whole grade level's worth of achievement in a single school year," Wilkins told CNN. "For kids, that can mean the difference between a remedial track and the college prep track."[9] Personally, I'd rather have my kid in a class with fifty other kids and a great teacher than getting one-on-one instruction from a bad one.

There are all types of studies out there on the subject of class size. Eric A. Hanushek, a professor of economics at the University of Rochester in New York, culled through a great number of these studies and came to this conclusion: size doesn't matter. He found that only 15 percent of these studies showed a positive improvement in achievement with smaller class size, 72 percent found no statistically significant effect, and 13 percent found a negative effect on achievement.[10] He also confirmed my theory that the quality of the teacher is more important than class size.

Hanushek writes: "Considerable evidence shows that by far the largest differences in the impact of schools on student achievement relate to differences in the quality of teachers. Thus, whether or not large-scale reductions in class sizes help or hurt will depend mostly on whether or not any new teachers are better or worse than the existing teachers."[11] Precisely.

A Louisiana Education Department study in 2003 confirmed that qualified teachers are far more important than class size. The study showed that as a district increased its percentage of highly certified teachers, its students' performance scores increased. The study also cited a correlation between teachers who received top grades on professional exams and higher performance scores for students.[12] These things taken into consideration, class size was virtually irrelevant compared to the other factors.

Instead of spending billions of dollars nationwide to reduce class size, it's obvious that money spent on such endeavors should be redirected toward rewarding higher-qualified teachers. Not paying them for their education, mind you, but paying them when they do a better job. The "tenure equals more money" mentality of the teachers unions won't cut it. Great teachers have to be able to break out of the pack and be rewarded for it. The teachers unions are unlikely to join the bandwagon. Reducing class size means more teachers. More teachers means more dues for the union.

Professor Hanushek also nailed it when it comes to teacher evaluations. "If we are to have a real impact on teaching," he writes, "we must evaluate actual teaching performance and use such evaluations in school decisions.

We cannot rely on requirements for entry, but must switch to using actual performance in the classroom."[13]

I know what some of you teachers out there are saying: "It's not fair to evaluate us, because each class is different and each school is different." Welcome to my world, friends. Let me tell you something about fair. You ought to take a trip with me to Laurel, Maryland, where the Arbitron Rating Service keeps the diaries filled out by radio listeners. You'll find people who can hardly string two sentences together trying to write down what they've listened to over the span of an entire week, when they can't even remember what they had for lunch. Some of these diaries are even filled out in crayon, for crying out loud. You think that's a fair way to evaluate my performance on the radio? It ain't fair but it's all we've got, and we live and die by the ratings. The only thing less fair than evaluating teachers is allowing our children to be subjected to a substandard education.

School Choice Empowers the Poor

If ever you needed evidence that liberals practice the politics of dependency, it is crystal clear in the debate over school choice. For clarification purposes, when I talk about school choice, my definition is limited to choice among public schools. When you include private or religious schools, the issue is vouchers, which have been used at various places across the country with mixed results.

School choice will produce the most immediate results because it absolutely changes the entire dynamics of the public school system. You must realize that one of the last bastions of noncompetitiveness in our nation is the public school system. Private schools compete against each other and the public schools for students. Public schools know no such competition. Principals and teachers have certain demands placed on them, for sure, but not like they would if their schools had to compete against other schools in the system for students.

Merely giving parents the ability to send their children to the best schools within a system would create more confidence among the parents as well as better principals, teachers, and schools. I know that in radio, were it not for competition, we probably wouldn't push ourselves to do our best each day. Making sure you kept your students instead of watching them march down the street to the next elementary school or across the hall to the next classroom would, quite naturally, produce better schools.

So who benefits most from school choice? The very poor. I'll give you an example, I once lived in an area of town zoned for a great elementary school. Not a mile away was a run-down section of town zoned for a bad school. Had my neighborhood been zoned for a bad school, I had options. I could either send my kids to a private school, home school them (since my wife stayed home with the kids), or move. A single working mother living in that bad section has none of those options. She can't afford to send her kids to a private school. She works, so home schooling is out. She can't move, because she's either already living in public housing or the house she owns in the run-down area where she lives is virtually unmarketable. So, she's stuck. She has to put up with her son navigating his way through the crack dealers and gangs on the way to and from school—and all because the liberals who claim to want to help her won't allow her school choice. Funny, isn't it, how they demand that a woman has a right to choose . . . except when it comes to where to send her kid to school?

We've spent billions of dollars trying to pull poor students up into the mainstream when the answer has been as close as the school right down the street. Every nearby business and every working parent who drops his or her child off at school each day experiences competition (except for the union workers). So, what's stopping these school systems from giving parents a choice? Governments, with encouragement from the teachers unions, are hesitant to allow it. But in some places schools are so bad that they really have nothing to lose.

Schools are best run by local people on the local level. If parents aren't happy with the way their children are being educated, they should be allowed to do something else, such as sending them to another public school or perhaps a charter school in the local district. Only then will we see widespread parental confidence return to the public schools.

20

TAX RATES should be flat and fair.

A wise and frugal government, which shall restrain
men from injuring one another, which shall leave
them otherwise free to regulate their own pursuits
of industry and improvement, and shall not take
from the mouth of labor the bread it has earned.
This is the sum of good government, and this is
necessary to close the circle of our felicity.

—*Thomas Jefferson, First Inaugural Address*

To MANY ON THE left, the terms *flat* and *fair* are mutually exclusive. Those who contend that the two cannot co-exist are unable to grasp the spirit of what made this country great. If the Founding Fathers were able to see how extensive and intrusive our tax structure has become, they might well wish to abandon the whole notion of America. Certainly they knew the power to tax is also the power to destroy. Not that we don't need taxes. They fund this wonderful nation of ours. However, tax dollars, in the wrong hands, grow governments beyond its intended boundaries, which is what has happened in our country.

I laid out a basic philosophy during the great Tennessee Tax Revolt in which people throughout the state rallied to prevent the legislature from enacting a state income tax. That philosophy came to be known as the Valentine Doctrine: government is there to do only what the private sector won't, can't, or shouldn't do. This simple principle of limited government is in keeping with the Founding Fathers' original intent. It also serves to keep our politicians in check. Understand that politicians will spend every dime they get their hands on. They're like teenagers. They'll blow our hard-earned dollars if we don't draw some parameters. It's up to us as the breadwinners to constantly audit their spending habits and keep them responsive to the good of the whole, not just a special few.

When I testified before the Tennessee Senate Finance Committee in 1999, I scolded that the "You scratch my back, I'll scratch your back" way of doing things had to end. I warned that it was breaking the back of the taxpayer. The problem is even more out of control on the federal level. Some politicians look at tax dollars as Monopoly money. The old adage that a billion here and a billion there and soon you're talking about some real money is truer than most realize. It takes such mind-boggling numbers before some elected officials begin to get nervous about spending it, and even then there are those who don't bat an eye. The only way to combat this total disregard for our tax dollars is to somehow impress upon our elected officials the value of a dollar. How one goes about doing that is the $6 billion question.

Less Is More

One thing I've learned about liberals is, there is some kind of mental block that keeps them from understanding why confiscatory taxes hurt the little guy. All they see is dollar signs. They equate higher taxes to swelling tax coffers. What they fail to see are the long-term implications of soaking the rich. They treasure the graduated income tax, one of the most inequitable forms of taxation ever devised by man. In what other facet of life are we required to pay a *greater* percentage the more income we have?

If you see a lawnmower at the hardware store, the price is the same for the person making twenty thousand dollars a year as it is for the person making two hundred thousand dollars. The same goes for any other goods or services we purchase, yet when the tax man comes, he wants money based on your ability to pay. It reminds you a lot of the familiar communist phrase "From each according to his ability, to each according to his needs," doesn't it? If that sounds a bit paranoid, most people in this country have forgotten a time when the government essentially put a cap on what you could make. Some of the very rich found loopholes in the tax code and were able to shelter a good deal of their wealth despite the money grab, but many were discouraged from making more money.

I heard a story once about Ronald Reagan wherein he

used his own personal experience to explain, quite succinctly, how exorbitant taxes choke off the economy.
When Reagan was making movies, the top marginal tax
rate was 91 percent.[1] That's not a misprint. Ninety-one
percent! Once he'd made his limit, it was futile for him to
go back out and make another picture knowing that he
would only be allowed to keep 9 percent of the money. So
he stayed home.

That didn't hurt Ronald Reagan. He was happy to
spend his leisure time at home or traveling, enjoying the
fruits of his labor. Who it *did* hurt were all of the people
who would have worked on that picture—the set design-
ers, the caterers, the electricians, the cameramen—all of
whom didn't come close to reaching the 91 percent tax
bracket. In its attempt to "soak the rich," the government
had unwittingly soaked the middle class. You see, like it or
not, it's the rich who create the jobs. Remember this:
when you soak the people at the top, everybody gets wet.

A similar situation occurred in the early 1990s with
the luxury tax on items such as yachts. Instead of paying
the tax, the wealthy either chose to forgo purchasing another vessel or they merely bought one offshore. The result
was devastation to the American yacht-building industry.
Sales dropped 70 percent.[2] Those who suffered were the
laborers who built the yachts.

You see, it's not enough to tax the income of the rich,
the Left wants to tax their toys into oblivion too. But each
time they fire an envy arrow at the rich, they miss their

mark and land a direct hit on the very people they claim to be helping.

Reagan wasn't the only one to understand how this worked. A man who has become an icon to modern-day liberals made the following statement:

> Our true choice is not between tax reduction, on the one hand, and the avoidance of large Federal deficits on the other. It is increasingly clear that no matter what party is in power, so long as our national security needs keep rising, an economy hampered by restrictive tax rates will never produce enough revenue to balance our budget, just as it will never produce enough jobs or enough profits. Surely the lesson of the last decade is that budget deficits are not caused by wild-eyed spenders, but by slow economic growth and periodic recessions, and any new recession would break all deficit records.
>
> In short, it is a paradoxical truth that tax rates are too high today and tax revenues are too low, and the soundest way to raise the revenue in the long run is to cut the rates now.[3]

That *wild-eyed radical* was none other than President John F. Kennedy. He proposed reducing the top marginal tax rate from 91 percent to 70 percent, reducing the lowest income tax rate from 20 percent to 14 percent, and cutting the corporate income tax rate from 52 percent to 47 percent. Kennedy sent his tax cut proposal to Congress on January 24, 1963. He would never live to see it enacted, but it passed Congress in early 1964. Just as Kennedy had predicted, the tax cut led to an increase in federal taxes, especially from the "evil rich," and a significant increase in economic growth.[4]

Who Really Pays the Taxes?

Instead of engaging in class warfare, let's fall back to that age-old crutch of the conservative movement—the facts. Remember that "Top 1 Percent" Al Gore kept accusing George W. Bush of wanting to help during the 2000 presidential campaign? That top 1 percent of wage earners in America pays more than 39 percent of the income tax. (It gets better.) The top 5 percent pay more than 59 percent. The top 10 percent pay more than 70 percent of the taxes. The top 25 percent pay more than 85 percent! Conversely, the bottom 50 percent of wage earners pay just 3 percent of income taxes![5] These figures come straight from that bastion of conservative propaganda, the Internal Revenue Service.

To put it in simple terms, how many folks making twenty grand a year ever gave you a job? Instead of begrudging the rich folks, we should be thanking them. Of course, I'm not suggesting that all rich people are angels, but the same can be said for any economic group. What I'm saying is, they're the ones creating the jobs, and if you have a job, chances are you're working for somebody who's got some money.

Ben Franklin once said, "It would be thought a hard government that should tax its people one tenth part." *One tenth!* Today, the average American taxpayer coughs up roughly 35 percent of his or her income in federal, state, and local taxes—and that's a conservative estimate. In some parts of the country, taxes take close to half, or more, of the income from working Americans. That's more than housing, food, and clothes *combined!*[6]

That is certainly not what the Founding Fathers envisioned. Perhaps you're thinking that they didn't envision all the roads and post offices and essentials that our wonderful government provides. You're right, but they also never envisioned 135 million tax returns each year. With all of those millions of people paying taxes, our individual tax burden should be going down, but it's not. Toll roads are a classic example of government greed. The tolls are levied to build the roads. Once they're built, it would stand to reason that the tolls would be reduced or eliminated. Instead, they go up because the government becomes dependent on them.

No doubt, times have changed quite a bit since 1776, but the principle is the same. Government runs most efficiently when it's lean, providing essential services instead of trying to be all things to all people. Government was never intended to be the primary breadwinner of otherwise able-bodied souls. It was never government's job to hand out money like candy to any individual or corporation with its hand out. It was designed to purchase goods and services that would serve our mutual benefit. It was also never meant to supplant the private sector. It was intended to do those things that were needed but would not get done otherwise. Remember, the government is there to do only what the private sector won't, can't, or shouldn't do.

With that in mind, all sorts of things become apparent that we, as keepers of the government, have no business funding. Sports stadiums (some prefer *stadia*), for example. Here's a clear example of something the private sector would do, could do, and should do, yet we have cities throughout the nation falling all over themselves trying to give sports teams a place to play. I understand that, in many cases, the citizens vote to subject themselves to such abuse, but that still doesn't make it right. Our Founding Fathers would be ashamed of our greed, using the government to satisfy even our most frivolous whims. Sure, I'm a huge football fan but I don't want some gray-haired little old lady living on a fixed income to have her taxes raised just so I can enjoy football. If I want football, or basketball, or any other sport, I should pay for it. It shouldn't become the burden on taxpayers that it is becoming across America.

What's Fair?

Let's address the issue of fairness. How much tax is fair? That's a difficult question to answer. As singer-comedian Ray Stevens once reminded us in song, *If Ten Percent Is Good Enough for Jesus (It Ought to Be Enough for Uncle Sam)*. Whether the percentage is right for government is not the point. The point is that the percentage should be the *same* for everyone, no matter how much you make. How is that fair, you ask? Let's take the 10 percent example. A guy making $30,000 per year would pay $3,000 in taxes. Ah, but what about the girl making $90,000 per year? She'd pay $9,000 in taxes. If she makes three times as much money, she pays three times as much in taxes. Is that fair? Absolutely. Where is it written that the more you make, the bigger chunk the government should take? Only in the U.S. Tax Code.

You want to know what the tax rate was when it first started in 1913? It was 1 percent on incomes over $20,000. What's that in today's money? About $425,000. Anyone making below that paid *nothing* in income tax. The top rate was 7 percent for those making more than $500,000.[7] That's equivalent to someone making $10.6 million a year today. *Seven* percent—top rate! Of course, once the government had its claws into that money, it couldn't resist taking more and more.

Any comprehensive attempt at tax reform is usually shut down by the demonizing demagogues on the left before it makes it out of the gate. To make the tax code fair, you must first start by lowering the top marginal rates, to wit, reducing the tax burden on the wealthy. The liberals scream bloody murder each time something like this is proposed. They'll even go so far as to say that the poor need a break from taxes first. That's the sentimental favorite refrain among the guilt-ridden populace; it sounds good to appear to be for the little guy.

Not to sound harsh, but the poor aren't paying much, if anything at all, in taxes as it is. Remember that figure from the IRS that I shared with you earlier? The bottom half of wage earners only pay about 3 percent of the income taxes. Besides, a good chunk of our federal, state, and local money goes to help the poor. They get food stamps, medical assistance, and even housing. What slays me is when a politician shouts about giving a tax break to some who don't even pay taxes! We should help those who can't help themselves, sure, but fixing the tax code has nothing to do with welfare. It's about fairness and keeping the wheels of commerce turning at optimum speed. You do that by making the tax rate fair.

Soon after President George W. Bush's tax-cut proposal came out, all sorts of groups gathered in Washington to oppose it. They claimed that the government needed to do more to help the needy and that the rich folks didn't need a tax cut. Forget that everyone who paid taxes was getting a tax cut; these demagogues would rather make political hay than actually solve problems. One of them, however, slipped up and said something that was quite revealing. Multimillionaire Justin Dart Jr., a leading activist for the disabled, said, "If I get a substantial reduction, as I would, I would not give it back (to the government). I would donate all of it to People for the American Way, the Leadership Conference on Civil Rights."[8]

Now, think about what ol' Justin said for a moment. He wants you to pay more taxes, but if he gets a tax break, he certainly isn't going to give it to the government. He's going to give it to private institutions he feels will do more good. Exactly, Justin. Then why don't you want to give the rest of us that option? That's what's known as "liberal logic." Justin Dart is going to scream and holler about tax cuts, saying the government needs the money, but when he gets a tax cut, he's not going to dare give that money to the government! Things like that make conservatives like me just throw up our hands. How do you even argue with someone like that?

You Buy, You Pay

Consumption taxes are probably the closest thing we have to a perfect tax. You buy something, you pay a tax, and everyone pays the same tax. If you buy a gallon of gasoline, you pay the same tax whether you drive a Rolls Royce or a Yugo. Is that fair? You bet. Gas taxes are primarily used to build and maintain roads (at least that's what they're supposed to be used for), and both cars take up about the same amount of roadway. When you buy a loaf of bread, the checker doesn't ask to see your W-2 and charge you according to your income. Everyone pays the same price for the bread, thus everybody pays the same tax on the bread.

You might conclude that I'm for abolishing the national income tax and replacing it with a national sales tax. That's certainly an idea I'm open to. The Fair Tax, as it's called, certainly has its merits. I love the idea of dismantling the IRS. The fact that people would have more control over how much they're taxed is also appealing. And I believe it would go a long way in retrieving some of our lost privacy. The IRS knows way too much about us. However, I'm concerned about some of the bugs in the Fair Tax proposal. For example, the Fair Tax on a new car would be 23 percent *plus* your state and local sales taxes. In my state that comes to almost 33 percent. If I buy a used car, under the Fair Tax proposal, I pay nothing. I'm concerned the Fair Tax, in its present form, would drive too many people out of the new car market, putting that industry in jeopardy. It also exempts the poor from paying any taxes. What constitutes poor seems to be a moving target, but whatever the number, it makes this an inherently *un*fair tax. I understand the reality of politics. The Fair Tax has absolutely no chance of gaining traction unless it panders to those who think poor people should be let off the hook. But everyone should be required to contribute, no matter how little they make. A flat consumption tax would ensure that they do. The Fair Tax, as it's now structured, does not.

However, as long as we have the federal income tax, it should be flat and it should be fair. Dick Armey, former congressman from Texas, was a big proponent of a flat tax. He suggested a rate of 17 percent. I haven't run the numbers to see just how much revenue that would produce, but I would advocate a zero-sum game. Suffice it to say that, in the spirit of fairness, the many tax shelters enjoyed by the wealthier taxpayers would have to go. In exchange, the lower income earners would have to pay a fairer share too.

As it stands right now, someone making $30,000 per year pays 15 percent in taxes, while someone making $358,000 pays 35 percent. That's not fair, no matter how you slice it. Forgetting deductions for the moment, that means the person who earns $30,000 per year would pay $4,500 in taxes, and the person who makes $358,000 would pay $125,300. Well, he ought to, you may be saying to yourself. Why? Do you think that just because he's making more money, the government has a right to take a bigger percentage of his earnings than it takes from you? If you answered yes, you suffer from class envy, and you need to get some help. Who knows? If you can get it declared a "condition," you might get some federal funding for a support group.

Here's why Dick Armey's 17 percent flat tax will never pass Congress: more than half of Americans right now are paying less than 17 percent. It's going to be awfully hard to convince the majority of taxpayers to vote themselves a tax increase just so they can make the tax code more equitable. The politicians have been counting on this for a long time. Why do you think the majority of us don't pay as much in taxes? That's right, votes. You keep lowering taxes on the majority and you buy their votes. Pretty soon, you only have a very small minority paying the taxes. Let me tell you something. That day is already here. As I told you earlier, the IRS says that the top 10 percent of wage earners already pay more than 70 percent of the taxes. That's just 10 percent of the population carrying the weight of more than half the tax burden, while clearly 50 percent of workers are only carrying a collective load of 3 percent.

Ayn Rand, in her classic piece of literature *Atlas Shrugged*, paints a scenario in which the country's leading innovators and industrialists suddenly begin to disappear, and those who have depended on them to carry the load suddenly find themselves running the country. The dependence mentality being the stubborn state of mind it is to shake, the country begins an ugly descent into materialistic cannibalism. With the producers gone, the nonproducers are left to use up all of the resources left behind without a clue as to how they can produce more.

In one scene, Francisco d'Aconia, one of the producers, overhears a gentleman at a cocktail party. This "intellectual" says of d'Aconia to a young lady, when he thinks d'Aconia is out of earshot, "Don't let him disturb you. You know, money is the root of all evil—and he's the typical product of money." Francisco turns to them "with a gravely courteous smile" and proceeds to unleash a torrent of a gentlemanly tongue-lashing that sums up our capitalist system like few have done before or since:

> "So you think that money is the root of all evil?" said Francisco d'Aconia. "Have you ever asked what is the root of money? Money is a tool of exchange, which can't exist unless there are goods produced and men able to produce them. . . . Money is not the tool of the moochers, who claim your product by tears, or of the looters, who take it

from you by force. Money is made possible only by the men who produce. Is this what you consider evil? Have you ever looked for the root of production? Take a look at an electric generator and dare tell yourself that it was created by the muscular effort of unthinking brutes. Try to grow a seed of wheat without the knowledge left to you by men who had to discover it for the first time. Try to obtain your food by means of nothing but physical motions—and you'll learn that man's mind is the root of all the goods produced and of all the wealth that has ever existed on earth. Wealth is the product of man's capacity to think. Then is money made by the man who invents a motor at the expense of those who did not invent it? Is money made by the intelligent at the expense of the fools? By the able at the expense of the incompetent? By the ambitious at the expense of the lazy? Money is MADE—before it can be looted or mooched—made by the effort of every honest man, each to the extent of his ability. An honest man is one who knows that he can't consume more than he has produced."

Francisco d'Aconia ends the conversation with this:

"Until and unless you discover that money is the root of all good, you ask for your own destruction. When money ceases to be the tool by which men deal with one another, then men become the tools of men. Blood, whips and guns—or dollars. Take your choice—there is no other—and your time is running out."

Although her novel was published back in 1957, its warnings certainly apply to our present condition more than they ever have. What if the top 10 percent of wage earners were no longer there? Two-thirds of the tax revenue would cease to exist. Quite a precarious situation we find ourselves in, and clearly not healthy for the nation.

Leveling out the tax structure will accomplish two major goals. First, it will transfer some of the undue burden from the few and spread it evenly among the wage earners, as is fair. Everyone should be made to contribute in some small way, no matter how small the paycheck. No able-bodied American should ever get a free ride. Paying your fair share connotes ownership, and ownership instills pride. Pride in this country is what we need, not a bunch of folks looking at it as a gravy train.

Second, it will free an amazing amount of capital that can be used to grow the economy. Remember, it's the folks at the top who create the jobs. Lessen their load and they'll unleash that money into the economy, which will in turn create more and better jobs for those on the lower rungs of the ladder. Taxes should be flat and fair, not just for the good of the wealthy, but for the good of the nation.

21

UNIONS have outlived their usefulness.

P LEASE ALLOW ME TO be blunt. Unions exist, plainly and simply, to protect the mediocre. Before any of you union folks throw this book down in disgust, understand one thing: I'm not saying that all union members are mediocre. If you're a great employee, if you're giving the company your best each day, you have little to fear from the company. I would also submit to you that if you're giving 100 percent each day, you don't need a union. It's those who don't give it their all who need protection by the union.

You may ask, How about those who *do* work hard and still get fired? Well, you don't want to be working for those folks anyway. Find someone who appreciates your dedication to your job. In the meantime, you need to concentrate on ways to make yourself a more valuable employee. That's my advice to people starting out in the broadcast business. Make yourself indispensable. Make it so the company would actually lose money if you weren't there performing your job. That applies to any vocation.

I found myself in a format change (which happens

quite often in radio) where everyone got blown out, from the program director on down. Since the station was going to be purely satellite-driven, the only position they needed to fill was a commercial-production guy. We had a lot of people on the air, but nobody had taken the time to learn the commercial-production side of the business. They were air personalities and knew nothing about how to write or produce commercials. Fortunately, I had taken the time to learn that side of the business, and I was the only member of the air staff who survived, all because I had tried to make myself a more valuable employee earlier in my career. If you strive to perform in a manner that benefits the company, you will, in most cases, reap the rewards.

Certainly there are exceptions. I've been fired in spite of doing all the right things and having great ratings. Some owners can't see the benefit of your talent, or want to take a radio station in "a different direction." I reminded one station that in a ratings-driven business like ours, there are only two directions—up and down. If they want to change directions, that's their prerogative. It's their station. If you're in a situation where someone doesn't appreciate your talents, you're better off leaving anyway, as I certainly was.

"It's My God-Given Right"

I had a guy who called my show one day during the Peterbilt Motors Company lockout saying that the company had locked him out of "his job." I tried to explain to him that it wasn't his job, it was the owner of the company's job to give to whomever he thought was going to do the best work. This old union guy became belligerent and argued that it was in fact his job, since he'd had it for thirty-three years. You see, that's the union mind-set. It's an "us against them" mentality that is utterly destructive to a business. If this guy had concentrated on doing a great job all those years and broadened his worth to the company, he might not have found himself locked out. Then again, being union, the company probably had no choice. The union offers employees as a package deal, bad apples included, and this company got sick of the package.

The fight at that particular company was over benefits. Peterbilt had been paying generously into employee pension and health plans. Competition, a soft economy, and changes within the trucking industry had forced them to look at ways to save money. They were offering more money in the way of salary but asked the union members to pick up some of the increase in benefit costs. The union said no, so the company had no choice but to lock the workers out.[1] After thirty-three years, this guy thought it was his God-given right to have his pension and health insurance plan fully provided by the company. He pointed to greed on the owners' part as the reason why the company was hitting hard times. There may have been some truth to that but, short of any illegality on the owners' part, it's theirs to run as they see fit. That's something the unions don't understand or accept.

You want to talk about greed? Nothing rivals the greed

of the unions. It's all about getting more and more out of the company, past the point of reason, until the company has to make some tough decisions. The high cost of labor and benefits puts the company at a disadvantage within the marketplace. The union is unyielding in its demands, always wanting more and never willing to give more. When the company finally does have to either lay off workers or close down, it's their fault and not the union's.

Let me give you an example of unreasonable wages. A caller to my show bragged that he knew of a union friend who was making eighty-one thousand dollars per year putting together boxes! I kid you not. The caller thought it was a great thing that this man could find such a job. It would be great, were the wages not artificially inflated. If the market demanded that the guy putting together boxes be paid eighty-one thousand dollars a year, then that's the going price for box building. However, the union, over years of demanding more and more, had pushed the pay to a ridiculously high level. I don't know the name of the company he was talking about, but I can imagine that it's not long for this world. Some nonunion competitor will eventually arrive, and the boxes will cost much less to manufacture. When that happens, the eighty-one thousand dollars box maker will be out of a job. I suspect the reason that hasn't already happened is because the shipping companies that buy the boxes are also union. These high-paying union jobs are putting marks on their backs.

Even as a private negotiator, I know not to ask for so

much money that I become a target. I negotiate what I think I'm worth, but I don't try to rape the company. If it comes to a point where my employers are not making money and I'm part of the problem, I'm out the door. Unions don't see it that way. It's all about getting more and more, with no regard to the corner into which they're pushing the company. It's short-term thinking, and it's one of the reasons so many companies have packed up and moved overseas or to Mexico.

Stay with Us, the Mediocre

Still another caller told a story of being offered a job in management. Although the pay was better, the benefits were not. The union officials at his company talked him into staying in his union job, thus further tightening their grip on his life. There's little doubt that the smart career move would have been to move into management, but he dared not leave the security of the union. The limousine liberals of the labor union movement preach safety in numbers while their exclusive club lives large on the backs of their members.

Once you go into management, you're persona non grata in a lot of union shops. You're suddenly the enemy. That's the attitude that so bugs me about the unions. If you're anything but a union worker, they're against you. Whatever happened to everyone pulling in the same direction? I know as a program director I never tolerated sorry attitudes. Radio is a very competitive business, and the one thing we didn't need were people eating us up from the inside. Bad attitudes are like poison; they contaminate the entire work area. I've found that the only way to fix the problem is to remove the poison. If you're a union shop, you're stuck with the poison.

Fortunately, I never had to fire too many people as a program director. The few I did fire certainly deserved it. One case involved the poison syndrome I just mentioned. As much as I tried to get along with this guy, the moment I turned my back, he was bad-mouthing me and everybody else in the company. He complained about every task I assigned him and acted like he'd rather be anywhere except there at work. After a couple of months of putting up with this behavior, I called the man into my office and told him it wasn't working out and that I was going to have to let him go. He was floored. It never dawned on him that he could be fired. For some reason, he thought his job was safe.

Never assume your job is safe. Always work as though there are ten people standing in line for your job. Knowing that you can be replaced keeps you honest and appreciative of what you have. On the other hand, if you're miserable in your job, get out. You're not doing you or your employer a favor by being unhappy. There are millions of jobs out there. Go find one that fits you.

Collective Extortion

In theory, I don't have a problem with employees banding together to address some grievance at work. For example, if a lot of people were getting sick because the boss refused to have the air filters changed at work, then perhaps you could make an argument for those workers refusing to come back until the problem was fixed. Doctors in New Jersey refused to show up to work in early 2003 to call attention to the high cost of malpractice insurance. I don't have much problem with that type of activity, when it's justified. Where the unions lose me is in collective bargaining over wages and benefits. That's the closest thing we have to communism in this country.

If I'm a widget maker and I can make thirty widgets a day, it doesn't make sense that I get paid the same amount as the guy who only makes ten. Instead of encouraging him to make more, the union asks me to slow down. Immediately, the incentive for excellence is greatly diminished. If I work harder, I should be able to reap the fruits of my labor instead of allowing this underperformer to drag the rest of us down. Unions aren't in the business of rewarding excellence. They're in the business of making everyone even. That sounds rather communistic to me.

Collective bargaining for wages and benefits runs contrary to every capitalist bone in my body. Union guys ask me how I expect a thousand different workers at a factory to "make their own deal" without a union. My answer is, it's done every single day, since the vast majority of workers in America are nonunion. You go to the department head who makes the hiring decisions and lay out your qualifications for the job. He or she tells you what the company will pay, and you either accept or reject the job. How hard is that? Once you're in, you work hard and prove yourself. If you're a good worker and bring value to your position, you can negotiate a raise. If you just shuffle through the day, you take what they give you and hope you don't get fired.

Under a union, both of those employees would be equally protected and equally paid. Any reasonable person knows that's just not right. Take away the risk or reward, and you take away the incentive. Take away the incentive, and productivity suffers. When productivity suffers, the company becomes less competitive and less profitable.

Daddy, Don't You Work So Fast

I can't tell you how many listeners have called to tell me stories about overproducing under the watchful eyes of the union. One guy told about loading a stack of freight in about two hours. The union representative came over and told him he was supposed to take four and a half hours. The man argued that he'd been raised on a farm and had learned to pace himself. "I don't care," the union guy responded. "Next time do it in four and a half hours." The worker couldn't believe his ears. Try as he may, the slowest he could do the job was about three and a half hours. Imagine how much more productive that company would have been if everyone were trying to keep up with his pace-setting two hours. Instead, they were urged to slow the pace, cutting productivity by more than half.

Stories like this are commonplace in union shops. The last thing the union boss wants you to do is show up everyone else. And once you're in, you're in. Some unions have a no-layoffs policy, giving union members de facto jobs for life. Such was the case in the Miami-Dade school system when conflict over a particular union came to a head in 2002. The state oversight board proposed privatizing maintenance work at twenty-seven schools in order to save millions of dollars a year that might be used to help educate the children. A district audit found that the maintenance division, a union shop, was full of problems and recommended cutting 209 custodians and seventy-one tradesmen.

The American Federation of State, County, and Municipal Employees and the Dade County School Maintenance Employee Council, two unions that represent the maintenance workers, went nuts. The audit found that the maintenance workers were charging eight dollars per square foot to maintain school facilities. That was three dollars more per square foot than private industry pays to maintain its buildings, on average. Despite the evidence in the audit, the local teachers union backed the bloated maintenance unions, even though cleaning them up would mean more money for education.[2] It doesn't take a genius to see that the teachers union was looking out for union interests and was unconcerned about the children.

This is a recurring theme, especially among unions that represent government employees. The objective never seems to be to save the company (or taxpayers) money. The objective is to get the most money for the least amount of work possible. That's the bottom line. And that's why union jobs keep slipping away.

Is It Love to Hate or Hate to Love?

There is quite an interesting contradiction between how Americans feel about unions and how they actually participate in them. About 60 percent of Americans support unions today.[3] However, only about 12 percent of workers belong to a union.[4] That means that 88 percent of us don't belong to unions. Makes you wonder how the polling questions are asked, doesn't it? Of course, the figures on actual union membership don't take into consideration how many people belong only because they feel like they have to in order to keep their jobs. When you break it down between the government and the private sector, you find that four in ten government workers are union as opposed to only one in ten in the private sector.[5] Half of the 16.3 million union members in America live in six states: California, Illinois, Michigan, New York, Ohio, and Pennsylvania.[6]

Since union membership was shrinking, unions were looking north for evidence that would secure their future. The ten-year love affair that many U.S. unions had with moving toward a Canadian-style union work force has died now that the facts are in and they've been exposed. The theory was that the Canadian model made for higher living standards for its workers, but the whole model proved to be a house of cards when productivity was taken into consideration. It seems that during the 1990s, according to the Centre for the Study of Living Standards (CSLS), a think tank based in Ottawa, Ontario, Canadian gross domestic product per person dropped from 86 percent to 80 percent when compared to that of their American counterparts.

According to the National Institute for Labor Relations Research (NILRR) in Virginia, "The two CSLS papers provide compelling evidence that, over time, there is an intimate link between the growth of employees' productivity and the growth of their incomes."[7] In other words, the more an employee produces, the more he can earn. But Canada's compulsive union system stunts that theory by dragging good workers down.

A comparison of productivity in right-to-work states—states that forbid union membership as a prerequisite to getting a job—and non-right-to-work states shows a startling difference. The NILRR points to U.S. Census figures that show that "on an inflation-adjusted, per manufacturing sector-employee basis, the value added by manufacture increased by 76.3 percent in Right to Work states between 1963 and 1996, compared to just 58.8 percent in non-Right to Work states." The NILRR says this mirrors the trend in per capita income: "Between 1964 and 2001, real per capita income grew 27 percent faster in Right to Work states than in non-Right to Work states." That would explain why non-right-to-work states see a net loss of a half million citizens annually who opt to move to right-to-work states.[8] It's hard to argue with those figures. Unions stifle your incentive to produce because they limit your potential to rise above the crowd.

A different study on the effects of unions on productivity and the economy provides insight into the underlying problem. A study by Florida State University concluded that although unions lined the pockets of their members, they had "deleterious" effects on performance. "The broad pattern that emerges from these studies," it said, "is that unions significantly increase compensation for their members but do not increase productivity." In other words, union members are overpaid for what they produce. It also pointed out that, "Following an accounting for company size and firm-level changes in labor, physical capital, and R&D (Research & Development), union firms are found to have substantially slower productivity growth than nonunion firms."[9] Also, "Empirical evidence points unambiguously that unionization leads to lower profitability," the study found. Higher costs, lower productivity, fewer profits. This is the legacy of unions.

You Got a Problem with That?

Probably the most distasteful aspect of unions is their historic ties to organized crime. As newsman Les Nessman on the old television show *WKRP in Cincinnati* once told his fellow employees who were urging him to join them in a union, "I'll join if you can tell me where Jimmy Hoffa is."[10] A great line, but it underscores the more sinister side of unions. I need not delineate here the examples of the

Mob's dominion over the unions. Organized crime's influence on unions is common knowledge and well documented. Its tactics are evident during the unions' darker moments, namely strikes. One need only look at their treatment of so-called scabs, workers who want to continue supporting their families, to see the Mob's influence. Slashed tires, thrown rocks, and worse sully almost every picket line that workers choose to cross in order to keep working. Although many union members downplay their union's affiliation with organized crime, it's a large part of the unions' history that cannot be ignored, and a reputation they have a hard time shaking. They've taken to putting a smiley face on unions in order to entice workers to join, but the ever-present gun in the ribs is always in the back of Americans' minds.

To beef up recruitment and flex its muscles during the 1996 presidential campaign, one of the unions launched an ad campaign entitled *Proud to Be Union*, which ran on the radio station for which I was working. I answered with my own parody, *Proud to Be A Union Thug*, which we use to this day as our union theme. When our version first aired, the outcry from the unions was deafening. Union members called me in hysterics. I made *The Wheel*, the local United Auto Workers newsletter, on several occasions and was practically branded public enemy number one. The letters and e-mails I received were laced with vitriolic venom and have yet to be duplicated. I used to follow *Proud to Be a Union Thug* with the theme from *The*

Godfather as the musical background to the union story I was reading. I was advised to drop that part when I moved to Philadelphia because, as one helpful station employee pointed out, "the Godfather lives *here*."

There are many different labor unions in this country. Some are better than others. Some hardly resemble labor unions at all but serve more as a social club for their members. Professional sports unions are probably among the most useless. They represent guys, many barely out of their teens, who are making hundreds of millions of dollars a year doing a thirty-second TV commercial for sneakers and have the audacity to threaten to go on strike because they say the owner of their team is making too much money. Why they need the union *and* an agent, I'll never understand.

Again, the guys who are really working and hustling and making money for the team don't need a union. I can imagine that if Michael Jordan complains the locker room is too cold, it wouldn't take a strike to fix that problem. So, why would a top player join the union in the first place? The big names purportedly support the union to take care of the not-so-fortunate players who aren't stars, yet I don't ever see any of the stars coughing up cash for the so-called poor players. In fact, because of salary caps, many of the stars eat up so much of the available money that less-fortunate players get cut so the team can stay under the cap. Doesn't sound very unionlike to me. Still, most people don't think of professional sports when they think of unions.

They think of the working man, the guy who struggles to make ends meet.

It's the Union Thugs, Not the Workers

I would suspect that most union employees are honest, hard-working, and resourceful. However, it's the few who run the unions who perpetually forge the negative image of the union thug in the public's psyche. I would also venture to say that the majority of union workers don't need the union, but their dues go to prop up the few who do.

There is little doubt that unions have played a major part in getting laws passed in this country regarding the number of hours in a work day, the hours in a work week, working conditions, workplace safety issues, and the like. However, this very well may be a case in which the cure has turned out to be worse than the disease. Regardless, I would suggest that it was the laws we really needed, not the unions. Now that labor laws are firmly in place, unions have long outlived their usefulness.

22

VIGILANCE is the price
of freedom.

IN CASE THE TITLE of this chapter sounds familiar—
and lest I be accused of ripping off one of our Founding
Fathers—it was Thomas Jefferson who said, "The price
of freedom is eternal vigilance." It was true when he said
it back in the eighteenth century, and it's still true in the
twenty-first. The freedom we as Americans enjoy today is
precious, but it's taken for granted, and it did not come
without a price. Many people have died protecting it,
and many have died seeking it. I literally thank God
every single day for all that He's given me, and I would
have nothing were it not for His wonderful gift of freedom. But forces internal and external threaten that freedom, and we'll devote this chapter to identifying some of
the bigger ones.

The Obvious Threat to Freedom

Is there any doubt after September 11 that terrorism is
one of the long-term threats to our national security and
our freedom? I'm both amazed and disturbed at how

quickly life got back to normal after three thousand people died and two monuments to our capitalist way of life were reduced to rubble. Sure, we cried. We memorialized. We waged war against those responsible. Then we went back to our lives. That's a blessing in one sense, a testament to our determination not to allow terrorists to change our way of life, but it's also a bit frightening that the anger subsided so quickly.

I guess, by nature, we're a forgiving people, but we must never forget how our sense of security was stripped away that day. We must reach way down deep inside ourselves and retrieve those raw emotions we experienced in the wake of September 11 that we now keep hidden. The pain. The anguish. The rage. The resolve. It's not necessary that we dwell on them every hour of every day; rather, we should keep them at the ready, to be brought out in those quiet moments of reflection. Evoke them when you hear our leaders speak of their convictions to end terrorism against this country.

It's easy to let our guard down when the explosion of a suicide bomber is muffled by thousands of miles of separation. It's hard to imagine that horror being part of a daily life in America, but it could be one day. It could be and it *will* be if we aren't ever mindful that each day we're not hunting down those who plot against us, they draw one step closer. Every day we allow someone to talk us into negotiating rather than annihilating, they draw one step closer. People that have never met you, that have never even seen you, hate you with every fiber of their being. They hate you because you're free. They hate you because you represent to them everything they want but can never have because they're slaves to an oppressive and consuming philosophy of hatred that drives them to the point of a yearning desire to die taking your freedom rather than winning their own.

These were the savages we saw on television celebrating the attacks on America in which innocent people died. These were the filth that celebrated when U.S. space shuttle *Columbia* and its seven-member crew fell from the sky. They rejoice at the death of Israeli and American children. They feed on the hatred of America and all she stands for. Remember. If their hatred is stronger than your resolve, they win.

The Enemy Within

How ironic it is that the very freedom and way of life these sick barbarians despise allow them to roam freely among us. You'd think we would have learned our lesson from September 11, but agents of terrorist states still remain inside this country. In the name of political correctness, we shy away from profiling so nobody gets his feelings hurt. The bad guys know there are enough members of the Neville Chamberlain Society in this country, unwitting accomplices in their grand scheme of terror, that they can chip away at us from within. They know the appeasers are the ones who would prefer to give another inch and wait another day rather than do what's necessary to shore up our borders.

We covered immigration in an earlier chapter, but it bears repeating that our porous borders may ultimately be our downfall. Without rigidly controlled immigration, those who would do us harm can exploit our leniency and freely hatch their plans inside our own country. If I don't drive any other point home in this book, please understand that our failure to secure our borders is the single most serious threat to our freedom.

Running a close second is the cavalier way in which we willingly choose to forfeit our freedom for security. Benjamin Franklin summed it up most succinctly: "They that can give up essential liberty to obtain a little temporary safety deserve neither liberty nor safety." Those words came back to me in the aftermath of September 11 when certain public officials started raising the specter of allowing law enforcement to be more intrusive than the Constitution might allow in order to ensure our safety. Now, I'm not talking about airport security, although some rules are a bit overboard. (No nail clippers?) When you make a reservation you agree to abide by the rules of the airline or you take some other mode of transportation. What I'm referring to are insidious programs like the Total Information Awareness program.

The Pentagon, under the direction of Iran-Contra figure John Poindexter, was, and probably still is, developing technology that will enable the government to know every purchase you make. They'll know every cash withdrawal, every gun purchase, every magazine, every book—every everything. The government claims it needs this information to fight terrorism. "The bottom line is, this is an important research project to determine the feasibility of using certain transactions and events to discover and respond to terrorists before they act," says Edward Aldridge, undersecretary of acquisitions and technology.

The Defense Advanced Research Projects Agency is in charge of the project, which Aldridge calls just an experiment. Chuck Pena, senior defense policy analyst at the Cato Institute, is alarmed by the "experiment." "What this is talking about is making us a nation of suspects, and I am sorry, the United States' citizens should not have to live in fear of their own government, and that is exactly what this is going to turn out to be," he said.[1] Eerily, the logo for the new organization is an eye scanning the globe. Warning signals are sounded by anyone making large cash withdrawals, booking a one-way air or rail trip, renting a car, or buying a gun. I was almost prompted to do all four the day I read the story.

I know what some of you are saying. "Well, Phil, what are they supposed to do? You said the government should be tightening up security. You said we should be vigilant." Indeed I did, but there are much better ways to maintain security without compromising our rights. First of all, every person from a terrorist-sponsoring nation who's in this country and is not a citizen should be asked to leave. You see, the government is looking at ways to trample on the rights of citizens, but it wouldn't dare offend people who have no right to be here in the first place. Sure, I know that not everyone from these countries is a terrorist, but we can't take chances. I'd much rather see these noncitizens inconvenienced than see American citizens subjected to this gross invasion of their privacy.

Heather MacDonald wrote a piece for the *Weekly Standard* in which she asserted that concerns raised by those of us who are worried about the Total Information Awareness program were merely the "ravings of privacy fanatics." We have nothing to worry about, she asserts, because, among other safeguards, researchers are "building numerous privacy protections into the system," she said, "such as concealing the names of people engaged in suspicious transactions until a threshold of probable cause is met."[2] It's how low that threshold might go that's alarming to me and should be to every American. This technology being used by the Bush administration seems benign, but can you imagine another Clintonesque administration where siccing the IRS on enemies might be commonplace? Can you imagine what such an administration might do with information provided by an apparatus like the Total Information Awareness program?

I sat on a panel discussion for *Talkers* magazine in December 2002 with a very intelligent, very articulate, and very pleasant Jewish rabbi and talk-show host named Shmuley Boteach. When I brought up this concern to the panelists, Shmuley commented that he didn't care if the government saw him at home in his underwear, he had nothing to hide. Although it got a chuckle from the group, the underlying attitude is one of total compliance and capitulation when it comes to your rights. I have nothing to hide either, but I'm not about to allow the government into my home and my life any old time it pleases.

I found the comment especially interesting coming from a man whose people have seen governments turn from benevolent to malevolent almost overnight with horrific results. Shmuley or one of the other panelists asked what the difference was between the government tracing your purchases and all of the grocery stores to which we gladly give our personal information in exchange for a discount card. My reply: "They don't have guns, the government does."[3] I would also add that using a discount card is voluntary. The TIA program, if we don't stop it, will not be.

On January 23, 2003, on a voice vote, the Senate passed an amendment to an appropriations bill that suspended funding for the Total Information Awareness program.[4] However, there's a big loophole in the amendment. It allows the president, any president, to approve continued funding for TIA. Only vigilance on our part will keep it from creeping back to life in the future.

The China Syndrome

The other big threat to our freedom looming on the horizon is China and its satellite countries like North Korea. It's interesting to note that just a couple of months before the September 11 attacks, ABC News commissioned a poll to see who Americans considered the biggest threat to world peace. China was far and away the winner with 35 percent. Iraq was a distant second with 13 percent. Compared to a 1991 poll that had China in third place with only 10 percent, behind Russia and Iraq, it's obvious at least some Americans were sitting up and taking notice.[5] September 11 changed our focus, but it did not reduce the Chinese threat. As I outlined in the chapter on oppression, China has taken full opportunity of our diverted attention.

The chilling image in 1997 of the Chinese communist flag draped over the railing at the New York Stock Exchange as Chinese president Jiang Zemin clanged the bell signaling the opening of trading was quite diabolically metaphorical. It was as if he were calling the eager, hungry wolves of Wall Street to dinner with copious quantities of cash tossed down to them like raw meat. What Wall Street didn't realize is that it was actually being led to slaughter.

The greed of corporate America continues to feed the Chinese war machine. Like the scrap metal sold to the Japanese prior to World War II that was turned into bombs dropped on Pearl Harbor, the cheap trinkets we buy from the Chinese will be turned into cash to buy a nuclear arsenal, and we'll have no way to stop this growing threat short of another major war.

Everyone looks to Taiwan as the "O.K. Corral" of Asia. How America reacts to the inevitable invasion of that island by China will determine the level of aggression displayed by the Red Chinese. If we rebuff them, as we've sworn to do in our treaty with Taiwan, then we may see a China rethinking its whole world policy. If we stand idly by while they waltz right in, then Katie bar the door. Once we've confirmed in their minds that we don't have the stomach for war with them, it will be the former Soviet Union all over again. They'll keep pushing until we push back.

Also, keep the name Spratly Islands in the back of your mind. This tiny island chain in the South China Sea has the potential for rich gas and oil deposits as well as explosive political consequences. Everybody and his brother claims these islands, including China, Malaysia, the Philippines, Taiwan, and Vietnam. China has built helicopter pads, a communications complex, and various other structures there over the last few years. If that conflict heats up, it could become a diplomatic nightmare for us. Certainly no one would expect us to jump into the middle of it, but how we react will send clear signals to China. My guess is, we'll give tacit approval to China's right to the islands, although the other nations seem to have a stronger claim. Such a move would embolden the Chinese to try Taiwan next—if they haven't already gobbled it up by then.

The America-Haters Among Us

America is like a number-one team in sports—everybody is gunning for us. Most of the animosity is rooted in envy.

There are people who hate everything we stand for. To them, America is wicked, perverted, and arrogant. They see us as the enemy of the world, the antagonist of the downtrodden, despite the fact that we give more in foreign aid than any other country on earth. They want us destroyed, and they're living right here inside our country. Let's talk about a few.

Jessica Quindel, president of the Graduate Assembly at the University of California at Berkeley, is one. "The flag has become a symbol of U.S. aggression towards other countries," she said, explaining why she and her comrades tried to ban the American flag from the university's September 11 remembrance ceremony. As noted conservative David Horowitz described her:

> Jessica Quindel is what I call a traitor of the heart, someone who shares with Osama Bin Laden the belief that America is the Great Satan and who would aid and abet any enemy . . . before she would embrace her own country and its defense. This is the creed of the sick fifth column in this country, whose base is the politically correct university and whose intellectual gurus are Noam Chomsky and Howard Zinn. To call these wretched people Benedict Arnolds would be an insult to a man who did betray his country, but at least did so on behalf of a tolerant democracy. These modern-day traitors do it on behalf of murderers and fanatics, on behalf of nothing more, really, than a blind, fanatical hate, which is really a self-hate.[6]

Filmmaker Michael Moore is another. This slovenly yellow journalist rose to prominence with his anti-capitalist, pro-union attack on General Motors called *Roger and Me*, which asserted that GM owed the people of Flint, Michigan, a living. Moore quickly became a darling of the Left. His comments on his Web site shortly after September 11 exposed him for what he is: an America-hating, bitter whiner who, instead of being angry at the terrorists, was angry at America. "Am I angry?" he asked on his Web site. "You bet I am. I am an American citizen, and my leaders have taken my money to fund mass murder. And now, my friends have paid the price with their lives. . . . Keep crying, Mr. Bush. Keep running to Omaha or wherever it is you go while others die."[7]

Joel Rogers, who teaches at the University of Wisconsin, wrote a column in the *Nation* magazine shortly after September 11. Of course, he blames America for the way we've conducted ourselves. "Our own government, through much of the past 50 years, has been the world's leading 'rogue state.' Merely listing the plainly illegal or unauthorized uses of force the U.S. was responsible for during the long period of cold war, and continued during the past decade of 'purposeless peace' . . . would literally take volumes. And behind that list reside the bodies of literally hundreds of thousands, if not millions, of innocents, most of them children, whose lives we have taken without any pretense to justice."[8]

These are but three examples, but they represent the

threat to our country from within academia and the entertainment industry. Vigilance denotes an outward attention, hands shading eyes affixed to the open sea. But vigilance is also about watching your back. It's about always being cognizant of those around you who would prefer the demise of this country over its continued status as the world's superpower. That's not to say that we should slink about, paranoid that some college egghead or second-rate filmmaker is going to steal our freedom. It's only a gentle reminder that the enemy is everywhere, especially in these times.

College campuses are filled with guilt-ridden brats whose minds are pliable in the hands of America-haters who afford them a way to "repent." Let us be ever mindful that there has never been a country founded that is impervious to destruction. I pray that America can last forever, but it will never last as long as we merely will it to do so. Longevity comes from vigilance because vigilance is the price of freedom.

Skewing the News to Tout Liberal Views

Media bias is certainly a big problem in this country. Fox News Channel has helped tilt the coverage back to the center. Talk radio and Internet sites such as NewsMax.com and WorldNetDaily.com have been quite effective in getting out the conservative point of view. Still, media bias is prevalent among many of the networks, and that's still where most Americans get their news.

I need not devote an entire chapter to the subject since books like *Bias* by Bernard Goldberg, a veteran CBS reporter, cover the subject better than I ever could. What I want to touch on is how pervasive the problem really is, and that most people don't even notice.

A few years ago, I was taking one of my sons to his preschool. He was looking out the window and asked me, "What are those?" "What are what?" I replied. "Those," he said, pointing out the back window at a fire hydrant. I explained what it was, and then I started thinking about fire hydrants. They were so commonplace that I didn't even notice them anymore. Media bias is much the same. This "fire hydrant" is so ingrained into our cultural landscape that we don't even notice it. It oftentimes takes someone pointing it out before you actually see it. Once you really start looking, however, you can see it everywhere. Part of being vigilant means looking for the insidious ways some members of the media try to sway you in their reporting.

A case in point: the morning after President Bush landed on the deck of the USS *Abraham Lincoln* to officially announce the end of the Iraq War, I was listening to a report on ABC Radio News. Terry Moran, the White House correspondent, noted that the banner behind the president read, "Mission Accomplished." He noted that some were questioning that claim since Saddam Hussein had not been found. Forget the fact that President Bush had made it crystal clear that victory was not contingent upon arresting or killing Saddam. The goal was a "regime change." Remember? Moran went on to report that President Bush would use the images from the carrier landing in the 2004 presidential campaign, and that the whole idea was the brainchild of Karl Rove. That was it. That was his full report. There was not one shred of factual information in it. What had the president said in his speech? How was he greeted? What other dignitaries were there? These were pertinent questions, totally ignored in order for Moran to make his political statement that the mission was a failure, that Bush was using the occasion simply for a photo op, and that Karl Rove was the real brains behind this president.

Remember this one thing every time you watch the news or pick up a newspaper: Look for the fire hydrants.

What Can WE Concerned Citizens Do?

Whether it's joining the military, giving blood, or volunteering in some capacity, we must all be prepared to pitch in and help when it comes to our national security. In times of crisis our military will certainly do the heavy lifting, but we cannot assume that everything else will be handled by someone else.

Vigilance doesn't mean vigilantly sitting in front of your television. It means getting involved, lending your talents and time to the cause of keeping our nation safe. By that I don't mean that everyone should join the military, but we must be prepared to respond when our country, state, or local community needs us. It may mean some sacrifice, but whatever we as ordinary citizens do pales in comparison to the sacrifice so many before us have made to ensure our freedom. Vigilance is indeed the price of freedom, but it's a very small expense for so great a nation.

23

WELFARE robs people of their dignity and is the poison of capitalism.

W ELFARE IS NEARLY AS old as time itself. In 70 BC, approximately 40,000 people were receiving food from the Roman food stores in Europe. By 44 BC, that number had grown to 150,000. In England, various laws were passed over the centuries to help the poor, including a poor tax in 1572 that was passed simultaneously with an order for relief administrators to put vagrants to work. That "poor law" was refined four years later, making the poor person's relief pay based on his work output, an early welfare-to-work program.

From the beginning of time, a certain portion of the populace has been poor. The question has always been, and still remains, what to do about it. Throughout human history, we've continued to make the same mistakes over and over again.

Before the American federal government became involved in dispensing assistance to impoverished citizens in the 1930s, welfare was handled on the state and local levels. That changed under Herbert Hoover's administration as he reluctantly attempted to have the federal government provide help during the Great Depression. Aid to Families with Dependent Children (AFDC) cleared Congress in 1935 as Title 6 of the Social Security Act. AFDC was replaced by the Personal Responsibility and Work Opportunity Reconciliation Act (PRWORA) in 1996.

AFDC seemed to work fine for many years. States, which still bore the responsibility for taking care of poor children, turned in their expenses to the federal government and Uncle Sam reimbursed them for part of the cost. Although the program was optional, during the cash-strapped 1930s few states turned the feds down. AFDC became progressively more inclusive in the number of people in a family it covered and more intrusive in the way the program was dictated to the states.

Prior to the '60s, AFDC concentrated on children. In 1961, AFDC-UP was introduced. The UP stood for Unemployed Parent. (You're starting to get that "oh, yeah" enlightened look on your face, aren't you?) The next year, a *second* parent in a family who was incapacitated or unemployed was allowed to receive benefits. In 1968, the "essential person" option went into effect, allowing "any other individual" in the home deemed essential to the child to receive money too. In the meantime, of course, the more babies you frumped up, the more money you got.

A working parent reduced the amount of welfare money a family could receive, so, since males couldn't give birth, they left the home—many of them by choice, I might add. After all, where's the guilt when Mom and the kids will get money from the government if you're not there? When viewed in this light, the skyrocketing illegitimacy rate starts to make sense. In 1981, the government began making payments to mothers during the last trimester of pregnancy, meaning the money began rolling in even before the child was born! All these rules and regulations began to be mandatory for the states in 1984.[1]

It's a . . . Nutritional Program. Yeah, That's the Ticket.

Believe it or not, the food stamp program was not considered to be welfare when it was first introduced, nor was it called by that name until later in its long, illustrious history. It was called a "nutritional program." The federal food stamp program dates back to the New Deal and was only expanded by a modest level in 1961 by the Kennedy administration.

The year 1968 was the turning point for food stamps. A documentary shown on Thanksgiving Day in 1967 focused on malnutrition and hunger in America. Hunger became a big campaign issue in '68, and as soon as Richard Nixon was in office, the program was once again expanded. In 1974, Congress required all states to provide the program. The food stamp program became joined with AFDC, and pretty soon more than 85 percent of AFDC recipients also got food stamps.

Does Welfare Help Poverty?

Dr. Kelly L. Ross of the department of philosophy at Los Angeles Valley College studied the effects of the welfare system on poverty and came to the conclusion that "what can and must be done is for Government to get out of the poverty business and for people to realize that poverty can be reduced only by the enterprise and industry of private individuals, both those who work hard for pay and those who invest capital in new business."[2]

What Ross found was that the poverty rate had drastically declined from 1950, when poverty statistics first became available, to 1966, the first year Lyndon Johnson's Great Society programs and the War on Poverty went into effect. During those years when capitalism, mind you, was the only factor, the poverty rate dropped from 30.2 percent to 14.7 percent. Quite a decline indeed. After the Great Society programs kicked in, the decline in the poverty rate almost came to a screeching halt. It dipped a little to 11.1 percent in 1973, then began its ascent, peaking in 1993 at 15.1 percent. That's higher than when the War on Poverty began! The poverty rate for 2006 was 12.3, about where it was in 1968.[3]

A *Los Angeles Times* article in 1997 tied poverty to single parenthood. The piece pointed out that although the poverty rate for the nation was, at that time, 13.7 percent, only 5.6 percent of married families were below the poverty level. It went even further, stating that of married families where "at least one partner works full time, year-round, no matter how menial the job," the poverty rate was just 1.8 percent. Conversely, "nearly one-third" of families headed by single women, and almost 14 percent of families headed by single men, were below the poverty level.[4]

This shouldn't come as much of a shock, since the government stepped in to become a parent during the Great Society. In 1964, prior to all this *help* from the government, the illegitimacy rate in America was 7.7 percent. By the end of the 1990s, that rate was 33 percent.[5]

Whose Responsibility Is It?

In 2001, Gordon Fisher presented a paper to the Annual Research Conference of the Association for Public Policy Analysis and Management in Washington, D.C. The paper was entitled "Enough for a Family to Live On?—Questions from Members of the American Public and New Perspectives from British Social Scientists." What the "cradle to grave" British could teach us about welfare is beyond me, but Fisher's paper presented questions from Americans. One, in particular, I found quite instructive. A young lady wrote:

I am a single Mother and work two jobs which equal about $18,000 per year. We barely afford rent, electric, cable, phone, water, food, taxes and vehicle expenses. [But] the federal poverty level is $11,060 [the 1999 poverty guideline for a family of two]. My daughter and I have zero, no, zilch money left after paying the bills for medical or clothing. How on earth does the Federal Government expect us to pay for cars. . . . There just is NOT enough money left at the end of the month for a car payment. . . . Please tell me . . . how they expect people to live on under $20,000 per year.[6]

Several things hit me when I read these comments. First, where's the father? Obviously there was a father involved at some point in time. Why isn't he helping out with raising his own child? She asks, "How on earth does the Federal Government expect us to pay for cars?" Why is she asking the government such a question? Why doesn't she ask herself that question, then find employment that fixes the problem? Instead, she looks to the government like the government is somehow responsible for the situation she obviously got herself into. Again, why isn't she asking the father these questions instead?

A minor point but one deserving of attention is her mention of cable. That somehow sneaked in there with food and water, as if it were one of life's essentials. Drop the cable, for crying out loud! My guess is that she probably has a cell phone too. Another one of life's essentials. Look, I'm not putting this woman down. The government is—and should be—there for those who genuinely need help. I'm merely trying to point out the problem here. The problem is, we have far too many people crying to the government about their problems instead of going about the task of fixing them.

I can certainly relate to this woman's plight. When I first started out in radio I was making $6,000 a year. That's equivalent to about $14,000 in today's dollars. By my third job in radio, I was working a consistent six-days-a-week, sixty-six-hours-a-week schedule for $8,000 a year. That worked out to about $2.33 per hour. Minimum wage was $3.10 per hour. By anybody's math I was poor, but I was doing exactly what I wanted to do and I was happy. My grandmother once asked me how I managed on the little money I made. I told her you just have to *act* like you have some money. She told me I ought to win an Oscar.

Even with an apartment payment and a car payment, I made it. It was tight, but I made it. My pay over the next couple of years increased from $8,000 to $10,000 as I became program director. There were lean times, but I was having the time of my life. I was out on my own, doing what I wanted to do with my career. I could've stood a little more money, but I was learning the business and paying my dues. Within three years, I snagged a job in Raleigh, North Carolina, making $16,000 per year. I thought I'd died and gone to heaven.

My point is, the lady with the kid making $18,000 per year is, hopefully, not in a stagnant situation. Poverty is a great motivator. It motivates you to try and better your situation. When you become dependent on the government, you give up that scary, uncertain feeling for a little security, but you also run the risk of getting comfortable in your poverty.

People on public assistance may know where their next meal is coming from because they're on food stamps (actually, it's a card nowadays). They probably don't worry about shelter because they have government housing. But they're also miserable because they see no future. You give up something when you become trapped in the seemingly endless cycle of welfare. You give up your dignity. Welfare is like a drug. You get lured in and then you're hooked. A lot of that has changed since the Republican welfare reform of 1996, but there are still those dependent on the government who can't break the cycle.

Welfare also poisons the capitalist system. When able-bodied people go on welfare, they're jerked out of the mainstream of society. People who might be productive citizens are many times trapped, as their children are and their grandchildren are, in a downward spiral of desperation. Today, there are many welfare advocates who scream "how dare you" when we ask welfare recipients to work for their money. As one Web site I read said, getting food stamps is a "nationwide entitlement." It explained that what that means is "you have a legal right to get them."

There should be no entitlements! The only thing you're entitled to is freedom. Many believe all of these government programs are God-given rights. If you ask people to work for them, they scream that they have a right to them because they're entitlements. You get to know a lot about a person when they accept something, whether it be from the government or charity, and act as though they're entitled to it. Not asking people to work, if they are able, in return for public assistance is, to me, the ultimate insult. Restoring lost dignity will go a long way in motivating people to do something about their plight. It'll also separate the needy from the greedy.

I remember a few years ago when the men from my Sunday school class were going to spend the night with the homeless at our church. We did this during the colder months, when the local homeless shelter was over-crowded. A friend of mine and I went to the shelter on a church bus and picked up the homeless folks. Once we were back at the church, everyone sort of found a place for themselves and settled in. Our wives had made sand-wiches, which were out on a table in the kitchen.

One man came through, acting very cocky, and looked down at the sandwiches. "Where's the pizza?" he asked.

"There's not any pizza," I told him. "We've got sand-wiches if you want one."

He became indignant. "I don't want no old sandwich. They promised us pizza."

"Who promised you pizza?" I asked.

"Well, the last church we stayed in. They had pizza."

I was bound and determined that this guy was going to eat a sandwich or nothing at all. I wasn't about to get him a pizza. My friend felt guilty and broke down and or-dered one.

A little while later, I was talking to a man who had come over to thank me for putting him up. I asked him about his situation, and he said he had been living too close to the edge. When he lost his job, he lost his house and had nowhere to turn but the shelter. He said that he'd found another job and was starting first thing in the morning on a construction site. This guy was deserving of our help. He appreciated it and understood that he wasn't entitled to anything. The first guy was a bum, plain and simple. He thought the whole world owed him, and he carried that chip around on his shoulder.

As a taxpayer, it's a lot more palatable to see humble people like the second gentleman I met at the church benefiting from my hard work. The problem is, we've created a monster, with citizens being drilled by the poverty pimps that they "deserve" money from the government, that they're "entitled" to handouts, that it's their "right" to get something for nothing. A little humility, a little embarrassment that you have to take a handout, goes a long way, but it's certainly rare these days.

Homeless vs. Bums

You scarcely hear the term *bums* anymore in this age of political correctness, but believe me, they're still there. They've just hijacked the pity train and have gotten in line, unnoticed, with the truly needy. There are ways to distinguish the bums from the needy, and teaching this lesson to your kids is a difficult but important task. The Reverend Carl Reasoner, who founded the Nashville Rescue Mission, had a great idea several years back. He provided tokens for motorists to hand to the bums standing at the stoplights at Interstate exit ramps. You know the ones—they have some sob story written on cardboard trying to shame you out of your money. Carl Reasoner's token indicated it was good for one free meal and one free night's rest at the mission.

Some bums are more aggressive than others, and we came upon just such a man one day. I usually try to ignore these guys, but this fellow came up to the car and began talking. I rolled down my window and asked him what he had said. He repeated that he needed some money to buy dinner. When I informed him that the mission, just three blocks away, served hot meals every night, he claimed he'd missed the cutoff time. Having worked with the mission while helping with their fund-raising efforts, I knew instantly that he was lying. When I called him on it, he stammered for a moment and then asked, "Well, can I have some money, anyway?" I refused, of course, and what followed was another Andy Griffith moment with my boys.

"Was he lying?" my ten-year-old asked.

"Yes, he was," I answered. I then proceeded to instruct my sons on the differences between bums and truly needy people. The truly needy, I explained, were over at the mission getting the services they needed. The bums were out on the streets trying to shake guilt-ridden citizens down so they could buy drugs or alcohol. Although it may seem compassionate just to give the man some money, all that will do is fuel his dependency problem, something the mission takes care of as well, with outstanding results.

My brother-in-law and I were having lunch at a little café in Greenwich Village a few years ago. As we enjoyed our meal on the patio, we were approached by a young fellow claiming to be hungry. He pleaded, in a haunting voice, that he hadn't eaten in three days and inquired if we would be so kind as to give him some money to buy food. I took a piece of bread from our table and offered it to the "poor fellow." His humble manner suddenly turned to rage. "F—you!" he shouted. "I don't need your f—ing bread." Then he stormed off.

What an eye-opening experience. One would think that if you hadn't eaten for three days, you'd be thrilled to have some fresh bread. Of course, the reality was, he had no intention of spending the money on food. From the looks of him, he was saving up for more heroin . . . or another body piercing. Either way, I wasn't interested in contributing.

We used to have a regular caller to the show named "Homeless Jim." That's what he called himself. He lived, by choice, in his truck. He took odd jobs and even managed to put out a CD during the 2000 presidential campaign, which we played. Before he was banned for using the F-word on the radio during a remote broadcast where we had no seven-second-delay, he would call us from his cell phone. That's right, a homeless guy with a cell phone. The same kind of guy you see standing by the roadside with a cardboard sign.

Don't get the wrong idea. I certainly understand that

there are people who need help. I've been around the mission enough to see the drug dependent, the mentally ill, and people who are just plain down on their luck. I once took a tour of the mission's new facilities with a guy who worked in their PR department as my tour guide. He was a very impressive, sharp individual with a degree from Auburn. We visited the various departments of the mission, from the drug rehab section to the dorms to the adult education wing, finally ending up in the kitchen.

My guide introduced me to the head of the kitchen, a guy who, I believe, had served time in the navy as a cook and seemed to have it all in one bag. My guide told me the kitchen supervisor had gone through the mission's program as a homeless man. When we were out of earshot, I turned to my guide and asked, "How in the world does someone like that end up homeless?" This nicely dressed college graduate answered matter-of-factly, "The same way I did."

I was floored. This man, who obviously was very intelligent and well-adjusted, had hopped a bus to Nashville after going through everything and everybody back in Alabama in order to support his addiction. Hitting rock bottom, he went through the Nashville Rescue Mission's rehab program and completely turned his life around. After completing the program, he was hired by the mission. He later was offered and accepted a larger position with one of Tennessee's charitable organizations. The man met his wife, who also worked at the mission, and they're now raising a family. He also served with me in the Tennessee State Guard.

I tell you all this so you will understand that I've seen firsthand that the most unlikely people can hit hard and desperate times. I've also seen that those who are willing to help themselves can pull themselves up from the depths of despair and start new and wonderful lives. But it has to be their decision to make the change.

Now for some ammunition on homelessness. Since it's quite difficult to survey homeless people, it's hard to get a bead on the problem. Many studies report that at least 25 percent to 30 percent are mentally ill. Another 40 percent or more are drug- or alcohol-dependent.[7] My personal observations tell me those figures are low. The estimates for how many people are actually homeless range from 500,000 to 1.3 million. However, here's the encouraging aspect of the homeless problem and probably the most important point to be made about this whole issue: 80 percent of the homeless people in America are homeless for only two to three weeks. Another 10 percent are homeless for up to two months. *Only 10 percent are chronically homeless.* Chronic is defined as being homeless for seven to eight months in a two-year period.[8]

Again, that's not to diminish the problems facing a homeless person or family. If you're homeless, it doesn't really matter much how many other people are in the same boat. Those statistics are intended to put the homeless problem in perspective. Despite the scare-mongers out there, you are not "just one paycheck away from being homeless." If you're not mentally ill or you don't abuse drugs or alcohol, your chances of ending up homeless are incredibly low. Also, the fact that the homeless rate actually rose throughout the economic expansion of the 1990s proves that it's not a money-driven problem. In all likelihood, the good times of the '90s afforded a lot more people the opportunity to screw up their lives with drugs.

I've also learned that government programs pale in comparison to private, charitable organizations in dealing with homelessness. Religious-based organizations are the very best at curing the problem because, in many cases, it's a matter of straightening out the homeless person's personal life before he can get back on his feet. That takes an unwavering dedication to walking the right path. Of course, there are those who cry that there's not enough affordable housing, or that the minimum wage is not high enough. If the truth be told, many of the people who find themselves in this situation are there because they made some bad life choices. Helping them make the right choices, not throwing more government money at the problem, is the long-term solution.

Corporate Welfare

This is one of those issues that really sticks in my craw. It's bad enough that we have people scamming the system for a few bucks a month, but corporate welfare has become a national disgrace. The first thing that comes to mind are all the rich sports franchises that insist that states and municipalities raise taxes to build state-of-the-art facilities they should be building themselves. Citizens often get caught up in "Pro Sports Fever" and vote these financing packages in. Meanwhile, the players make more and more money and the owners get filthy rich and then threaten to move the franchise unless the city builds them another facility—this time bigger and better.

I fought just such a move back in 1996 when the then-Houston Oilers approached Nashville about possibly moving that National Football League team here. City leaders and citizens fell all over themselves kissing owner Bud Adams's feet. I was all for the move. In fact, I had put a down payment on four PSLs, or personal seat licenses, that would enable me to purchase tickets. What I was vehemently against was public funding of such a venture. Look, I don't blame Bud Adams for trying to get the best deal he could. I blamed the mayor and the "NFL Yes" crowd, who were acting like bumbling fools, ready to take any deal just to get a team.

The mayor mentioned that he wanted to put Nashville on the map. I was dumbstruck. A football team is going to put Nashville on the map? We're already on the map. We're one of the most recognized names in the world. I surmised that the whole city was suffering from an inferiority complex, and for the life of me, I couldn't figure out why. The public funding issue was forced to a referendum. The corporate world dumped a ton of money into the campaign, and the proposal passed by about a three-to-two margin. I was fine with that. The people had spoken and this is what they wanted. Fine.

First, the mayor had to raise property taxes. Then he had to take money from the Water Department. Soon he had to raise taxes again and then again. Pretty soon people had had enough and started heading for the suburbs. Now all the counties surrounding Nashville are growing while Nashville is actually losing population.[9]

The *Boston Globe* did a series on corporate welfare in 1996. The paper exposed some outrageous payments made to corporations for items for which the government surely should not have footed the bill. For example, Walt Disney Corporation received $300,000 in federal assistance to perfect fireworks displays![10] At the time the article went to press, defense contractor Lockheed Martin was expected to get $1 billion to help the company with its $10 billion merger. Included in the funds: more than $16 million in pay and performance bonuses for top executives while nearly fifty thousand employees had been laid off between 1991 and 1996. All told, the *Globe* reported that an estimated $150 billion in taxpayer money is paid in corporate welfare. That's more than all the core programs of the welfare state combined![11]

Before you jump to the defense of these corporations, saying they deserve the money because they create jobs, think about what you're saying. You're allowing Congress to contaminate the free-market system by showing favoritism to their biggest contributors. Stephen Moore writes about corporate welfare for the Cato Institute. He observed, "The point is, we have very efficient capital markets in this country. The government has never been good at picking winners and losers. The Commerce Department and Congress are influenced by lobbying more than the market. That makes for a corruption of the market. And this in the long run is bad for the national economy."

It's rather unseemly, don't you think, if we criticize the welfare queens who ride around in Cadillacs and collect a few hundred dollars a month and don't criticize the welfare kings who ride around in Learjets and collect millions.

Welfare for the New Millennium

I want to touch on a side issue for a moment, a related subject that threatens to further divide this country. No doubt, one of the hottest perennial issues on my show is slavery reparations, the welfare program of the new millennium. No matter what else I talk about afterward, if I relay a story in the news about reparations, there is no getting away from it for the rest of the show. I don't want to talk about the motivations behind those who want to *receive* the reparations at this point, because I believe those motivations are numerous and varied. Some are honorable, some are not. What I want to cover here is the motivation behind non-blacks in wanting to *pay* the reparations.

The fact is, there's a lot of white guilt on the left. There's a feeling among many liberals that they somehow don't deserve the life they've been dealt, almost as if their prosperity is something for which they must atone. They're ashamed. I am like most white folks I know. I'm neither proud nor ashamed of being white. I simply am. Many whites who push for reparations are also ashamed of the way their ancestors treated blacks. Certainly the history of America is stained with the blood of slavery. No one could ever rationally argue that slavery was a good thing, nor could they argue that blacks in this country have not been treated abhorrently in the past. It disturbs me greatly that black people, even in my lifetime, were relegated to the back of buses and forced to use separate but unequal facilities. The question is now; what do we do about it?

The short answer is, we've already done what needed to be done. The abolition of institutionalized racism was a major step. There are still pockets of racism that will only continue to dissipate through the passing of time and the regeneration of those who do not hate. Each new generation brings with it a greater understanding between the races and, subsequently, a lessening of bigotry. Racism will never be obliterated completely. There will always be those who try to elevate themselves by belittling others. What we as a society must do is stand firm and reject that ideology as unacceptable. We have outlawed discrimination. We have opened the doors to all sectors of our society in hopes of correcting the misdeeds of the past. However, feeling shame for the actions of one's ancestors is irrational. Payment for the sins of the father should not fall on the son, much less the great-great-grandson.

Although we can all agree that slavery was abominable, the notion of paying *money* for that suffering is at once unworkable and an insult to the legacy of those who suffered. If we could pay directly those who were held in bondage, that might be an amenable solution. But we can't. Paying the offspring of slaves is becoming increasingly impossible, given that just a handful are still around. Surprised? Oh, yes. There are still a few around, believe it or not, and the sniffing, sue-happy, guilt-trippers of the Left have tracked them down.

In 2002, there was a news story about two surviving sons of a slave, Chester and Timothy Hurdle, who filed suit—or rather, had a suit filed on their behalf—against a laundry list of who's who in the corporate world who profited from slavery.[12] Chester, the younger brother, had been born in 1927. His father, Andrew Jackson Hurdle, was born a slave in 1845, which means he was eighty-two when he fathered Chester. (He should've gotten money for that, alone.) During the Civil War, sixteen-year-old Andrew Hurdle escaped after being beaten by his master. He joined the Union army and tended horses. Over the course of his eighty-nine years, Andrew Jackson Hurdle had two wives and twenty-five children, Timothy and Chester among them.[13]

I certainly believe that the Hurdle brothers might have a case against their father's master. However, they have no claim against any company that may have profited from what at the time was a legal enterprise. How many of us could go back in our lineage and find some ancestor who was wronged by someone else's ancestor? If injustice to an ancestor justifies monetary reimbursement to his descendants, then we'd all be suing each other.

Activist Deadria Farmer-Paellmann, who filed the lawsuit on behalf of the Hurdles against twelve corporations, has no direct claim to the money. But if you don't think this issue is about money, then consider that California reparations activist Morris "Big Money" Griffin helped file the Hurdles' suit.[14] Farmer-Paellmann, Big Money Griffin, and other activists were merely trying to extort money from successful corporations like J. P. Morgan Chase & Co., Lehman Brothers Holdings Inc., and Brown Brothers Harriman under the guise of helping blacks "deal with the vestiges of slavery that 35 million African-Americans still suffer from, like housing, education, and economic development in our communities."

The truth is, slavery did not cause many of these problems. They stem largely from the so-called solutions to the injustice, like the welfare state, rather than the "vestiges of slavery." The Hurdles modeled their lawsuit after the successful suits against German and Swiss firms that stole from the Jews during the Holocaust. The primary difference is, those reparations were paid either directly to the victims or their children. The Hurdles sought $1.4 trillion (yeah, that's trillion with a *t*) to compensate every black person in the country.

Aside from the Hurdles and a handful of others, the advocates of slavery reparations are trying to gain money for those far removed from the actual act of slavery. Not to mention that those asked to pay are just as remotely removed from the slave owners or profiteers as the ones who want to profit from reparations.

Simply put, slavery reparations are wholly unworkable because it is impossible to separate the victims from the innocent bystanders. By that, I mean that the whites alive today have no ties to slave ownership, nor can a case be made that all whites alive today are descendants of slave owners. The truth is, most are not. In my case, my ancestors were poor dirt farmers from North Carolina, as far removed from slave ownership as one could be without actually being a slave. To confiscate money from me and millions like me to pay for something my ancestors had no part in is clearly wrong. Conversely, there were freed slaves who, in turn, became prosperous enough to own slaves of their own. Is it fair to award money to blacks whose very own ancestors may have kept those of their own race in bondage? And what about blacks who have immigrated to this country from African nations since the Civil War? Chances are, some of their ancestors sold other blacks into slavery. Countless whites, Hispanics, Asians, and others who arrived in America long after slavery was abolished don't even come close to having ties to the issue, yet they would be asked to pay as well.

The most salient argument against reparations is the fact that the Civil War was fought, at least in part, to free the slaves. The conquering forces who achieved this goal gave their lives for the cause. Their blood was shed on battlefields throughout this country, and in the end they were victorious. Reparations have been paid with the blood of American soldiers. Is that not payment enough?

The whole slavery reparations issue, from the standpoint of whites in this country eager to participate, is a solution that will only exacerbate the problem. Whenever our government has attempted to right wrongs with cash, it has been met with disastrous results. I hearken back to that ancient Chinese proverb I mentioned earlier: "Give a man a fish, he eats for a day. Teach a man to fish, he eats for a lifetime." That pretty much sums up why welfare is a bad idea. In an effort to right the wrongs of the past, our government developed a plan that would ultimately trap generations in the vicious cycle of government dependency. It's time we as a society started teaching people how to fish.

The Welfare Reform Act of 1996 went a long way toward turning that misguided ship around, but that same philosophy should be applied to all government charity, because that's what it really is. The word *entitlement* should be stricken from every government document. It sets the stage for the whole attitude that a person is owed something by the government. The government owes me nothing but to get out of my way and allow me to make a living within the legal confines of our society. The sooner we wean ourselves and our fellow citizens from the government trough, the sooner we'll all become as productive as is humanly possible.

24

XENOPHOBIA is at the root of protectionism.

BUY AMERICAN. THAT'S A slogan that has echoed throughout this country for the past few years, especially since the passing of the North American Free Trade Agreement (NAFTA) in 1994. What irks me about this slogan is that if it is blindly followed, it will do more harm than good to America and Americans. Competition is good, whether it be domestic or international. It's good for American consumers and it's good, believe it or not, for American companies and their workers.

In the 1970s, when imports began to make a dent in American car sales, what do you think spurred Americans' thirst for foreign automobiles? It was the shoddy workmanship on products coming out of Detroit. Many of those American-made cars were, quite frankly, junk. Had it not been for the Japanese and German imports, Detroit would never have been prompted to get its act together. Today, many American-made cars are on a par with the imports (although some would argue they still have a ways to go), which has resulted in a healthier automotive industry in America.

When I say xenophobia is at the root of protectionism, I don't mean that in the context of racism. I use the word in its truest sense. Phobia means *fear*, and I think many in this country fear foreigners, largely because of issues involving immigration or trade. Many Americans have a "raise the bridge and put alligators in the moat" mentality. The seemingly invasion-like influx of foreigners and foreign goods into this country very much frightens people. They like America the way it is, or maybe the way it was, and don't want it to change.

I can certainly understand their concerns. I share with them the fear that unbridled immigration will result in irreparable damage to this country. I am all for protecting our borders, as I explained earlier in the chapter on illegal immigration. To many, that concern over the massive influx of immigrants, illegal and legal, spills over into trade. They're afraid that all of our jobs will, eventually, be shipped overseas. What I fear more is that lack of true competition will force us to accept second best, in turn making us uncompetitive on the international market.

Some point to America's trade deficit as a sign that we're in trouble. However, a trade deficit can also be evidence of a prosperous people with enough personal resources to purchase more than they manufacture. That's not to say that we shouldn't be concerned about our trade deficit, but it should be viewed in conjunction with other economic indicators to determine the well-being of our nation.

Value Drives the Market

I make my consumer decisions based on one simple premise—value. When I make a purchase, whether it be a car or a pair of pants, I choose the best product at the best price. I pay no attention to the country of origin. (One notable exception is products made in China, which I covered in a previous chapter.) When I make a purchase decision based on a quality-to-price ratio instead of where the item is made, I contribute to the competitive nature of the free-market system. Those buying only American products short-circuit the free-market system and allow mediocre companies to sustain their mediocrity instead of getting better. Now, that's not to say that all American products are mediocre. Not by a long shot. It *is* to say that lack of competition breeds inferior products, and I don't intend to reward manufacturers of substandard products with my business just because they happen to make them here.

I have to shake my head when I hear people complaining that their company pulled up stakes and went overseas as a result of NAFTA. Remember, the NA in NAFTA stands for North American. The jobs going overseas have nothing to do with NAFTA, although there's no doubt that many companies have moved their operations to take advantage of the cheaper labor in Mexico.

I bought a Fender Stratocaster guitar a few years back. I looked at two guitars that were seemingly identical except for price. One was a few hundred dollars and made in

Mexico, while the other was over a thousand bucks and manufactured in the United States. I asked the guy at the guitar shop if there was a discernable difference in the two instruments. He chuckled and said one was made in Mexico by Mexicans and the other was made in California . . . by Mexicans. Some of my more professional musician friends would argue that point.

Even my limited musical abilities told me that the Strat made in America was probably a bit better, but for my purposes, the Mexican version would do just fine. Again, it's all about value. For me, the Mexican Strat was a better value. That's why I chose it over its American sister. Fender surely understands this. That's why they offer the choice. Finer musicians will choose the finer Strat. Less accomplished guitarists like me will opt for the cheaper version as long as it provides a reasonable amount of quality.

This brings me to a very important point, one that should bring some comfort to those who have seen their jobs go south of the border. The free market is a wonderful thing. It not only loves competition, it also detests inferior products. I believe the very same market forces that allowed imported cars to flourish in America will bring many of those jobs lost to Mexico and overseas back to America.

Let me explain. A few years ago, I noticed that the particular brand of underwear I had been buying for years was beginning to fall apart, literally at the seams, after relatively little wear. Out of curiosity, I checked the label. "Made in the Dominican Republic," it said. I checked an older pair I had that was still in pretty good shape, and the label read "Made in USA." It was the same brand, only the company had moved its plant overseas. Needless to say, I went to the department store in search of a pair of underwear made in America and have never bought another pair made in a foreign country. I had to pay more for the American-made product, but I figured it was well worth it since I wouldn't have to replace it as often.

You see, checking labels for country of origin is fine as long as you do it because you want better quality and not out of some false sense of patriotism. I believe that eventually many of these manufacturing plants will come back home because the workmanship abroad simply isn't up to our standards. The old adage "You get what you pay for" is quite true, and American consumers won't accept inferiority in clothing or any other product any more than they would accept the inferior cars coming out of Detroit in the '70s.

If we're smart about manufacturing goods that people will buy, we have absolutely nothing to fear from foreign competition. Competition of any kind, foreign or domestic, makes companies stronger. Foreign goods flooding our stores should not be cause for alarm. A bigger cause for concern would be lack of choice in the marketplace.

Labor Pains

Let's face facts. One of the main reasons American companies are moving out is because of the high cost of labor, in many cases union labor. The artificially high cost of labor caused by collective bargaining has run these companies off. If the current trend of shrinking labor unions continues (except government unions, the only unions actually growing these days), the climate will be safe for these companies to return. Perhaps then the price of labor will be decided as it should be—by the market and not the unions.

Although the America First Party folks had their hearts in the right place, some of the planks in their platform that were supposed to protect the American worker would ultimately damage consumers. If the American worker wants to be protected, it will be up to him or her to be more productive for the money. One of their planks advocated a trade policy that "safeguards American labor, health, safety, and environmental standards from cheap imports."[1] Many of these "cheap imports" have made life better for Americans and have forced American companies to make better products. By the way, there was nothing in their platform to protect American consumers from the high cost of union labor.

Protectionist trade policies are no longer realistic. We are so intertwined in the world market that it would be impossible at this point to extract ourselves from it. If we were to pull back within our borders, no other country on earth would follow suit. The foreign markets for which American workers now provide goods would quickly buy products from other countries to fill the void. Foreign makers of consumable goods sold in America would suffer, but they, too, would adjust as any market does. What we'd accomplish in the meantime would be higher unemployment here and fewer quality goods on the market for consumers, which would translate into a lower quality of life.

I look at my own situation. As I write this, I own four automobiles, three Japanese and one German. I'm convinced that Japan and Germany make some of the best cars on the planet. The computer I used to write this book was made in South Korea. We could stop trading with these countries, but why? Why would I want to make my life less convenient? There's nothing to stop an American car manufacturer from building a better car than the ones I drive. Heretofore, that just hasn't happened. It's not about cheap imports. It's about value. If American manufacturers want to compete, they're going to have to understand that first.

Many U.S.-based companies have gotten the message. Harley-Davidson is a prime example. The company was getting creamed by Japanese motorcycle manufacturers until management figured out it could no longer rely on the Harley name to bring customers through the door. The employees bought the company, returned the product to its glory-years standards, and took it public. Now Harley-Davidson dominates the large motorcycle industry with 56 percent of the market. The firm also exports to foreign countries about 22 percent of the bikes it makes at its York, Pennsylvania, facility. Ironically, one of Harley-Davidson's largest overseas markets is now Japan.[2] It's all about value. Customers don't mind paying more for better quality, but they refuse to pay more when foreign competitors can make a better product for less. Protectionism protects those companies that refuse to provide that value. The free market washes those folks out, but the protectionists want to prop them up.

I will agree that we can be smarter about the trading partners with whom we climb in bed. Their markets need to be as open to our companies as our markets are to theirs. We can't dictate government policy on every trading partner, but the ideals of those countries should reflect our ideals as closely as possible. Communist China is a glaring example of a bad trading partner. We refused to trade with Cuba all those years because of its communist regime, yet we freely and eagerly deal with one that is far more brutal. We have awesome power in our trade. Our selection of trading partners should actually mean something.

There are two roads we need to watch in the next few years: the further demise of labor unions, and the American public's distaste of inferior products. Where these roads intersect, we'll find a path that will lead American companies back home.

Are Foreigners Buying Up This Country?

During the 1980s, fear spread as Americans heard story after story of how the Japanese, drunk with the newfound wealth generated by their automobile and electronics industries, were gobbling up everything American. One of their more high-profile acquisitions was Rockefeller Center. The famous sale in the late 1980s set off a virtual panic and a great deal of xenophobia. The impression was that the Japanese were in the process of buying our entire country. Interestingly enough, between 1978 and 1987, Japanese investors only bought 94 American companies. I say "only" because that put them in fifth place behind the British, who bought 640; the Canadians, who bought 435; the Germans, who acquired 150; and the French, who bought 113 U.S. companies.[3]

There were two major points I tried to make at that particular time of uneasiness. First, it takes two to tango. There has to be a willing seller in order for the Japanese, or anybody else, to buy. Second, the prices being paid, by the Japanese in particular, were way out of line. Sure enough, six years after their infamous purchase of Rockefeller Center, the Japanese sold most of the property's assets for about half what they had paid for them.[4] During the 1990s, the shoe was on the other foot as foreign interests gobbled up choice pieces of real estate in downtown Tokyo at bargain-basement prices.

The Japanese are not, nor have they ever been, the top investors in American property and businesses. Since colonial times, the British have been the primary investors in America, followed by the Dutch.[5] Foreign investment means more capital, a whole heap more if you can find some pigeons like the Japanese were back in the '80s. More capital means more jobs and higher wages. A foreign company setting up shop or buying an established company need not be feared unless too much of a vital industry is being scooped up by one country, or a malevolent regime seizes interest vital to national security, such as a huge defense contractor. Otherwise, we should take advantage of the opportunity that additional capital affords us.

Just to give you some peace of mind as to just how much control foreign investors have over Americans, according to government figures, only about 3.9 percent of the work force in America is employed by foreign companies.[6] Still, some politicians have loved making political hay out of scaring the heck out of everybody.

One campaign stop by Michael Dukakis during the 1988 presidential campaign was particularly humorous. Dukakis addressed a gathering at an automotive parts plant in St. Louis. Trying to juice up the crowd, he said, "Maybe the Republican ticket wants our children to work for foreign owners . . . but that's not the kind of a future Lloyd Bentsen and I and Dick Gephardt and you want for America!" Italians had owned the plant for eleven years.[7] Whoops.

Proceed with Caution

A constant reassessment of our trade deficit and of foreign investment in American companies is prudent. Knee-jerk reactions to foreigners purchasing businesses or opening satellite facilities here is not only xenophobic, it's counterproductive to good business. Their desire to do business here is a testament to our strong and lucrative economy. When they start pulling up stakes, that's when it's time to worry.

We can't close the borders to foreign investors, nor should we want to. However, a healthy, critical look at each transaction is certainly in order. Trends that run counter to our national interests should be noted, and reciprocal open trade with other countries must be demanded. Other than that, let the free market run. By doing so, we remain a beacon of capitalism to the rest of the world. The more they see things our way, the better off we'll be.

25

You and you alone are ultimately responsible for your own destiny.

I'VE NEVER BEEN AN advocate of haphazardly amending the Constitution, but if I could, I would add one simple line—the title of this chapter. Like the Tenth Amendment, which was designed to be a catchall amendment elucidating the express wishes of the Founding Fathers that any rights not covered in the Constitution belong to the states, my amendment would clarify all ambiguities in the law with regard to personal culpability. Excuses like "My parents never understood me, so I simply *had* to kill the convenience store clerk to get fifty dollars" would be summarily dismissed. Currently, we coddle people and try to justify their unseemly actions.

If everyone took personal responsibility for his or her deeds, all of our lives would be much simpler. I certainly realize that one of the easiest things to do is to blame others for your failure. Most of us have done that at least once or twice in our lives. We transfer the responsibility for our own shortcomings to someone else. It's a form of rationalization. We rationalize that someone else is responsible for the problem, and thus absolve ourselves. Blaming others every once in a while is human nature, but there are those in America who have turned the blame game into an art form. For these folks, it's become a way of life. They seem to speak an entirely new language—Whinese.

Big Tobacco Made Me Do It

Consider the numerous lawsuits that have been filed against the tobacco companies. In many of these cases, the families blamed the tobacco firms for the death of a relative—some of them four-pack-a-day smokers—who had smoked for thirty, forty, even fifty years. Now, I'm not defending smoking, don't get me wrong. However, we've known for decades that cigarette smoking will kill you. I remember seeing a cartoon from the 1940s that depicted cigarettes as coffin nails and showed a man smoking and smoking, only to end with his funeral. At least since the early 1960s, when the surgeon general issued a report on the dangers of smoking that was international news for weeks, we've known full well the hazards of smoking. Heck, the warnings are printed in large letters on the side of each pack, yet these people continued to smoke for all those years. When they developed lung cancer, they blamed the evil tobacco companies instead of their own actions.

Oh, I don't want to hear all that noise about cigarettes being too addictive to quit. Former Surgeon General C. Everett Koop once claimed that they were more addictive than heroin. Let me blow that assertion out of the water right now. If you've ever seen someone try to kick smack you'd know how ridiculous that statement was. Now, I've never been hooked on heroin, but when heroin addicts who also smoked were asked if quitting cigarettes was as tough as quitting heroin, only 3 percent said yes.[1] I'm certainly not suggesting that dropping the cigarette habit is easy. Some people struggle for years with it, but the only way you'll ever really quit smoking is if you really *want* to quit. You have to be mentally prepared to quit. Your resolve must be absolute. Merely knowing the dangers or having loved ones nag you isn't going to do it.

Those who pick up a cigarette weeks or even months later and claim to be addicted are lying to you and to themselves. They may be psychologically dependent, but the physical effects of nicotine are completely gone from the human body within seventy-two hours of smoking that last cigarette.[2] It's a matter of personal responsibility and commitment, two attributes that our society today is dearly lacking.

That goes for more than just kicking the cigarette habit. Too many of us give up in life—and sometimes *on* life—because we won't take responsibility for our own destinies. I know life sometimes places us in circumstances that are beyond our control. I understand that. (Geez, I don't want to be accused of being a cold-hearted conservative.) I'm talking about general day-in and day-out excuses as to why life isn't fair and you're just a victim. When you look around you and see other people overcoming much greater obstacles, that should be enough to stop the whining. But, unfortunately, it's not.

Choose Your Crutch

Racism is one of the most frequently heard excuses for failure. I'm not blind, mind you. There's still a lot of racism, even today. This may sound trite coming from a white guy like me, but you can either choose to let it cripple you or you can work around it. That probably enrages some of you, but you know it's true. There are certain realities, and racism, for some, happens to be one of them. You can either use it to motivate you, or you can allow it to defeat you.

I like what Colin Powell said when he encountered racism in the 1960s. He said racism was the other man's problem, not his. "I was not going to let bigotry make me a victim instead of a full human being," Powell wrote in his autobiography. "I occasionally felt hurt; I felt anger; but most of all I felt challenged. I'll show you!"[3] He was determined that nothing or no one was going to deny him his dreams.

We've all had times of discouragement in our lives. Some have encountered people who tried to keep them down. I know that when I first got into radio there were few who would tell me that leaving college to begin a career where my starting salary would be six thousand dollars per year was a good idea. The more people doubted my future success, the more I was determined to make it happen. One of the first station owners I worked for fired me, but not before completely excoriating me. He said, "Your on-air presence is horrible, your production (commercials) is horrible. You don't have the talent or the voice for radio. You've made a terrible mistake getting into this business, and you should do yourself a favor and go back to college before it's too late." For years, every time I would get a new job in a bigger market, I'd send him the press clippings. Looking back, I actually drew strength from the skepticism. That's the choice you have. You can either choose to use adversity as your excuse, or you can choose to use it as your motivation.

I won't pretend that I grew up in abject poverty. My father was an attorney, and we lived comfortably. However, we weren't given everything we wanted either. It wasn't until I was actually making it on my own that I learned to appreciate my father's philosophy of earning money. He encouraged us to work and to save for things we wanted. He made a deal, starting with my eldest brother, Steve, that he would match us dollar-for-dollar if we saved to purchase a car. For some of my friends, a car on their sixteenth birthday was automatic. Not for us. Steve worked summers in tobacco, for a furniture manufacturer, and did other manual-labor jobs. He was able to save enough to buy, with my father's matching funds, a brand-new Pontiac Firebird.

By the time it came my turn, I bought a ten-year-old Opel station wagon for five hundred dollars. I, too, had worked summers but had blown my money on partying. Steve had his Firebird for ten years. I had that Opel less than three days. The engine was shot, as it turned out, and we had to talk the former owner into taking it back and giving me a partial refund (another of my father's life lessons—the art of negotiation). I learned many things from that experience: among them, the value of a dollar, saving for the future, and prioritizing. The biggest lesson was about personal responsibility. The fact that my brother was driving a Firebird and I had purchased a dud was no one's fault but mine. Some might see that as unfair, but I learned I wouldn't reach my goal unless I worked for it. It's a lesson that has served me well in my career in radio.

Personal Irresponsibility Horror Stories

Nowhere is personal responsibility thrown out the window more than in cases involving a firearm. It's always the gun's fault. There are countless lawsuits against gun manufacturers for crimes committed by humans. They even put a handgun on trial in Florida (they lost, by the way). If there's no gun to sue, people will sue anybody or anything else, just so long as they don't have to take responsibility for their own actions.

An Australian man sued the mental hospital that released him instead of taking personal responsibility for his own despicable actions. At the request of police, he had checked himself in voluntarily after an altercation with a friend. He admitted to heavy alcohol and marijuana use.

Hospital personnel examined him and said that although he was "displaying some signs of mental unwellness," he was not psychotic. Furthermore, a counsel for the mental health facility testified that the man and his brother insisted he be released immediately. After it was determined that the hospital had no legal authority to hold the man, he was released. Several hours later, he stabbed his brother's fiancée to death.[4]

Then there's the "I'm hooked on fast-food" lawsuits in which people sued because of health problems. In New York, a class-action suit was filed on behalf of several "fast-food addicts," including a woman who had eaten at fast-food restaurants at least twice a week since 1975. She'd ballooned from a size six to a size eighteen and said the restaurant had inflicted her with all sorts of ailments, including a thyroid problem, hypertension, and high cholesterol. Another plaintiff in the suit said the restaurant had made him fat and unable to walk without a cane. "I got addicted to it," he said.[5] Fortunately, the case was thrown out.

Here's an inventive criminal. A man who robbed a bank in Pittsburgh entered of plea of insanity. No, he didn't claim that he's crazy about money, although that's probably coming. He said *racism* had driven him crazy. He insisted on having a black psychologist examine him for the court because a white person wouldn't have the "empathy, moral courage, and responsibility, as well as the intellectual depth or the peculiar understanding . . . of the African-American's unique humanness, sensitivity, and the traumatically acquired psychological aberrations . . . (of) White Racism." Yeah, whatever. By the way, he was wearing a dress when he robbed the bank.[6]

Things have gotten out of hand, folks! We are witnessing the death of personal responsibility. Whatever has gone wrong in your life, it's never your doing. It's always somebody else's fault. I've grown very tired of it all. We're turning into a "no-fault" society, a nation full of victims. It's pathetic! Take control of your life, for crying out loud. If you come upon an obstacle, don't stop. Go over it, under it, or around it. Don't look for excuses. Make opportunities for you to succeed. It's time we returned to that colonial spirit of rugged individualism, of self-made instead of self-pity. It's time we turned our backs on the whiners and the wimps, the excuse-makers and the bellyachers, and the constant drumbeat of victimization that permeates our society.

Are you with me?

26

ZERO TOLERANCE is the only way to effectively deal with crime.

LET'S FACE FACTS. IF we want to stop a certain crime, we can. It's not a matter of *if* we can do it, it's a matter of resolving ourselves to make it happen. We know we can virtually wipe out any crime we wish by making the penalty severe enough. If we wanted to end jaywalking, for instance, we could. Allowing the death penalty to be carried out by the arresting officer would bring jaywalking to a screeching halt. Yes, that's a bit extreme, but my point is, we can eradicate most any crime we choose if we're serious enough as a society to do so. In our system of plea bargaining, few crimes are punished with the severity they deserve. When we do get serious about particular crimes, we usually get results.

Take driving under the influence, for instance. Once we decided to do something about vehicular accidents caused by drunken driving, the results were impressive. According to Mothers Against Drunk Driving, alcohol-related deaths have dropped about 40 percent since 1980.[1]

Of course, not all of that success can be attributed to MADD, but stiffening the penalties for DUI and DWI have certainly gotten results.

In nineteenth-century America, they used to hang horse thieves. Was that because stealing a horse was as bad as murder? No, it was because horses were an essential part of everyday life. Horse thieves were hanged not just because of the value of the horse but because horse stealing was so easy that there had to be a penalty strong enough to deter the activity. Certain death did the trick, for the most part. Sure, there were still horse thieves. There's always somebody who thinks he can get away with the crime, no matter how harsh the penalty. The point is, you can put a serious dent in a crime if you truly punish the perpetrators.

Drug dealing is one of those crimes that everyone admits is detrimental to society, but when it comes to actually doing something about it, few have the stomach to do what's necessary. As I mentioned in an earlier chapter, my plan for drug dealers is simple. I call it "Last Chance." First-time offenders would be sentenced to hard labor for six months. No frills, no fun.

At the end of the six months, the prisoner would be reminded that if he's convicted of dealing drugs again, this will be his life, forever, with no chance of ever getting out. Think that wouldn't have an effect on drug dealers? The trouble is, we talk a big game about wanting to rid our society of drugs, but nobody's proposing stiff enough penalties to actually do something about the problem. The punishment has to be severe enough that doing the crime just isn't worth doing the time.

In 1994, California signed into law the toughest "three strikes" law in the nation. Twenty-one other states quickly followed its lead. In the first five years of its three-strikes law, which calls for mandatory life imprisonment of criminals on their third conviction, California saw violent crime decline by 38 percent.[2] Other states have had varying degrees of success with this approach, depending on how rigorously the laws have been enforced. Critics of the three-strikes law point to other factors, but as Bill Jones, author of the California legislation, notes, "I don't see any time frame in the history of California where you've seen this dramatic a drop."[3]

Zero tolerance, when it comes to crime, produces results. Personally, I think three strikes is probably at least one too many. I prefer my last-chance approach instead, but at least Three Strikes is a step in the right direction.

For those critics of three-strikes laws, let's consider the opposite. Let's say you lessened the penalty for armed robbery, murder, rape, et al. Do you think you'd have more or fewer of those crimes? The answer, of course, is obvious. Therefore, it makes sense that if you stiffen the penalty for a certain crime, you'll have fewer people committing it. This notion is lost on the left-leaning bleeding hearts who constantly make excuses for criminals and their crimes. These are the same folks who would have you reason with a three-year-old, arguing that a firm swat to the fanny is child abuse.

I would contend that if you really want to screw up a child, don't discipline him. For those of you who've never had to lay a hand on your kids, God bless you. If your children are predisposed to unusually docile behavior, then you're one of the lucky ones. For the rest of us, a little spanking now and then has helped to mold and shape our children into good citizens. Once our kids grow up, there is a code of conduct they're expected to follow. If they don't follow that code, they will pay the price.

Laws and punishment aren't about rehabilitating criminals, although rehabilitation has its place. The purpose of laws and punishment is to make the criminal pay for his or her crime. It sends a message to the rest of society that if you commit such-and-such a crime, the price you pay will be this. The less ambiguity, the better. Plea bargains and parole just muddy the waters. If there's a clear understanding of what the penalty is, there's a much better chance of deterrence.

Boot Camps

The first military-style correctional boot camp for adults opened in Georgia in 1983. The first juvenile version was developed in Orleans Parish, Louisiana, in 1985.[4] Although popular when they first opened, the juvenile boot camps have begun to lose their luster. Critics cite abusive instructors, inconclusive results, and at least one death. However, even press reports that are critical of boot camps admit that part of the problem is that many Americans don't have the stomach for them. They think they're too tough. According to Jason Ziedenberg, a policy analyst with the Justice Policy Institute's Washington, D.C., branch, "What we've seen on youth issues in the last two years is that there's some public support for second chances for kids."[5]

My feeling is, such facilities are not tough enough. There's also no imminent threat that offenders will be returned for an extended stay if they don't behave. Those of you who have been through a real military boot camp probably never want to go back. Had you been told that you would be sent straight back to the "hell hole" if you screwed up, it's doubtful you'd do anything to warrant your return.

In all the studies on boot camps I've read, not one mentions that the consequence of recidivism would be returning the offender to the camp for a protracted period of time. To my knowledge, such a study has yet to be done. It seems that's the key. When we *talk* about zero tolerance, we should *mean* zero tolerance.

What We Need Is a Singapore Cane

Remember the outcry in this country when juvenile delinquent Michael Fay was sentenced in Singapore to caning for vandalizing cars? Man, you'd have thought they were going to torture Mother Teresa. Despite a personal plea from President Clinton, the Singapore police put the wood to Fay's backside, saying they couldn't make an exception just because he was an American. They argued that they had to be strict to keep crime low and the tourists coming in.

Their approach must be working—Singapore has twelve times the population of Vancouver but just half the crime rate.[6] For the sake of comparison, America's crime rate per 100,000 citizens is around 4,100; Singapore's crime rate per 100,000 citizens is around 1,200.[7] One of the reasons is more cops. Singapore ranks second in the world in terms of cops per capita, while America ranks thirtieth.[8] The point is that Singapore is obviously serious about reducing crime. We're much less so. Oh, yeah, we complain about it, but compared to other countries around the globe that have less of a problem with crime, we don't take the steps necessary to deal with it. That's not to say that I'd rather live in Singapore, but we could certainly learn a lesson or two about dealing with crime. They could probably use a lesson or two about personal freedom.

Crackin' the Whip in America

Crime statistics show that when we crack down on crime here in the States, we get good results too. The crime rate here took a tremendous dive starting in 1990. The experts have been scratching their heads as to why. Overall crime was at 3,808 incidents per 100,000 citizens in 2006. That's the lowest rate since 1969. Violent crime was at its lowest level in more than thirty years, and the murder rate hadn't dipped as low since 1965![9] Why? One obvious answer would be the strong economy prior to the slowdown of 2008; however, we had a booming economy in the '80s but the crime rate then continued to rise unabated.

The first year we began to see a drop since 1972 was in 1992. The difference between those two declines is that the '72 drop was an aberration. By 1973, crime was on the rise again and continued to increase for twenty years. So why did that trend turn around in 1992? If you're thinking Bill Clinton was the reason, think again. Clinton didn't take office until 1993. The real reason was the "get-tough" posture of the courts, which moved away from rehabilitation and toward throwing the book at criminals. That doesn't mean there's no place for rehabilitation. It simply means that evidence and experience have proven that longer sentences are an effective deterrent to future crimes.

The National Center for Policy Analysis has conducted several studies on crime and punishment. The think tank's papers provide invaluable proof that getting tough on crime is the answer, not pandering or pampering or feeling sorry for the criminal. All of the information cited in this section is from their study.[10] I've also cited their sources for particular interesting tidbits, just to give you additional ammunition.

For example, a survey of convicts provided some very interesting observations on deterrence. One criminal, who had done time for robbery, opted for burglaries instead. "After [serving] eight years for robbery, I told myself then I'll never do another robbery because I was locked up with so many guys that was doin' twenty-five to thirty years for robbery, and I think that's what made me stick to burglaries, because I had learned that a crime committed with a weapon will get you a lot of time."[11]

As I was doing research for this section, I came across a Web site run by whiners complaining that sentencing in American courts is too tough. They described an eighteen-year-old who decided to sell LSD because (grab your tissue) he needed to make his car payment. Hey, kid. Ever thought about working another job? Anyway, this drug dealer got a mandatory ten-year federal sentence.[12] The site was full of boo-hoo stories and pleas to reduce the sentences, but the fact of the matter is, more people in prison for longer periods of time means a decrease in crime.

In 1980, there were 139 sentenced inmates incarcerated under state and federal jurisdiction per 100,000 citizens. By 2000, that number had jumped to 478.[13] By 2007 it was 751 per 100,000. Concurrently, the crime rate went down from 5,960 crimes per 100,000 in 1980 to 3,808 in 2007. Coincidence? I don't think so. Economist Steven Levitt concluded that for each additional criminal locked up, approximately fifteen crimes are eliminated.[14] If you focus on the really bad criminals, that number skyrockets. Marvin Wolfgang, a criminologist at the University of Pennsylvania, and some of his colleagues conducted a study of crime in Philadelphia and found that roughly 7 percent of the criminals were committing two-thirds of the violent crime in the city.[15] You put guys like these in the slammer for a good, long time and you'll see crime plummet.

Enough Is Enough

All this hand-holding psychoanalysis does nothing to prevent an innocent teenager from being raped or a grandmother from being robbed and killed. What works is tracking down the animals who commit these crimes and locking them up—for a very long time. The other criminals will start to get the message. In my last-chance scenario, if a criminal sees a fellow drug pusher on the street get arrested and then never return to peddle his poison, the word will soon start to spread that crime is a dead-end street.

We're heading in the right direction with stiffer sentences, but we still could do better in making sure violent criminals never again see the light of day. Everybody has a study to shove in your face showing that we need to be compassionate with these monsters because of their financial background or because their mama didn't love them enough, blah-blah-blah. The bottom line is, we must send a message to the violent offenders—the murderers, the rapists, et al.—that there can be no excuse for committing such crimes. We can talk about it until the cows come home, but if we want to get serious about making America a better place in which to live, then zero tolerance is the only way to effectively deal with crime.

Epilogue

THE ROAD THAT LIES ahead of America is lined with uncertainties. Crime rates fluctuate, fads come and go, prosperity can be fleeting, and too many of our citizens do without. Like each of us individually, America still has room for improvement. All things considered, though, we're what the rest of the world strives to be. We stand as a beacon of freedom and promise to the oppressed, the downtrodden, and the hopeless. Despite all its faults, America is still the greatest nation on the planet. Many have come before us and many have become victims of their own success. What sets us apart is our self-determination and a power structure that flows from the people on up to our leaders instead of the other way around. We must never forget that important point if we are to survive.

We hold the key to our own destiny. Winston Churchill noted, "The empires of the future are the empires of the mind." Genius in the hands of totalitarianism is either stifled or becomes a tool for evil. Creativity becomes either a stooge for propaganda or something to be feared and extinguished. It's freedom that breathes life into brilliance. It's freedom that nurtures creative minds. But we must be ever watchful. We must not let our intellect rule our principles; rather, we must let our principles rule our intellect.

It's easy to act high and mighty when we're the world's lone superpower, but conservative values keep us grounded. They keep us heading in the right direction. They inspire us to settle for nothing but the best. They teach us tolerance for people but intolerance for intolerable behavior. They instill in us the spirit of our forefathers, of independence and self-sufficiency. They demand compassion for those who cannot help themselves and repugnance for the opium of dependency.

Conservative values remind us of how precious our liberties really are and how steadfastly we must stand to defend them. They also remind us that these liberties are gifts from God, not from men. But to whom much is given, much is expected in return. We are the keepers of the eternal flame of hope. It is our job, our sacred responsibility, to see to it that the flame is never extinguished.

Appendix
Notes
Index

Appendix

Civil Rights Act of 1964

Who Supported It? • Who Opposed It?

Republicans For: 163
Democrats For: 199

Republicans Against: 41
Democrats Against: 112

HOUSE OF REPRESENTATIVES

ALABAMA
Andrews–N
Elliott–N
Grant–N
Huddleston–N
Jones–N
Rains–N
Roberts–N
Selden–N

ALASKA
Rivers–Y

ARIZONA
Senner–Y
Udall–Y
Rhodes–Y

ARKANSAS
Gathings–N
Harris–N

Mills–N
Trimble–N

CALIFORNIA
Burton–Y
Cohelan–Y
Edwards–Y
Hagen–Y
Hanna–Y
Johnson–Y
Leggett–Y
McFall–Y
Miller–Y
Moss–Y
Sheppard–Y
Sisk–Y
Van Deerlin–Y
Baldwin–Y
Clausen–Y
Gubser–Y
Mailliard–Y

Martin–N
Talcott–Y
Teague–Y
Utt–X
Wilson–N
Younger–Y
Los Angeles Co.
Brown–Y
Burkhalter–Y
Cameron–Y
Corman–Y
Hawkins–Y
Halifield–Y
King–Y
Roosevelt–Y
Raybal–Y
Wilson–Y
Bell–Y
Clawson–N
Hosmer–Y
Lipscomb–N

Smith–N

COLORADO
Aspinall–Y
Rogers–Y
Brotzman–Y
Chenoweth–Y

CONNECTICUT
Daddario–Y
Giaimo–Y
Grabowski–Y
Monagan–Y
St. Onge–Y
Sibal–Y

DELAWARE
McDowell–Y

FLORIDA
Bennett–N

Republican members are listed in **bold**

Y = Yes   N = No   ? = Absent   + = Paired For   x = Paired Against

433

Fascell–N
Fuqua–N
Gibbons–N
Haley–N
Herlong–N
Matthews–N
Pepper–Y
Rogers–N
Sikes–N
Cramer–N
Gurney–N

GEORGIA
Davis–N
Flynt–N
Forrester–N
Hagan–N
Landrum–N
Pilcher–X
Stephens–N
Tuten–N
Vinson–N
Weltner–Y

HAWAII
Gill–Y
Matsunaga–Y

IDAHO
Harding–Y
White–Y

ILLINOIS
Gray–Y
Price–Y
Shipley–Y

Anderson–Y
Arends–Y
Findley–Y
Hoffman–Y
McClory–Y
McLoskey–Y
Michel–Y
Reid–N
Springer–Y
Chicago/Cook Co.
Dawson–Y
Finnegan–Y
Kluczynski–Y
Libonati–Y
Murphy–Y
O'Hara–Y
Pucinski–Y
Rostenkowski–Y
Collier–Y
Derwinski–Y
Rumsfeld–Y

INDIANA
Brademas–Y
Denton–Y
Madden–Y
Roush–Y
Adair–Y
Bray–Y
Bruce–Y
Halleck–Y
Harvey–Y
Roudeush–Y
Wilson–N

IOWA
Smith–Y
Bromwell–Y
Gross–N
Hoeven–Y
Jensen–N
Kyl–Y
Schwengel–Y

KANSAS
Avery–?
Dole–Y
Ellsworth–Y
Shriver–Y
Skubitz–Y

KENTUCKY
Chelf–N
Natcher–N
Perkins–Y
Stubblefield–N
Watts–N
Siler–N
Snyder–N

LOUISIANA
Boggs–N
Hebert–X
Long–N
Morrison–N
Passman–N
Thompson–N
Waggonner–N
Willis–N

MAINE
McIntire–Y
Tupper–Y

MARYLAND
Fallon–Y
Friedel–Y
Garmatz–Y
Lankford–?
Long–Y
Sickles–Y
Mathias–Y
Morton–Y

MASSACHUSETTS
Boland–Y
Burke–Y
Donohue–Y
Macdonald–Y
McCormack
O'Neill–Y
Philbin–Y
Bates–Y
Conte–Y
Keith–Y
Martin–Y
Morse–Y

MICHIGAN
O'Hara–Y
Staebler–Y
Bennett–?
Broomfield–Y
Cederberg–Y
Chamberlain–Y
Ford–Y

Griffin–Y
Harvey–Y
Hutchinson–Y
Johansen–N
Knox–N
Meader–N
Detroit/Wayne Co.
Diggs–Y
Dingell–Y
Griffiths–Y
Lesinski-Nedzi–Y
Ryan–Y

MINNESOTA
Blatnik–Y
Fraser–Y
Karth–+
Olson–Y
Langen–Y
MacGregor–Y
Nelsen–Y
Quie–Y

MISSISSIPPI
Abernethy–N
Colmer–N
Whitten–N
Williams–N
Winstead–N

MISSOURI
Bolling–Y
Hull–N
Ichord–Y
Jones–N
Karsten–Y

Randall–Y
Sullivan–Y
Curtis–Y
Hall–N

MONTANA
Olsen–Y
Battin–N

NEBRASKA
Bermann–N
Cunningham–Y
Martin–Y

NEVADA
Baring–N

NEW HAMPSHIRE
Cleveland–Y
Wyman–N

NEW JERSEY
Daniels–Y
Gallagher–Y
Joelson–Y
Minish–Y
Patten–Y
Rodino–Y
Thompson–Y
Auchincloss–Y
Cahill–Y
Dwyer–Y
Frelinghuysen–Y
Glenn–Y
Osmers–Y
Wallhauser–Y

Widnall–Y

NEW MEXICO
Montoya–Y
Morris–Y

NEW YORK
Dulski–Y
O'Brien–Y
Pike–Y
Stratton–Y
Barry–Y
Becker–Y
Derounian–Y
Goodell–Y
Grover–Y
Horton–Y
Kilburn–X
King–Y
Miller–+
Ostertag–Y
Pillion–Y
Pirnie–Y
Reid–Y
Riehlman–Y
Robison–Y
St. George–Y
Wharton–Y
Wydler–Y
New York City
Addabbo–Y
Buckley–Y
Carey–Y
Celler–Y
Delaney–Y
Farbstein–Y

Gilbert–Y
Healey–Y
Kelly–Y
Keogh–Y
Multer–Y
Murphy–Y
Powell–+
Rooney–Y
Rosenthal–Y
Ryan–Y
Fino–Y
Halpern–Y
Lindsay–Y

N. CAROLINA
Banner–N
Cooley–N
Fountain–N
Henderson–N
Kornegay–N
Lennon–N
Scott–N
Taylor–N
Whitener–N
Broyhill–N
Jonas–N

N. DAKOTA
Andrews–Y
Short–N

OHIO
Ashley–Y
Feighan–Y
Hays–Y
Kirwan–Y

Secrest–Y
Vanik–Y
Abele–Y
Ashbrook–N
Ayres–Y
Betts–Y
Bolton, F. P.–Y
Bolton, O. P.–Y
Bow–Y
Brown–Y
Clancy–Y
Devine–Y
Harsha–Y
Latta–Y
McCulloch–Y
Minshall–Y
Mosher–Y
Rich–Y
Schenck–Y
Taft–Y

OKLAHOMA
Albert–Y
Edmondson–Y
Jarman–N
Steed–Y
Wickersham–X
Belcher–N

OREGON
Duncan–Y
Green–Y
Ullman–Y
Norblad–+

PENNSYLVANIA
Clark–+
Dent–Y
Flood–Y
Holland–Y
Moorhead–Y
Morgan–Y
Rhodes–Y
Rooney–Y
Corbett–Y
Curtin–Y
Dague–Y
Fulton–Y
Goodling–Y
Johnson–Y
Kunkel–Y
McDade–Y
Milliken–Y
Saylor–Y
Schneebeli–Y
Schweiker–Y
Weaver–Y
Whalley–Y
Philadelphia
Barrett–Y
Byrne–Y
Green–Y
Nix–Y
Toll–Y

RHODE ISLAND
Fogarty–Y
St. Germain–Y

S. CAROLINA
Ashmore–N

Dorn–N
McMillan–N
Rivers–N
Watson–N

S. DAKOTA
Berry–N
Reifel–Y

TENNESSEE
Bass–Y
Davis–N
Everett–N
Evins–N
Fulton–Y
Murray–N
Baker–N
Brock–N
Quillen–N

TEXAS
Beckworth–N
Brooks–Y
Burleson–N
Casey–N
Dowdy–N
Fisher–N
Gonzalez–Y
Kilgore–N
Mahon–N
Patman–N
Pickle–Y
Poage–N
Pool–N
Purcell–N
Roberts–N

Rogers–X
Teague–N
Thomas–Y
Thompson–N
Wright–N
Young–N
Alger–N
Foreman–N

UTAH
Burton–Y
Lloyd–+

VERMONT
Stafford–Y

VIRGINIA
Abbitt–N
Downing–N
Gary–N
Hardy–N
Jennings–N
Marsh–N
Smith–N
Tuck–N
Broyhill–N
Poff–N

WASHINGTON
Hansen–Y
Horan–Y
May–Y
Pelly–Y
Stinson–Y
Tollefson–Y
Westland–Y

WEST VIRGINIA
Hechler–Y
Kee–Y
Slack–Y
Staggers–Y
Moore–Y

WISCONSIN
Johnson–Y
Kastenmeier–Y
Reuss–Y
Zablocki–Y
Byrnes–Y

Laird–Y
O'Konski–Y
Schadeberg–Y
Thomson–Y
Van Pelt–N

WYOMING
Harrison–N

SENATE

ALABAMA
Hill–N
Sparkman–N

DELAWARE
Boggs–Y
Williams–Y

IOWA
Hickenlooper–N
Miller–Y

MICHIGAN
Hart–Y
McNamara–Y

ALASKA
Bartlett–Y
Gruening–Y

FLORIDA
Holland–N
Smathers–N

KANSAS
Carlson–Y
Pearson–Y

MINNESOTA
Humphrey–Y
McCarthy–Y

ARIZONA
Hayden–Y
Goldwater–N

GEORGIA
Russell–N
Talmadge–N

KENTUCKY
Cooper–Y
Morton–Y

MISSISSIPPI
Eastland–N
Stennis–N

ARKANSAS
Fulbright–N
McClellan–N

HAWAII
Inouye–Y
Fong–Y

LOUISIANA
Ellender–N
Long–N

MISSOURI
Long–Y
Symington–Y

CALIFORNIA
Engle–Y
Kuchel–Y

IDAHO
Church–Y
Jordan–Y

MAINE
Muskie–Y
Smith–Y

MONTANA
Mansfield–Y
Metcalf–Y

COLORADO
Allott–Y
Dominick–Y

ILLINOIS
Douglas–Y
Dirksen–Y

MARYLAND
Brewster–Y
Beall–Y

NEBRASKA
Curtis–Y
Hruska–Y

CONNECTICUT
Dodd–Y
Ribicoff–Y

INDIANA
Bayh–Y
Hartke–Y

MASSACHUSETTS
Kennedy–Y
Saltonstall–Y

NEVADA
Bible–Y
Cannon–Y

NEW HAMPSHIRE
McIntyre–Y
Cotton–N

NEW JERSEY
Williams–Y
Case–Y

NEW MEXICO
Anderson–Y
Mechem–N

NEW YORK
Javits–Y
Keating–Y

N. CAROLINA
Ervin–N
Jordan–N

N. DAKOTA
Burdick–Y
Young–Y

OHIO
Lausche–Y
Young–Y

OKLAHOMA
Edmondson–Y
Monroney–Y

OREGON
Morse–Y
Neuberger–Y

PENNSYLVANIA
Clark–Y
Scott–Y

RHODE ISLAND
Pastore–Y
Pell–Y

S. CAROLINA
Johnston–N
Thurmond–N

S. DAKOTA
McGovern–Y
Mundt–Y

TENNESSEE
Gore–N
Walters–N

TEXAS
Yarborough–Y
Tower–N

UTAH
Moss–Y
Bennett–Y

VERMONT
Aiken–Y
Prouty–Y

VIRGINIA
Byrd–N
Robertson–N

WASHINGTON
Jackson–Y
Magnuson–Y

WEST VIRGINIA
Byrd–N
Randolph–Y

WISCONSIN
Nelson–Y
Proxmire–Y

WYOMING
McGee–Y
Simpson—N

Notes

AMERICA is good.

1. Amy Chua, *Day of Empire: How Hyperpowers Rise to Global Dominance—And Why They Fall* (New York: Doubleday, 2007).

2. Ibid.

3. David Barton, "Were all of America's Founding Fathers racists, pro-slavery, and hypocrites?" ChristianAnswers.net.

4. Ibid.

5. Tony Blair, address to British ambassadors in London, January 2003.

6. Global Integrity Index, Global Integrity Report, 2007.

7. Bernard Wasow, "Greasing Palms: Corruption in Mexico," TheGlobalist.com, June 27, 2005.

8. Gordon Sinclair, CFRB radio, June 5, 1973.

9. Ralph Dannheisser, "Aid efforts continue well after devastating 2004 tsunami," America.gov, October 29, 2007, http://www.america.gov/st/washfile-english/2007/October/20071029081347AKllennoCcM0.4600946.html.

10. "A 'tsunami' in private giving," *Christian Science Monitor*, January 24, 2005, http://www.csmonitor.com/2005/0124/p08s01-comv.html.

11. "U.S. image up slightly, but still negative," Pew Global Attitudes Project, June 23, 2005.

12. Jaroslaw Anders, "United States Is Largest Donor of Foreign Aid, Report Says," America.gov, May 24, 2007.

13. "United States, Canada World's Strongest Economies," Demographia.com, December 18, 2007.

14. Sean M. Lynn-Jones, "Why the United States Should Spread Democracy," Discussion Paper 98–07, Belfer Center for Science and International Affairs, Harvard University, March 1998.

15. Jerry Ropelato, "Internet Pornography Statistics," Internet-filter-review.toptenreviews.com.

BELIEF IN GOD is a cornerstone of our republic.

1. North Carolina Constitution, sec. 32, 1776.

2. Thomas Jefferson, "Rights of British America," 1774.

3. Thomas Jefferson, letter to John Wayles Eppes, 1813.

4. Jason Pierce, "Senate Passes Resolution Against Pledge Ruling," CNSNews.com, June 26, 2002.

5. Lawrence Jones, "Newdow Brings New Challenge to Pledge of Allegiance," *Christian Post*, November 5, 2007.

6. Soviet Union Constitution, chap. 7, art. 52, sec. 2, "In the USSR, the church is separated from the state, and the school from the church."

7. Anne Gearan, "Supreme Court won't review case allowing student-led graduation messages," Associated Press, December 10, 2001; case cited: *Adler v. Duval County School Board*, 01-287.

8. Michael Kranish, "Court bars suit on faith-based plan," *Boston Globe*, June 26, 2007.

9. Carl Limbacher, "Supreme Court Okays School Vouchers," NewsMax.com, June 27, 2002.

CHARACTER is the single most important attribute in a leader.

1. Robert Windrem, "The Man Behind the China Trouble," MSNBC, entered into the *Congressional Record* under the heading "Establishing the select committee on U.S. national security and military/commercial concerns with the People's Republic of China" (House of Representatives, June 18, 1998).

2. U.S. Department of State, news release, "Customs Service Probe Hits Loral with $20 Million Fine: Loral passed technology to China to

improve missile systems," January 10, 2002.

3. "U.S. official: Chinese test missile obliterates satellite," CNN, January 19, 2007.

4. Gallup Poll, February 12–13, 1999.

5. Gallup Poll, March 20–22, 1998.

6. Ibid.

7. "Former House Speaker Newt Gingrich acknowledges having affair during Clinton impeachment," Associated Press, March 8, 2007.

8. "Warren Harding: The Return to Normalcy President," about.com.

9. Thomas C. Reeves, *A Question of Character* (New York: Free Press, 1991), 418–19.

10. "Teapot Dome," infoplease.com.

11. Aristotle, *Politics*, bk. 1, pt. 13.

12. Reeves, *Question of Character*, 12.

13. John Podhoretz, "The Little Lies Al Gore Tells," London *Times*, September 28, 2000.

DRUG LEGALIZATION will cripple America.

1. Department of Health and Human Services, Substance Abuse and Mental Health Services Administration, *2006 National Survey on Drug Use and Health*.

2. Office of National Drug Control Policy, Fact Sheet, June 1999, based on information from *2001 National Household Survey on Drug Abuse*.

3. U.S. Department of Health and Human Services. *Monitoring the Future Survey*, December 19, 2001.

4. Health and Human Services, *National Survey on Drug Use and Health 2006*.

5. Office of National Drug Control Policy, Fact Sheet, March 2000, based on information from *National Household Survey on Drug Abuse*.

6. U.S. Bureau of Justice Statistics, *Comparing Federal and State Prison Inmates*, 1991.

7. U.S. Department of Health and Human Services, *National Survey on Drug Use and Health*, 2006.

8. Adding 119 million heroin addicts and 94 million cocaine addicts.

9. Bureau of Justice Statistics, *Sourcebook of Criminal Justice Statistics 1999*, 455.

10. Bureau of Justice Statistics, *Criminal Justice Statistics 1999*, 442.

11. 2006 Federal Sentencing Guidelines, par. 2C1.1, "Offering, Giving, Soliciting, or Receiving a Bribe; Extortion Under Color of Official Right."

12. 2006 Federal Sentencing Guidelines, par. 2P1.2, "Providing or Possessing Contraband in Prison."

13. National Drug Control Strategy Budget Summary, FY 2009.

14. The Regional Drug Initiative, "Employer's guide for preventing substance abuse in the workplace," 2001.

15. National Institute on Drug Abuse, *The Economic Costs of Alcohol and Drug Abuse in the United States 1998*, sec. 1.8, "Who Bears the Costs of Alcohol and Drug Abuse?"

ENTREPRENEURS are our economic lifeblood and deserve every penny they make.

1. Dun and Bradstreet, *Business Failure Record: A Comparative Statistical Analysis of Geographic and Industry Trends in Business Failures in the United States*, 1998.

2. "Ted Turner: 'I am a socialist at heart,'" *Drudge Report*, September 29, 1999.

3. Forbes 400, *Forbes* magazine, 2007.

4. "Ted Turner's Gift to Department Called 'a Joke,'" *World-Herald*, October 2, 2000.

FAMILIES are the basic building blocks of society.

1. Fred Jackson and Jim Brown, "Census Bureau Stats Indicate Staggering Moral Decay in America," Agape Press, May 15, 2001.

2. Michael Foust, "'Living together' before marriage a statistical

risk," Baptist Press, March 26, 2008.

3. National Center for Health Statistics, *National Vital Statistics Report*, vol. 48, no. 16, October 18, 2000.

4. Centers for Disease Control, *National Vital Statistics Report*, vol. 56, no. 6, December 2007.

5. *Wall Street Journal*, "How to Be Happy," September 29, 2002.

6. Alan Guttmacher Institute.

7. FBI Violent Crime Statistics, *FBI Uniform Crime Report*, 2001.

8. National Center for Health Statistics, *Vital Statistics of the United States, Mortality (Annual 1950–90)*, 1998.

9. David G. Blanchflower and Andrew J. Oswald, "Well-Being over Time in Britain and the USA," Dartmouth College, November 16, 1999.

10. Lee A. Lillard and Constantijn W. A. Panis, Rand Center for the Study of Aging, *Marital Status and Mortality: The Role of Health*, 1998.

Guns are good.

1. "O'Donnell defends bodyguard's gun permit," Associated Press, June 8, 2000.

2. Don B. Kates and Gary Kleck, "The Frequency of Defensive Gun Use," in *The Great American Gun Debate: Essays on Firearms and Violence*, ed. Don B. Kates and Gary Kleck (San Francisco: Pacific Research Institute for Public Safety, 1997).

3. Kates and Kleck, *Gun Debate*, criminologist Kleck's analysis of national crime victimization surveys, 1997.

4. Robert A. Waters, *The Best Defense* (Nashville: Cumberland House, 1998).

5. CNN, October 2, 1997, 2:40 p.m. EST.

6. Reuters Newswire, April 26, 1998.

7. Maria Glod and Fredrick Kunkle, "Va. Town, Law School Linked in Mourning," *Washington Post*, January 18, 2002.

8. Rick Montgomery, "Gun Lobby says media downplayed role of gun owners in subduing shooter," *Kansas City Star*, March 6, 2002.

9. Roger Alford, "Shooting rampage kills three at law school," Associated Press, January 17, 2002.

10. Bill Douthat and Kathryn Quigley, "Gun used to kill teacher on trial," *Palm Beach Post*, October 7, 2002.

11. Ibid.

12. John R. Lott Jr. and William M. Landes, "Multiple Victim Public Shootings, Bombings, and Right-to-Carry Concealed Handgun Laws: Contrasting Private and Public Law Enforcement," Chicago School of Law, April 1999.

13. Ibid.

14. Jacob Sullum and Michael W. Lynch, interview with economist John Lott, *Reason*, January 2000.

15. Stephen P. Halbrook, "An Armed Society," *American Guardian*, January 1998.

16. Gerard Jackson, "Switzerland: Europe's gun centre where kids don't kill kids," *New Australian*, no. 124, June 21–27, 1999.

17. Thomas Harding, "Handgun crime soars despite Dunblane ban," *Electronic Telegraph*, no. 2057, January 11, 2001.

18. *The International Crime Victims Survey*, conducted by Leiden University in Holland; Jon Dougherty, "Britain, Australia top U.S. in violent crime," WorldNetDaily.com, March 5, 2001.

19. Dougherty, "Britain, Australia top U.S. in violent crime."

20. National Center for Health Statistics, *Deaths: Final Data for 1997*, table 19.

21. *FBI Uniform Crime Report*, 2006.

Hyphenated labels are divisive and destructive.

1. Lee Williams, "Activist quits fight against Indian mascots," *Argus Leader*, March 14, 2002.

2. "Diversity in Newspaper Newsrooms," American Newspaper Editors Association, 2007.

ILLEGAL IMMIGRATION **is dangerous to this country.**

1. Larry Huss, "Illegal Immigration Victims—The Working Poor," OregonCatalyst.com, January 16, 2008.

2. Nathan Burchfiel, "Illegals aren't criminals, Cardinal McCarrick says," CNSNews.com, April 11, 2006.

3. Debra Saunders, "Arellano's Overdue Departure," RealClearPolitics.com, August 21, 2007.

4. Louis Sahagun, "Illegal immigrant invokes church sanctuary," *Los Angeles Times*, June 4, 2007.

5. Ibid.

6. Frontier.net.

7. J. J. Johnson, "Sen. Phil Gramm Moves to Sell Out US, Says Pro-American Organization," SierraTimes.com, January 12, 2001.

8. Ibid.

9. Ibid.

10. Bob Moser, "White Heat," *Nation*, August 28, 2006.

11. Dictionary.com, s.v., nativist.

12. "In an Absolut world all men are created 'equal' and gay marriage is a celebrated reality," PRNewswire, April 7, 2008.

13. "California in Mexico? Absolut-ly," *Brisbane Times*, April 8, 2008.

14. Anna Gorman and Susana Enriquez, "Ad putting L.A. in Mexico called slap in face," *Los Angeles Times*, April 27, 2005.

15. Edward Hegstrom, "'English Only' lands cabbie in trouble," *Houston Chronicle*, September 17, 2002.

16. "The Estimated Cost of Illegal Immigration," Federation for American Immigration Reform, February 2004.

17. Deborah Schurman-Kauflin, "The Dark Side of Illegal Immigration," Violent Crimes Institute, 2006.

18. Joseph Farah, "Illegal aliens murder 12 Americans daily," WorldNetDaily.com, November 28, 2006.

19. Valerie Richardson, "Lawmaker feels heat for deportation effort," *Washington Times*, September 19, 2002.

20. Carl Limbacher, "GOP Targets Pro-borders Tancredo," News-Max.com (quoting the newspaper *Roll Call*), November 20, 2002.

21. Mark Krikorian, "Not our kind of people," NationalReviewOnline.com, February 9, 2007.

22. Charles Zehren, "Teen jobs are going to illegal immigrants, analyst says," *Newsday*, July 23, 2005.

23. "National Teen Summer Employment Rate Drops to New Low," Center for Labor Market Studies, Northeastern University, 2007.

JUNK SCIENCE is behind the global warming scare.

1. Clare Nullis, "Report details risks from global warning," Associated Press, February 19, 2001.

2. Carl Limbacher, "Scientists Pour Cold Water on Global Warming Stats," NewsMax.com, January 15, 2001.

3. Roger Harrabin, "Global warming 'dips this year,'" BBC, April 4, 2008.

4. Michael Asher, "Temperature Monitors Report Widespread Global Cooling," DailyTech.com, February 26, 2008.

5. Richard Harris, "The Mystery of Global Warming's Missing Heat," *Morning Edition*, National Public Radio, March 19, 2008.

6. Marc Morano, "Global Warming Models Labeled 'Fairy Tale' by Team of Scientists," CNSNews.com, May 14, 2002.

7. Ibid.

8. William P. Hines, "The Exxon Valdez Oil Spill," National Marine Fisheries Service, National Oceanic and Atmospheric Administration, 1994.

9. ValdezScience.com, "10 Years After the Valdez Oil Spill: An Environmental Update," *Fish and Wildlife Recovery*, 1999.

10. Ker Than, "Sun Blamed for Warming of Earth and Other Worlds," LiveScience.com, March 12, 2007.

11. "The Sun Also Sets," *Investor's Business Daily*, February 7, 2008.

12. Alex Kirby, "Animals retreat as Antarctic cools," BBC News, January 14, 2002.

13. John McCaslin, "Inside the Beltway," *Washington Times*, June 21, 2001.

14. Ibid.

15. Thomas Sowell, "Global Hot Air," *Jewish World Review*, June 21, 2001.

16. Andrew C. Revkin, "Expert revises view of global warming," *New York Times*, August 20, 2000.

17. Dennis Newman, "Astronomers hatch plan to move earth's orbit from warming sun," CNN, February 5, 2001.

18. Pete Winn, "Glass Particles in the Sky Studied as 'Global Warming' Fix," CNSNews.com, April 10, 2008.

19. "Space Sunshade Might Be Feasible in Global Warming Emergency," *Science Daily*, November 5, 2006.

20. Miles Weiss, "Gore's wealth soars in 7 years," *Nashville Tennessean*, March 9, 2008.

21. Marcus Baram, "An Inconvenient Verdict for Al Gore," ABC News, October 12, 2007.

22. "Al Gore's Personal Energy Use Is His Own 'Inconvenient Truth,'" Tennessee Center for Policy Research, February 26, 2007.

23. Peter Schweizer, "Gore isn't quite as green as he's led the world to believe," *USA Today*, August 9, 2006.

24. Christopher Monckton, "Why 'Global Warming' Is Not a Global Crisis," *Hawaii Reporter*, January 22, 2008.

25. "Gore's 'carbon offsets' paid to firm he owns," WorldNetDaily.com, March 2, 2007.

26. "Earth Gases—Carbon Dioxide," BBC Weather, April 10, 2008.

27. John Berlau, "Al Gore's Live Earth: Has Global Warming Hysteria 'Jumped the Shark,'" AmericanThinker.com, June 6, 2007.

28. "Gore makes Nashville home more 'green,'" Associated Press,

October 12, 2007.

29. Cliff Kincaid, "Bush-Bashing Left Pushes Global Taxes," News-Max.com, April 10, 2002.

30. Ibid.

31. "Global Carbon Tax Urged at UN Climate Conference," U.S. Senate Committee on Environment and Public Works, December 13, 2007.

32. Robin McKie, "Sun's rays to roast Earth as poles flip," *Observer*, November 10, 2002.

33. Based on the earth's age of 60,000 years and keeping temperature records for 100 years; actual scale is 416.6 years to 1 minute.

KILLING through partial-birth abortion is murder.

1. "What is Surgical Abortion? Fact Sheet," Planned Parenthood Federation of America, 1996.

2. "What the Nurse Saw," National Right to Life Committee Web site at NRLC.org.

3. David Brown, "Late Term Abortions: Who Gets Them and Why," *Washington Post*, September 17, 1996.

4. "Reasons for partial-birth abortions," National Right to Life Committee, http://www.nrlc.org/abortion/pba/pbafact10.html.

5. Douglas Johnson, *Partial-Birth Abortions: Behind the Misinformation*, National Right to Life Committee, March 27, 1996.

6. John-Henry Weston, "Abortionist Tiller Admits to Performing Abortions the Day Before Delivery," LifeSiteNews.com, March 19, 2008.

7. Johnson, *Behind the Misinformation*.

8. Douglas Johnson, *Benchmarks in the Debate*, National Right to Life Committee, September 17, 1996.

9. Ibid.

10. *Doe v. Bolton*, 410 U.S. 179 (1973), majority opinion.

11. Bill Clinton, letter to Arkansas Right to Life, September 26,

1986, quoted by Cal Thomas in "Elizabeth Dole's Choice," *Jewish World Review*, April 14, 1999.

12. Congressman Al Gore's letters to constituents mailed from September 15, 1983, to August 22, 1984, quoted by Thomas in "Elizabeth Dole's Choice."

13. "Laci's unborn baby in abortion debate," WorldNetDaily.com, April 21, 2003.

14. U.S. Congress, 108th Congress, Partial-Birth Abortion Ban Act of 2003, sec. 1, par. 1.

15. Ibid., sec. 1, par. 13.

16. Ibid., sec. 1531(a).

17. "Supreme Court Upholds Partial Birth Abortion Ban Act," Associated Press, April 18, 2007.

18. Dinesh D'Souza, *Ronald Reagan: How an Ordinary Man Became an Extraordinary Leader* (Washington: Free Press, 1997), 212–13.

19. *Los Angeles Times* Poll, Studies no. 302, October 1992, no. 387, October 1996, and no. 442, June 2000.

20. ABC News–*Washington Post* Poll, January 22, 2003.

LIBERALISM is an ideology doomed to failure.

1. Rhoda Thomas Tripp, ed., *The International Thesaurus of Quotations* (New York: Crowell, 1970), 76.

2. Dean Smith, *A Coach's Life* (New York: Random House, 1999).

3. John Fonte, "Conservatives Can Be Proud of Their Civil Rights Record," *National Review*, January 9, 2003.

4. Jim Sparkman, "Letter Sets Record Straight on GOP's Civil Rights Stand," ChronWatch.com, January 2, 2003.

5. "Major Features of the Civil Rights Act of 1964," http://www.congresslink.org/print_basics_histmats_civilrights64text.htm.

6. Ibid.

7. Everett Dirksen, *Issues and Answers*, ABC, July 3, 1966.

8. Associated Press, "Second shootings stun Wichita," *Topeka*

Capital-Journal, December 17, 2000; Scott Rubush, "The Wichita Horror," *FrontPage*, January 12, 2001.

9. Wendy Orent, "Still a Scourge," Proto (Spring 2006), http://www.protomag.com/issues/2006_spring/polio_scourge.html.

10. Ibid.

11. "HIV/AIDS in the United States," Center for Disease Control and Prevention, March 2008.

12. Ed Vitagliano, "Homosexual Leader Calls AIDS: 'A Gay Disease,'" OneNewsNow.com, April 2008.

13. CDC, National Vital Statistics Reports, vol. 56, no. 10, January 2008.

14. "The Relation Between Funding by the National Institutes of Health and the Burden of Disease," *New England Journal of Medicine*.

15. Steve Kangas, Liberalism Resurgent, http://www.huppi.com/kangaroo/tenets.htm.

16. Ibid.

MILITARY STRENGTH deters aggression.

1. Norman Schwarzkopf, *It Doesn't Take a Hero* (New York: Bantam, 1992), 300.

2. Pauline Jelinek, "Air Force readiness hits lowest level in 15 years, official says," Associated Press, May 2, 2000.

3. Ibid.

4. "North Korea Has Three Nuclear Weapons, South Korean Spy Chief Says," United Press International, October 29, 2002.

5. "North Korea refuses demands to end nuclear program," Associated Press, October 30, 2002.

6. Nicholas Kraley, "N. Korea offers to dismantle nukes," *Washington Times*, April 29, 2003.

7. "Bush official: Libya's nuclear program a surprise," CNN, December 19, 2003.

8. George Washington, first annual address to Congress, January

8, 1790.

9. George Washington, fifth annual address to Congress, December 13, 1793.

10. Thomas Paine, "Thoughts on Defensive War," *Pennsylvania Magazine*, July 1776.

11. Daryl Kimball, "Chronology of Key Events," Reaching Critical Will: Reaching for a Critical Mass of Political Will for Nuclear Disarmament, http://www.reachingcriticalwill.org/legal/ctbt/ctbtest.html.

NATIONAL SECURITY is the first responsibility of the federal government.

1. Tom Bailey Jr., "Adding state immigrant ID license for disaster, foes say," *Memphis Commercial Appeal*, February 20, 2002.

2. Tom Bailey Jr. and Richard Locker, "Smith led low-impact life until arrest, fiery end," *Memphis Commercial Appeal*, February 15, 2002.

3. Bill Dries, "Flaming death no accident, FBI says," *Memphis Commercial Appeal*, February 14, 2002.

4. Yolanda Jones, "Medical examiner attacked, tied to bomb outside office," *Memphis Commercial Appeal*, June 2, 2002.

5. Yolanda Jones and Thomas Jordan, "Body found downriver may be missing scientist's," *Memphis Commercial Appeal*, December 21, 2001.

6. Illegal Immigration Reform and Immigrant Responsibility Act, Sec. 235(a)(2).

7. Michelle Malkin, "Who Let Lee Malvo Loose?" *Jewish World Review*, October 25, 2002.

8. Mary Pat Flaherty and Scott Higham, "John Lee Malvo; Smuggled into This Country, A Transient Life in Shelters," *Washington Post*, October 24, 2002.

9. NewsMax.com, "Northern Command General Endorses Posse Comitatus Review," July 22, 2002.

10. Ibid.

11. Reuters, "Officials say Nokors could hit U.S. with nukes," ABS-CBN News, February 13, 2003.

12. Carl Limbacher, "McCain: North Korea Is 'Clinton's Greatest Failure,'" NewsMax.com, February 15, 2003, reporting on McCain's exchange with Katie Couric on NBC's *Today* show.

13. Caspar Weinberger and Peter Schweizer, *The Next War* (Washington DC: Regnery, 1996), 59.

14. Jonathan Watts, "N Korea threatens US with first strike," *Guardian*, February 6, 2003.

15. Andrew P. Napolitano, "How Congress Has Assaulted Our Freedoms in the Patriot Act," LewRockwell.com, December 16, 2005.

OPPRESSION should not be fueled by American capitalism.

1. Paul Sperry, "China's Little Secret," WorldNetDaily.com, May 24, 2000.

2. Rudolph Rummel, "Rudolph Rummel Talks About the Miracle of Liberty and Peace," *The Freeman: Ideas on Liberty*, July 1997.

3. *Congressional Record*, April 24, 2001.

4. Christopher Ruddy and Stephan Archer, "Chinese Company Completes World's Largest Port in Bahamas," NewsMax.com, January 19, 2000.

5. Wes Vernon, "China Shows Contempt for U.S. Concerns," NewsMax.com, February 28, 2002.

6. Walter Pincus and John Mintz, "White House: Chinese Launches Aid U.S.," *Washington Post*, June 19, 1998.

7. "US Awash in Satellite Scandal," Reuters, June 12, 1998.

8. Peter Grier, "The China Problem," *Air Force Magazine* 82, no. 8 (August 1999).

9. Hudson Institute, *China's New Great Leap Forward: High Technology and Military Power in the Next Half-Century* (Washington DC: Hudson Institute, 2005).

10. Pamela Hess, "CIA: China, Iran, Terrorism, pose worst threats,"

United Press International, February 7, 2001.

11. "Chinese ammo found in al-Qaida hideouts," WorldNetDaily.com, December 18, 2001.

12. "Chinese fighters killed in U.S. strikes," WorldNetDaily.com, October 22, 2001.

13. *Hindustan Times*, October 22, 2001.

14. *Guardian*, October 20, 2001.

15. 1979 Taiwan Relations Act, Sec. 3301b, par. 3.

16. Ibid., par. 4.

17. Ibid., pars. 5–6.

18. Greg Torode, "Increased weapons to Taipei opposed," *South China Morning Post*, September 17, 1999.

19. Barry Schweid, "Ex-CIA director accuses Clinton administration of appeasing China," Associated Press, October 26, 1999.

20. "Bush Pledges to Stand 'Steadfast' by Taiwan," Reuters, April 25, 2001.

21. Oliver Chou and Reuters, "Fight for Taiwan tops PLA's list of priorities," *South China Morning Post*, September 21, 1999.

22. Stanislav Lunev, "Dangerous New Developments in Chinese Policy," NewsMax.com, December 21, 1999.

23. T. Kumar, "Human Rights in China: The Attacks on Fundamental Rights Continue," Amnesty International, February 11, 1999.

24. Lunev, "Dangerous New Developments in Chinese Policy."

25. Anthony C. LoBaido, "Harry Wu on the Real China," WorldNetDaily.com, April 5, 2001.

26. Edward Jay Epstein, *Dossier: The Secret History of Armand Hammer* (New York: Random House, 1996).

POLITICAL CORRECTNESS is the liberal version of fascism.

1. "The Origin of Political Correctness," Agape Press, January 16, 2001.

2. Dave Clark, "Dodge Ball Challenged," *Focus on the Family*, January 3, 2001.

3. Sherry Jones, "Teacher reprimanded for word choice," *Wilmington (NC) Star*, September 4, 2002.

4. Mark Waligore, "Eugene's tree ban ignites wide debate," *Seattle Post-Intelligencer*, December 25, 2000.

5. "Islam studies required in California district," WorldNetDaily.com, January 11, 2002.

6. Abdon Pallasch, "Delegate for Obama quits over remark," *Chicago Sun-Times*, April 8, 2008.

7. Jon Dougherty, "New book decries PC medicine," WorldNet-Daily.com, March 13, 2001.

8. Ibid.

9. Julie Foster, "Forcing doctors to ask kids about guns," WorldNet-Daily.com, May 1, 2001.

10. Scott Stafford, "Carrollton: No Toy Guns in Public," *Dallas Morning News*, November 20, 2002.

11. Mary Ann Lickteig, "Politically correct pet owners in San Francisco may soon be 'guardians,'" Associated Press, October 20, 1999.

12. Diana Lynne, "Say the 'N' word, go to jail," WorldNetDaily.com, February 20, 2002.

13. J. J. Stambaugh, "UT frat suspended over incident," *Knoxville News-Sentinel*, October 31, 2002.

14. "Auburn fraternity members suspended indefinitely over blackface Halloween costumes," Associated Press, November 15, 2001.

15. Paul Sperry, "Screening system ignored nationality," WorldNet-Daily.com, March 18, 2002.

16. Paul Sperry, "Arab flight students streaming into U.S.," World-NetDaily.com, November 1, 2001.

17. "Airline ticket agent recalls Atta on 9/11," Associated Press, March 7, 2005.

18. Ann Coulter, "Would Mohamed Atta Object to Armed Pilots?" FrontPageMagazine.com, May 30, 2002.

QUOTAS are wrong.

1. Borgna Brunner, "Timeline of Affirmative Action Milestones," infoplease.com, http://www.infoplease.com/spot/affirmativetimeline1.html.

2. Stephen Cahn, "Stephen Cahn on the History of Affirmative Action," Affirmative Action and Diversity Project, University of California at Santa Barbara, 1995, http://aad.english.ucsb.edu/docs/Cahn.html.

3. Ibid.

4. Brunner, "Timeline of Affirmative Action Milestones."

5. Ibid.

6. Ibid.

7. Nancy E. Roman, "Merit-based college admissions earn scorn of Justice nominee," *Washington Times*, November 13, 1997.

8. Ibid.

9. Balint Vazsonyi, "Creative biography," *Washington Times*, February 17, 1998.

10. Paul Craig Roberts, "Reverse Racism," NewsMax.com, March 6, 1999.

11. Bob Zelnick, *Backfire* (Washington DC: Regnery, 1996), 3.

12. American Association for Affirmative Action, affirmativeaction.org.

13. "Cochran says black coaches held to different standard," Associated Press, October 1, 2002.

14. Colin Powell, *My American Journey* (New York: Random House, 1995), 608.

REAGAN was right.

1. Ronald Reagan, *An American Life* (New York: Simon and Schuster, 1990), 105.

2. Franklin Delano Roosevelt, State of the Union Message, January 11, 1944.

3. Ronald Reagan with Richard Hubler, *Where's the Rest of Me?* (New York: Dell, 1965), 160.

4. Nancy Reagan with William Novak, *My Turn: The Memoirs of Nancy Reagan* (New York: Random House, 1989), 129.

5. Ronald Reagan, national television address on behalf of Barry Goldwater, October 27, 1964.

6. Reagan, *An American Life*, 145.

7. Cato Policy Analysis no. 261, October 22, 1996.

8. U.S. Bureau of Labor Statistics, "Consumer prices in the 1980s: the cooling of inflation."

9. Ibid.

10. Budget Message of the President, Fiscal Years 1981–1989; Budget of the United States, FY 1993, pt. 5, table 1.3, 5–18.

11. U.S. Budget, Historical Tables, Table 1.1, "Summary of Receipts, Outlays, and Surpluses or Deficits: 1789–2005."

12. U.S. Budget, Historical Tables, Table 8.3, "Percentage Distribution of Outlays by Budget Enforcement Act Category: 1962–2005."

13. John Kenneth Galbraith, "A Visit to Russia," *New Yorker*, September 3, 1984.

14. Strobe Talbott, "The Case Against Star Wars Weapons," *Time*, May 7, 1984.

15. Dinesh D'Souza, *Ronald Reagan: How an Ordinary Man Became an Extraordinary Leader* (Washington DC: Free Press, 1997), 4.

16. Ibid., 75.

17. Lou Cannon, *President Reagan: The Role of a Lifetime* (New York: Simon & Schuster, 1991), 95–96.

SCHOOLS are best run by local people on the local level.

1. Applied Research Center, "Historical Timeline of Public Education in the US."

2. Ibid.

3. Ibid.

4. "Tennessee Yearbook 2002: Documenting Our Public Schools," WNPT Nashville Public Television, October 15, 2002.

5. Average SAT scores 1980–2005, InfoPlease.com.

6. Martin B. Solomon, "The Case Against John Stossel," EdNews.org, June 4, 2006.

7. Gerald Bracey, "How to Destroy Trust in Public Schools," Education Disinformation Detection and Reporting Agency, December 12, 1999, http://www.america-tomorrow.com/bracey/EDDRA/EDDRA12.htm.

8. Diane Long, "Principals emerging as keys to better schools," *Nashville Tennessean*, May 18, 2001.

9. Jim Morris, "Schools face challenges for class-size reduction," CNN, November 12, 1999.

10. Joel Turtel, "Surprise-Public School Class Size Doesn't Matter," NewsWithViews.com, October 21, 2006.

11. Ibid.

12. Michelle Krupa, "Class size is not so important, study says," *New Orleans Times-Picayune*, February 10, 2003.

13. Hanushek, "Evidence on Class Size."

TAX RATES should be flat and fair.

1. Daniel J. Mitchell, *Time for Lower Income Tax Rates: The Historical Case for Supply-Side Economics*, Heritage Foundation Study, no. 1253, February 19, 1999.

2. Steven Cole Smith, "Been ogling that land yacht? Tax on them just fell," *Orlando Sentinel*, January 2, 2003.

3. John F. Kennedy, speech to the Economic Club of New York, December 14, 1962.

4. U.S. Congress, House Committee on the Budget, Joint Economic Committee, and Congressional Research Service, Economic Stabilization Policies: The Historical Record, 1962–76, Joint Committee Print, 95th Cong., 1st sess. (Washington DC: Government Printing Office, 1978), 6–9, 15–19, 70–91.

5. Internal Revenue Service, Tax Year 2005, figures compiled by the National Taxpayers Union.

6. Doug Bandow, "Still Paying for Government," *Investor's Business Daily*, May 12, 1998.

7. "Federal Individual Income Tax Rates History: Income Years 1913–2008," Tax Foundation, http://www.taxfoundation.org /publications/show/151.html.

8. Peter Roff, "Analysis: Bush Tax Proposal—Pros and Cons," United Press International, March 2, 2001.

UNIONS have outlived their usefulness.

1. Bush Bernard, "UAW reinforcements join picketing Peterbilt workers," *Nashville Tennessean*, February 14, 2003.

2. Charles Savage, "Private maintenance work pits school board vs. unions," *Miami Herald*, May 14, 2002.

3. Gallup Organization, "Public Approval of Labor Unions," August 13–16, 2007.

4. U.S. Bureau of Labor Statistics, "Union Members Summary," January 25, 2007.

5. Ibid.

6. Ibid.

7. National Institute for Labor Relations Research, "Trouble in Big Labor 'Paradise.'"

8. Ibid.

9. Barry T. Hirsch, "Unionization and Economic Performance: Evidence on Productivity, Profits, Investment, and Growth," Department of Economics, Florida State University, 1997.

10. *WKRP in Cincinnati*, Episode 69, "The Union," written by Blake Hunter, directed by Linda Day.

VIGILANCE is the price of freedom.

1. Carl Limbacher, "Why Pentagon Wants to Spy on Your Shop-

ping," NewsMax.com, November 21, 2002.

2. Heather MacDonald, "Total Information Unawareness," *Weekly Standard*, vol. 8, issue 22, February 17, 2003.

3. *Talkers* magazine year-end review, held at the Heritage Foundation in Washington DC, December 16, 2002.

4. "Making Further Continuing Appropriations for Fiscal Year 2003," U.S. Senate, January 23, 2003, Amendment No. 59, S1412.

5. Dalia Sussman, "Dubious Honor: China Tops List of Most Threatening Nations," ABC News, July 24, 2001.

6. David Horowitz, "American Haters," *FrontPage*, September 10, 2002.

7. L. Brent Bozell III, "American-Haters at Home," Creators Syndicate, October 5, 2001.

8. John Podhoretz, "American-Haters Within," *New York Post*, September 19, 2001.

WELFARE robs people of their dignity and is the poison of capitalism.

1. U.S. Department of Health and Human Services, "A Brief History of the AFDC Program," 1998.

2. Kelley L. Ross, "Historical Statistics and Analysis on Unemployment, Poverty, Urbanization, etc., in the United States," 2002, Los Angeles Valley College, Van Nuys, CA.

3. U.S. Census Bureau, "Poverty in the United States: 2001."

4. Ronald Brownstein, "Promise of Reducing Poverty May Be Found Inside Marriage Vows," *Los Angeles Times*, October 6, 1997.

5. National Center for Health Statistics, vol. 48, no. 16, October 18, 2000.

6. Gordon M. Fisher, "Enough for a Family to Live On? Questions from Members of the American Public and New Perspectives from British Social Scientists," 23rd Annual Research Conference of the Association for Public Policy Analysis and Management, Washington

DC, November 2, 2001.

7. "Who Are the Homeless?" Arizona Department of Education–Arizona State University West College of Education.

8. Ibid.

9. U.S. Census Bureau, Population Percentage Change, April 1, 2000–July 1, 2001, Davidson County down 0.8 percent; average growth for surrounding counties for same period was 2.9 percent.

10. Charles M. Sennott, "The $150 Billion 'Welfare' Recipients: U.S. Corporations: First of three parts," *Boston Globe*, July 7, 1996.

11. Ibid.

12. Bill Rigby, "Blacks File Slavery Suits Against Firms," Reuters, September 3, 2002.

13. NBC11–TV (San Francisco, Oakland, San Jose), "Slave's Sons Sue for Reparations," September 8, 2002.

14. Nisa Islam Muhammad, "New trillion-dollar reparations lawsuit filed," *Final Call*, September 24, 2002.

Xenophobia is at the root of protectionism.

1. Platform of the America First Party, pt. 2; Trade; Trade Policy; item 3.

2. White House, "Harley-Davidson: A Success Story for American Trade," November 10, 1999, http://clinton3.nara.gov/WH/New/WTO-Conf-1999/factsheets/fs-002.html.

3. Mack Ott, "Foreign Investment in the United States," Concise Encyclopedia of Economics, http://www.econlib.org/LIBRARY/Enc/ForeignInvestmentintheUnitedStates.html, referencing Eric Rosengren's work.

4. Trends in Japan, "Buying Up Japan: Foreign Firms Snap Up Real Estate Bargains," June 4, 1998, http://web-japan.org/trends98/honbun/ntj980601.html.

5. Ott, "Foreign Investment."

6. U.S. Bureau of Economic Analysis.

7. Ott, "Foreign Investment."

You and you alone are ultimately responsible for your own destiny.

1. Philip J. Hilts, "Relative Addictiveness of Drugs," *New York Times*, August 2, 1994.

2. "Motivation, Education and Support for Cold Turkey Nicotine Cessation," http://www.whyquit.com.

3. Colin Powell, *My American Journey* (New York: Random House, 1995), 43.

4. Leonie Lamont, "Patient sues hospital for letting him out on night he killed," *Sydney Morning Herald*, October 15, 2002.

5. Michael Y. Park, "Ailing Man Sues Fast-Food Firms," Fox News Channel, July 24, 2002.

6. "Suspect in Pennsylvania robbery claims racism made him insane," Associated Press, December 23, 1999.

Zero tolerance is the only way to effectively deal with crime.

1. Jeff Frank, "Plenty of reasons to be glad for MADD," *North County Times*, September 24, 2000.

2. Daniel B. Wood, "The impact of 'three strikes' laws," *Christian Science Monitor*, March 8, 1999.

3. Ibid.

4. U.S. Department of Justice, *Juvenile Justice Reform Initiatives in the States 1994–1996: Juvenile Boot Camps.*

5. Nate Hendley, "The shine is off boot camps," *Eye Weekly*, January 20, 2000.

6. Pam Soltani, "Crime and Punishment in Singapore," Pacific Rim Magazine (2003), http://www.langara.bc.ca/creative-arts/publishing/prm/2003/singapore.html.

7. U.S. figures from FBI Uniform Crime Report; Singapore figures

from "Singapore sees drop in crime rate in 2001," Kyodo News, February 25, 2002; 1998 is the last year for full numbers from Singapore, thus its numbers were compared to U.S. figures for 1998.

8. *UN Global Report on Crime and Justice*, 1999, 384.

9. FBI Uniform Crime Reports, 1960–2006.

10. Morgan O. Reynolds, "Does Punishment Deter?" National Center for Policy Analysis, Policy Backgrounder no. 148.

11. Richard T. Wright and Scott H. Decker, *Burglars on the Job* (Boston: Northeastern University Press, 1994), 8; see also Eugene H. Methvin, "Mugged by Reality," *Policy Review*, July–August 1997, 32–38, esp. 34 describing sociologist James A. Inciardi's study of 611 high-crime youngsters in Miami.

12. Families Against Mandatory Minimums, "Mandatory sentencing was once America's law-and-order panacea. Here's why it's not working."

13. U.S. Bureau of Justice Statistics, Correctional Populations in the United States.

14. Steven D. Levitt, "The Effect of Prison Population Size on Crime Rates: Evidence from Prison Overcrowding Litigation," *Quarterly Journal of Economics*, May 1996, 319–51; see also Steven R. Hanke, "Incarceration Is a Bargain," *Wall Street Journal*, September 23, 1996.

15. Paul E. Tracy, Marvin E. Wolfgang, and Robert M. Figlio, *Delinquency Careers in Two Birth Cohorts* (New York: Plenum Press, 1990).

Index